BLACK LEGACY PRESS™
WWW.BLACKLEGACYPRESS.ORG

SLAVE NARRATIVES

VOLUME X
MISSOURI NARRATIVES

By
United States.
Work Projects Administration

Copyright © 2024 by BLACKLEGACYPRESS.ORG

All rights reserved. No part of this publication may be reproduced or transmitted in any form or by any means electronic or mechanical, including information storage and retrieval systems without permission in writing from the publisher, except for student research using the appropriate citations.

ISBN: 978-1-63652-215-9

SLAVE NARRATIVES

A Folk History of Slavery in the United States.
From Interviews with Former Slaves

**UNITED STATES.
WORK PROJECTS ADMINISTRATION**

TYPEWRITTEN RECORDS PREPARED BY
THE FEDERAL WRITERS' PROJECT
1936-1938
ASSEMBLED BY
THE LIBRARY OF CONGRESS PROJECT
WORK PROJECTS ADMINISTRATION
FOR THE DISTRICT OF COLUMBIA
SPONSORED BY THE LIBRARY OF
CONGRESS

WASHINGTON 1941

VOLUME X
MISSOURI NARRATIVES

Prepared by
The Federal Writers' Project of
The Works Progress Administration
For the State of Missouri

CONTENTS

James Monroe Abbot	1
Betty Abernathy	7
Hannah Allen	9
Aunt Hannah Allen	15
W.C. Parson Allen	19
Charles Gabriel Anderson	21
Jane Baker	25
Mary A. Bell	27
William Black	33
George Bollinger	37
Annie Bridges	47
Betty Brown	55
Steve Brown	61
Richard Bruner	63
Robert Bryant	67
Alex Bufford	75
Harriet Casey	79
Joe Casey	83
Lula Chambers	87
Emmaline Cope	91
Peter Corn	93
Ed Craddock	103
Isabelle Daniel	105
Henry Dant	109

Lucy Davis	111
Mary Divine	113
Mary Douthit	117
John Estell	119
Smoky Eulenberg	121
Ann Ulrich Evans	125
James Goings	131
Rachael Goings	133
Sarah Frances Shaw Graves	139
Emily Camster Green	153
Lou Griffin	157
Louis Hamilton	159
Fil Hancock	161
Dave Harper	173
Clara McNeely Harrell	179
Joe Higgerson	181
Delia Hill	187
Louis Hill	191
Rhody Holsell	199
Henry Johnson	211
Hannah Jones	219
Emma Knight	223
Harriet Lee	227
Mattie Lee	229
Wes Lee	233
Perry McGee	237
John McGuire	243

Eliza Madison	247
Drucilla and Richard Martin	249
Hattie Matthews	257
Letha Taylor Meeks	261
Wylie Miller	267
Lewis Mundy	269
Malinda Murphy	273
Margaret Nickens	275
Eliza Overton	279
Delicia Ann Wiley Patterson	283
Marilda Pethy	289
Susan Rhodes	295
Charlie Richardson	301
Madison Frederick Ross	311
Alice Sewell	317
Perry Sheppard	323
Frank Sides	325
Mollie Renfro Sides	327
Jane Simpson	329
Clay Smith	335
Gus Smith	339
Ann Stokes	353
Edward Taylor	361
Tishey Taylor	365
Louis Thomas	373
Jane Thompson	377
Sarah Waggoner	379

Minksie (Minksy) Walker 387
James Wilson 393
Mintie Gilbert Wood 397
Ellaine Wright 401
Sim Younger 403

JAMES MONROE ABBOT

Interview with James Monroe Abbot,
Cape Girardeau, Missouri.

"I's born on December 25, 1854. My muthuh wuz Allie Ann Lane. Aftuh 'mancipation I tuk my daddies name Abbot—he wuz Anthony Abbot, an' belonged to Ole' Joe Abbot, a neighbor. Our Mastuh wuz Joe Lane an' our Missus wuz Jane Knox Lane. Dey had a girl, Barbara Ellen, an' two boys, Tom en' Ed. Latuh years dey had more boys but I nevuh knowd dem.

"De white folks house wuz big, wid porches, an flowers all aroun', an sweet locust trees in de do' yard. Dis wuz up in Perry County, a few miles fum Seventy Six Landing.

"When Ole Mastuh died, dat wuz de fathuh ob young Mastuh Joe—he war sick a long time. Dar he lay fum openin' o' spring, 'bout de time flies cum, 'til wheat-sowin' time in de fall. An' it's de God's trufe, all dat time he made me stan' side o' his bed—keepin' de flies offen him, I wuz jes seben year ole but dere I had tuh stan, day en night, night en day. Co'se I'd sleep sumtimes wen he wuz sleepin'. Sumtimes when I'd doze, my bresh ud fall on he's face, den he'd take he's stick an' whack me a few across de haid an' he'd say, 'Now I dare you to cry.' I cried, but he didden see me do it.

"But at las' he died. Jane came in an' said, 'He's daid. You can go out to play now James.' She ustah come in to Ole Mastuh an say, 'Why don' you let him go out tuh play an' let someone else stan' here?' But Ole Mastuh say, 'No! I want James.' So now I runs outside—I meets ma sister an I says: 'By God, he's daid.' I didden know I wus cussin', she say 'I gonna tell Muthuh on you,' but I's so glad to be out, I runs till I meet Uncle Rube an' I says, 'By God, he's daid,' den I runs an meets ma Muthuh, an' I tells her 'By God, he's daid.' She jes kinda turned her back tuh me an' I cud see her shakin'. She war laffin'!

"Aftuh de buryin' was over, Young Joe an' Jane stood dar on de porch an' dey call de darkies up one at a time. Fust dey calls ma Grampa an' young Joe says, 'Yo ole Mastuh's daid. Now I's you' Mastuh, an' Miss Jane here is your Missus. Do you unnerstan dat?' Grampa say 'Yessir' an pass on. Nex' he call Lucy, den Aunt Hanna. To each one he says de same, 'I's yore Mastuh and Miss' Jane here is yore New Missus'—sum ob' em says 'Yessir', sum ob' em jes kinda bows dey haid an' pass on. Wen he call mah Muthuh up an' say de same tuh her—she look at him a minit den she say, 'I know'd yuh all dese year as Joe an' her as Jane, an' I ain't gonna start now callin' you Mastuh or Missus. I'll call you Joe an' Jane like I allus done,' an' she walked away.

"One time 'fore dat she puddin near kill young Joe. She wuh hoeing corn in de field an he cum ridin'—I spect he war jes tryin' to be smaht but he tells her to swallow dat tobbaccy she got in huh mouth. She don' pay him no mind an' he tell her agin. Den she say, 'You chewing tobaccy? Whyn't yuh swaller dat?' Dat make him mad and he take a double rope en whack her cross de sholders. Den she grab huh fingers roun' his throat, an his face wuh all black es my own 'fore dey pulls her offen him. Den Ole Mastuh try tuh whup her, but he couldn' by hisself, so he sends fo' three nigger-buyers dat's close by. When one o' em tells muthuh to put her han's togedder so he tie em, she grab him by de collar an' de seat o' he's pants an knock's his haid agin a post like a battern' ram. Den Ole Mastuh say, 'Men, yo' better go on home. I don' want my cullud folks to git hurt.' He said it like dat.

"My Muthuh wuz big an' strong. She nevuh worked in de house none but dey warn't nothin' on de place dat she couldn' do. She cud cut down a big tree en chop off a rail length an' use a wedge an' maul an' make rails as good as anybody. Pore Muthuh, she shore did have a hard time. Dey warn't never nuthin' for her but work hard all de time, she neveh came in fum de fiel' 'til dark, den had to feed wid a lantern.

"George Swan, a neighbor used tuh whup ole Felix with a cat-o'-nine-tails til we'd hear him holler over at our place.

"I 'member one time de snow wuz a foot deep an I had tuh gathuh corn. I wuz barefooted an' barehanded. Mah feet hurt so bad an' mah hands got so stiff I couldn' work mah fingers, but ah had tuh keep on breakin' off de corn. Dat night mah feet crack open an' nex' mahnin' when I had tuh make de fires I lef' a track o' blood across de' flo.' Dey shore wuz mean to us but God Bless you, dey's all daid an' gone an' de Lawd has spared me.

"Wen de war cum, lots o' cullud men went off to fight fo de Government. Young Mastuh Joe nevuh went but whenever de sojers cum aroun' Mastuh Joe couldn' nevuh be foun.'

"One time a passel a' sojers cum to de place, dey didden go to de big house, but dat night dey spread straw fum de straw pile on de flo ob our cabin—an' slep dar. We slep in de loft. Nex' mornin' dey went to de barn an' took de bran' new wagon an' de bes' team o' mules an' dey went to de smoke house an' hep deysefs. Dar wuz one man standin' on de wagon cuttin' down de hams an' side meat an' de udder packin' it in de wagon. Jane cum out on de porch an' start raisin' a ruccus 'bout 'em takin' her meat. De sojer whut wuz cuttin' down de meat pull out he's gun an' say 'Whut dat she say?' Jane run in de house quick—but he got mad de way she talk an' den' he take all a de meat an' cans o' lard, an a barrel of molasses. We ain't nevuh seed dat wagon agin an' it wuz bran' new.

"Dey wuz a battle a few mile away an' dey said you couldn' walk on de groun' wifout steppin on daid men.

"Wen de war wuz over dey didden want us to know 'bout it. Dey want to keep us es long es dey could. But it cum out in de papers dat de Guvment men wuz gonna cum round an' see so dey had tuh turn us loose.

"Abe Lincoln wuz de honestest President we evuh had. Ef it warn't fo' him we'd still be in bondage.

"If you puts two hoss-shoes above youh door—one up an' one down—it'll shore catch de wiches if dey tries tuh come through.

"One time it wuz in de evenin' I wuz puttin hay in de pen fo de hosses at night, an I see a big white light a-cummin' up de lane jes a little above de top o' de fence. It wuz big an' shiny white. I wuzn' rightly skeered but I stood dere watchin' it. It cum up an followed de' fence to de road. I watched to see did it go to de graveyard, an' shure nuf it did. It meant sumpin' but I don' know whut. An den one day, 'bout noon I seed sumpin. I wuz out side dar an a little dog cum towards me. It wo' a bright collar, shinin' like, an' pretty. I ain't nevuh seed nuthin' like it. I goes to it an calls, 'Heah puppy, heah puppy.' It stan dere n' look at me fir a minit den turn an' jump ovuh dat ten rail fence an' is lost in de tall weeds. Now you know no natchel puppy could jump ovuh a ten-rail fence. I goes in an tells Hanna de cook 'bout it an' she say, 'Lawd ha' mercy! dat's a token fo' sumpin. I don' know whut—mebby somebody gonna die, but it sho' is a token.'"

United States. Work Projects Administration

BETTY ABERNATHY

Interview with Betty Abernathy,
Cape Girardeau, Missouri.

"My muthuh brought me to Cape Girardeau in 1862, an' I was 'bout ten yeah ol' at dat time. Huh name was Malissa Abernathy an' she tole' me that 'Ole Massa' John Abernathy was mah daddy. 'Ole Massa' was mean to his cullud folks and so was 'Ole Missis Willie'.

"We lived up in Perry County. The white folk had a nice big house an' they was a number of poor little cabins fo' us folks. Ours was one room, built of logs, an' had a puncheon floor. 'Ole 'Massa' had a number of slaves but we didden' have no school, 'ner church an' mighty little merry-makin'. Mos'ly, we went barefooted the yeah 'round.

"My muthuh an' some of the othuh women done the weavin' an' sewin'. I learned to spin, I could fill broaches and spin as good as any of 'em. One time 'Ole' Tom Johnson, the 'nigger-buyer' come up frum Little Rock. He was go'in to buy muthuh an' her family, and take us to Arkansas, but 'bout that time they was so much talk 'bout freein' the slaves, he was 'fraid to.

"Mostly we had right fair eatin's. We didn't go into the big house much, jes' on cleanin' days an' such like.

"Ole Massa' often hired his cullud folks out to neighbuh farmuh an' he didden' care how they was treated.

One time my two brothers was hired out an' in the evenin' they came an' tole muthuh they was goin' to run away 'cause they's treated so mean. She begged 'em not to come there to hide 'cause they'd find 'em 'shore, an' most likely kill 'em right before her eyes. They got away an' 'Ole Massa' come to the cabin to search fo' 'em. When muthuh tole him she didn't know where they was, he tied a rope 'round huh neck, an' tied the other end to the raftuhs. Then he beat her to make her tell.

"Aftuh this we was treated so mean that a neighbor helped us escape. We-all got in a big wagon, 'bout ten or twelve of us, an' druv us to the Cape, where they's sojers who'd protect us.

"I remembuh when we got there, they put us in a long, low, frame house, that stood on the cornuh where Mr. Hecht now lives. Here we lived fo' a long time. Muthuh an' I had no trouble findin' work to do. She hired me out fo' twenty-five cents a week an' I was so proud to be earnin' money that I nevuh thought 'bout learnin' to read or write."

HANNAH ALLEN

> Interview with "Aunt" Hannah Allen,
> Fredericktown, Missouri.

God Got A Hold On Her

One of the oldest ex-slaves encountered in Missouri is "Aunt" Hannah Allen of Fredericktown, who claims she is 107 years old. According to Madison County records, Aunt Hannah gave her age as 82 when she made application for a marriage license in Fredericktown in 1912.

In spite of her extreme age, Aunt Hannah is able to do all of the work around her house and she frequently walks up town and back, a distance of several blocks. Her eyesight is very good and even at her advanced age she does not have to wear glasses. She claims her grandfather was a white man and she attributes her unusual health to several causes. She was well treated as a slave during her younger years when she was under the ownership of a family named Bollinger. She is childless and has been content to live on the same spot during the last 71 years. Being a Negro, she naturally does not take life seriously but as she expresses it "jes' lives it like it comes".

In reviewing the incidents which she was able to recall on the occasion of the writer's recent visit to her home, she outlined her story as follows:

"Down in Pocahontas, Arkansas, a man had 400 slaves

and de boss would allow an old colored man to have meetins every Saturday night and of a Friday night dey would have a class meeting. Several of dem got religion right out in de field and would kneel down in de cornfield. De boss went home and told his wife he thought de slaves was losin' their minds 'cause dey was all kneeling down in de field. De boss' daughter also got religion and went down to de mourners' bench. De colored church finally made de boss and his whole family get religion. De old white mistress would sing and pray while she washed dishes, milked de cows, and made biscuits. So dey called de doctor and he come and said dat God had got a hold on her.

"One of de darkies had a baby out in de field about eleven o'clock one morning. De doctor come out there to her. She was sick a long time 'cause she got too hot before de chile was born. After dis happened de boss got to be a better man. Dis old boss at first would not let the darkies have any church meetins.

"On Sunday dere at home de colored folks could get all de water dat ran from de maple trees. De slaves would get through their work for de boss and den dere would sometimes be three days when dey could work for themselves. Den dey would get paid for working for others and den buy clothes. Dey had de finest boots.

"Dey did not want de mistress to tell me when we was free 'cause dere was only two of us slaves left there. De other slaves already done run off. I did not want to leave. When I was a slave I learned to do a job right or do it over. I learned to sew, cook, and spin. We set by de fireside and picked a shoe full of cotton and den we could go to bed. But you did a lot before you got dat shoe full of cotton when it was pressed down. Dis was almost enough to pad a quilt with. De white children would be getting their lessons den and dey used a pine torch for a light to see by.

"I was paid nothin' after slavery but just stayed with de boss and dey gave me things like a calf, clothes, and I got to go to church with dem and to camp meetings and picnics. Dey would have big basket meetings with pies, hogs, sheep and de like. Dey did not allow me to go with other colored girls if dey had no character. We all set down and ate at de same table with de white folks and tended de sick together. Today if de parents would make their children do like dey did in slavery, den we would have a better race. I was better off dan de free people. I think dat slavery taught me a lot.

"In Fredericktown I worked for my mistress' sister and made $10 a month. My father told me to always keep myself clean and nice and to comb my hair. When I lived in Fredericktown de people I worked for always tried to keep me from going out with de low class. After I washed de supper dishes, I would have to go upstairs and cut out quilts and I did not like it but it was good for me.

"My first husband gave $50 for dis lot I am living on. Dat was just at de end of de war. He hauled de logs and chinked and white-washed dem and we had two rooms and a hall. It was a good, nice, warm house. He was a carpenter. About twenty-five years later my husband built him a frame house here and dug him a well. He had 4 dozen chickens, 15 head of hogs, 2 horses, 2 wagons, and a buggy to go back and forth to de church at Libertyville, New Tennessee, or Pilot Knob. We lived together fifty years before he died. He left me dis home, three horses, 3 milk cows and three hogs.

"We had no children but 'dopted a little boy. He was my husband's sister's child. De boy's mother took a notion that she wanted to work out and she was just a young girl so we took de boy at about de age of three and he was with us about six years. He went to a colored school den but a white teacher taught him. We adopted a girl too from Marquand. De girl's father was a colored man and de mother was a white woman. De woman den married a white man in Marquand and her husband did not want de child so we took her at about three years old. We did not have her no time 'til she died. We have helped to raise about a dozen children. But I have quit doing dat now. I now has my second husband; he always liked to have children around but we ain't had none of our own.

"When my first husband died, he did not owe fifteen cents. He just would not go in debt to nobody. He attended de Masonic lodge. After he died I went to work. I brought wood, washed, ironed, and cooked. I have made as high as $15 a week and keep. I took care of a man's children after him and his wife separated. We have had two houses burn down right here. One of our houses was a little too close to Saline Creek and it was condemned and we tore it down and built de one we have now, thirteen years ago. Harry Newberry has a mill and he give us de lumber to build dis house.

"We have a lot in de colored graveyard. I have no insurance but Mr. Allen has some kind of insurance, so if he gets hurt traveling he will get something. We is getting, together, $25 in pensions a month and we is living pretty well right now. Some months we spend from seven to eight dollars on food. Almost everything is cash for us. I been going barefoot about ten years. I come mighty near going barefoot in de winter time. We been getting a pension about two years and we was on relief for two or three years before dat. Our biggest debt is a doctor bill of about $60.

"Some of de colored folks is better off now and some is worser. De young race says we who was slaves is ten times worse off den dey 'cause we had bosses and couldn't read or write. But I say de young race is got all dis to go by and dey ought to be much better off dan dey is. We is better off in one sense dan de young race 'cause about half of dem don't know how to raise their children and dey don't know how to do nothing. I think our folks has just as good a chance now as de white folks but dey don't get cultivated. Dey say today dat I don't know nothing 'cause I was a slave and all I learned was what de master learnt me. But I know enough to keep out of devilment. I think all dis speed shows dat people ain't got no sense at all."

United States. Work Projects Administration

AUNT HANNAH ALLEN

> Interview with Aunt Hannah Allen,
> aged 107, Fredericktown, Mo.
> Interviewed by J. Tom Miles.

"I's born in 1830 on Castor River 'bout fourteen miles east of Fredericktown, Mo. My birthday is December 24. Yes, sir, I is 107 years old dey say and dey got de records up there in de court house to prove it. De first time I married Adam Wringer in 1866 and was married by Squire Addison in Fredericktown. In 1912 on August 11 me and de parson was married in de Methodist church here and dis was de largest one in Fredericktown. 'Bout six or seven hundred come for de celebration. I guess I is 'bout de oldest person in Madison County.

"My father come from Perry County. He was named Abernathy. My father's father was a white man. My white people come from Castor and dey owned my mother and I was two years old when my mother was sold. De white people kept two of us and sold mother and three children in New Orleans. Me and my brother George was kept by de Bollingers. This was in 1832. De white people kept us in de house and I took care of de babies most of de time but worked in de field a little bit. Dey had six boys.

"Our house joined on to de house of de white folks. Many times I slept on de floor in front of de fireplace near de mistress. Dey got hold of a big buffalo rug and I would sleep on it. De Bollinger boy, Billy Bollinger, would go to de cabin and sleep with George, my brother. Dey thought nothing of it. Old man Bollinger sent some colored folks up to his farm in Sabula and Billy cried to go long with dem. He let Billy go. I stayed with old Aunt Betsy on Castor River.

"Before de Civil War broke out we were at Sabula and a Mr. Schafer and Mr. Bollinger started to take de slaves to Texas. Dey got as far as Rockport, near Hot Springs. A man by de name of John Higdon from Colorado married Olive Bollinger and he was injured in de arm in de Battle of Fredericktown. Den John Higdon went to Rockport after he was shot and had taken de oath of allegiance. Higdon's wife died in Rockport and she had a child two years old. I took de baby to care for. De wife was to be buried back home so dey took de body in a wagon with just a sheet over it towards Little Rock. I was sitting in de wagon holding de two year old baby. On de way 'bout ten miles out we were captured by Federal soldiers and took back to Rockport. De body was put in a room for two weeks and den placed in a vault above de ground and stayed dar for 'bout eight years before Mr. Higdon took it back home to bury.

"Higdon took me and his child to 'bout eight miles from Hot Springs to a hotel he had bought. Once he come up to de hotel with two government horses and put me and de child on a horse and we were on de way to Little Rock. We rode dat way for 'bout two weeks and was captured again near Benton. Higdon had on a Union cape. De soldiers asked us all 'bout de horses, guns, child, etc. De soldiers let him keep his gun 'cause dey said it wouldn't kill a flea. But dey cut de buttons off de coat, and took de spurs off of his heels and said he could not go any further.

Dey took me and de baby and made us sit on de ground. De soldiers took Higdon to de river. It was late in de day. Dey said dey was going to transfer him back to Missouri and sell de horses. Higdon had papers from Col. Lowe and Chambers. De soldiers were Masons and after a while dey all come back just a-laughing and shaking hands.

"We were put on a boat at Little Rock going toward St. Louis. De child took de small pox from a lady on de boat. When we got on de boat dey were firing at the wheels of de boat from across de river. I was feeding de baby and de chamber-maid come out and said, 'I would drown him'. I said, 'If you do dat you will have to drown me too'. Dey had Higdon locked up on de boat and he did not get to see de baby for two weeks when we got to St. Louis. Just as we got to St. Louis, two white ladies saw de baby who was so sick and dey went out and got some clothes for it. De doctor come on de boat and vaccinated me. De sores on the baby were as big as half dollars.

"Den after we got to St. Louis we went to Whitworth's in Ironton, Missouri. Higdon was on de back porch and a soldier shot at him and took him to headquarters dat night. Whitworth had some soldiers take us to Sabula, twenty-five miles away. De soldiers den took Higdon back to Ironton until de war was over. Higdon married three times.

"John, the baby, was raised by his grandmother and step-mother in St. Louis. John married the daughter of a county clerk in Luxemburg, Missouri. And he became county clerk for thirty years in dis county. John died 'bout two years ago this July.

"I 'member how dey would treat one slave. De master

took two boards and tied one to de feet and another to de hands and tied her back with ropes and whipped her with a cat-o'-nine-tails till she bled and den took salt and pepper and put in de gashes. I can 'member when I was in Iron County de soldiers stole de boss' horse and de boss had to go to Patton to git it. Once de soldiers made me get up in de smoke house and throw down some ham. De authorities 'gaged de soldiers for stealing from de people. I had to carry some stuff out for Sam Hildebrand to eat.

"I've been living here since de Civil War. Dis is de third house that I built on dis spot. What I think 'bout slavery? Well we is gettin' 'long purty well now and I believe it's best to not agitate."

W.C. PARSON ALLEN

> Interview with W.C. Parson Allen,
> aged 78, Fredericktown, Mo.
> Interviewed by J. Tom Miles.

"I's born in Harrison County, in 1859 and was raised in Georgetown, Scott County. Yes, I was born a slave. My boss was John McWiggin, a Scotch-Irishman, who raised hogs, sheep, hemp, and darkies. He had 'bout 230 darkies on de place. We lived in log cabins. Dey had slip doors for de windows. Man, what you talkin' 'bout? We never saw a window glass. Had 'bout fourteen cabins and dey was placed so dat de old master could sit on his porch and see every one of dem. My mistress was Alice McWiggin.

"I was kep' busy shooin' flies off de table with a peafowl brush, watching de chickens, and gettin' de maple sugar from de root of de trees. We made a pocket at de base of de tree and dipped out de sugar water with a bucket. Had 'bout 40 or 50 trees along de road. Had all kinds of berries. We never got no whippin', only a little boxin'. In church we sat on one side and de whites on de other. De white preacher always read a special text to de darkies, and it was this, 'Servants, obey your master.'

"John McWiggin was a son of a Federal. His brother, Keenie, was a Confederate. When de Confederate army come Keenie took de silver goblets down to de creek and gave de soldiers water to drink. Den when de other soldiers come Johnie would help his crowd. De soldiers took

Mac's iron-gray saddle hosses to Lexington, and de boss had to pay $500 to get de hosses back. He got some of his mules back. De bushwackers and nightriders were here. But de boss got 'round it this way. He had de slaves dig trenches 'cross de road and tie grape vines over it. Den have de darkies go up on de hill and sing corn songs. Den de nightriders come a-rushing and sometimes dey would get four or five whites in these raids. It would kill de men and horses too, when dey fell into de trench. On Saturday night we had a shindig. We would eat chicken and pound cake and of course whiskey made in Kentucky. De jail was called de watch-house.

"After de war de government instituted religious trainin' 'mong de colored people and gave dem white teachers. I was in Lexington, Ky., when I learned my letters. Just how dese latter-day children learn to read without de letters is a mystery to me.

"I's one of de preachers of de church here and am a deacon, too. I studied at de University of Louisville, where I was a theological student, and was one of de main orators in de school.

"I've married a lot of 'em, in Poplar Bluff, Kennett, Farmington, and Fredericktown, and have preached quite a few funerals. Have preached some brush arbor sermons and stood under a arbor when we was married. I baptized 42 in Pennsylvania.

"I ain't eligible enough to express 'bout slavery. I ain't sayin' nothing."

CHARLES GABRIEL ANDERSON

Interview with
Charles Gabriel Anderson,
St. Louis, Missouri.

Hale And Hearty At 119

Charles Gabriel Anderson, 119 years old, lives at 1106 Biddle Street in St. Louis alone. He is 5 feet, 3 inches in height, has mixed gray hair and weighs 145 pounds.

He is slightly bent, but does not have to wear glasses, and is able to go anywhere in the city without assistance. He has a good memory, and cheerful attitude. Seated in the church of God in Christ, a store front church, next door to his home, where he attends because of the convenient location, he tells the writer the following story:

"I was born January 5, 1818 in Huntsville, Alabama de son of Sallie McCree and George Bryant. My owner's name was Miss Margaret Tony. She sold me to Edmond Bryant while I was quite young. I sometimes go by de name of Bryant.

"I was just big enough to carry water and help a bit with farming while Miss Tony had me, but I jedge I was 'bout 14 years old when Mr. Bryant got me, 'cause I was old enough to plow and help with de cotton and I done a man's size work in his field. I was his slave when de war broke out. I joined de army in 1864. I used to git a pension of $65 a month, now I only git $56 a month but last month I didn't git no check at all. I don't know why. Wish I could find out 'cause I needs it bad to live on. I used to nurse de white folks children when I was a little boy. I made a better nurse dan most girls, so jest kept on at it till I was old enough to be a field hand.

"I had a hard time till de war broke out. Soon as I got a chance, I run off and went to de army. I served two years and six months. I come out in 1866. 'Course I was in de hospital till '66. I don't know how long I was in der wounded. But I do know when I got better, I was such a good nurse de doctors kept me in de government hospital to help nurse dem other soldiers and dere sure 'nough was a heap of 'em up dere. Dat was in Madison, Wisconsin. After dey turned me loose from de hospital, I went to work in a barber shop up dere. I worked in it one year to learn de trade. After I learned de barber trade I don't remember how much longer I stayed dere. I left dere and went to Dodgeville, Wisconsin and opened a barber shop of my own and run it about two or three years. Den I went to Dubuque, Iowa, and stayed about one year and barbered in a hotel dere.

"I come to St. Louis in 1876 and started being a roustabout and firing on boats. I changed from dat after awhile and went to driving private carriages and done glass cleaning.

"I got what little education I got, 'tending night school here in St. Louis. I got 'nough to git ordained in de Chamber Street Baptist Church for a preacher. Den I come in holiness in Elder Jones, Church of God in Christ on Kennerly Avenue. I pastored the Macedonia Spiritual Church eight years in East St. Louis, Ill. I been married twice and am de father of three children, all dead, and both wifes dead. I don't know how long none of 'em been dead. My mother died while I was in de army and my father got drowned before I was born. I only had two sisters and three brothers, and dey is all dead. My brother, Jim Bryant, died in de army. He enlisted one year before I did, but in a different regiment. I has voted many times in my life time, and always voted Republican till dis last election, I decided I better vote de Democrat ticket and I did, and I don't regret it either.

"I gits my washing done by de neighbors dat do washing and I eat at de restaurant on de corner. De Ku Klux never bothered me none 'cause I stayed up north out of dere reach.

"I 'member de old slaves used to sing: 'Amazing Grace How Sweet De Sound'; 'I want to be a Soldier, Since de Lord has set me Free'; 'Fighting for Liberty'; 'Why Should We Start, and Fear to Die'; 'Death is the Gate to Endless Joy and Yet We Dread to Enter There'; 'The pain, the groan, the dying strife, rights our approaching souls away'; 'Jesus can make a dying bed, soft as downy pillows are, whilst on his breast, I lean my head and breathe our lives out sweetly there'.

"Sister, I just think dis younger generation is gone totally. Dey ain't taught right in de home, and de teachers can't do a thing with 'em. If it wasn't for de prayers goin' up to de throne of grace from all us old saints what's got sense enough to trust in nothin' else but Jesus, de whole business would be gone plum to rack. Dey ain't even got sense enough to know dat. De young folks' mind is on worldly goods and worldly pleasures and dere ain't no good in none of it, just misery and woe, to all it touches.

And still dey don't seem to see, and don't want to see and nobody got any sense, can't make' em see. God help dis generation is all dat I can say.

"I figure I lived dis long 'cause in de first place, I obey God, I never did drink liquor or smoke in my whole life. I never wore glasses but precious little and dat was when I did what little reading and writing I knowed how to do; 'cause after my children went to school long enough to read and write for me I just stopped doing dat little bit. Now dey's all dead so I just makes marks, and lets it go at dat. I am a member of The Kennerly Avenue Church of God in Christ."

JANE BAKER

Jane Baker,
Farmington, Missouri.
Interview with Chas. Baker.

"Ma muther wuz in a log cab'n east ob Farmington an when Price's soldiers com thru frum Fredericktown, one ob de soldiers climb'd ober de fence an robbed de hen house ob eggs an he put de eggs in his boots. Den when he climb'd ober de fence to git back to de road he mashed de eggs in his boots. De soldier tok off his boots an turned dem upside down to git de broken eggs out an ma muther ran out ta de fence an hollored, 'Goody, goody.'

"Ma muther say dat de worse side ob slabery wuz when de slabes war 'farmed out'. A master or slabe holder wud loan or sublet slabes ta a man fur so many months at so much money. De master agreed ta supply so many clothes. De man who rented de slabes wud treat dem jus lik animals.

"Ma muther wuz sole twice. De furst time she wuz 14 years ole. She wuz tak'n 26 miles to de new owner, an hit took all day. She tied all her belongings up in a red bandanna handkerchief an went on horseback. One stream wuz so high dat when dey cross'd hit dey got all wet. Den as soon as she got to de new owner she wuz ship'd de follin' day. One ob ma muther's owners wuz so good ta her dat she wuz treated as one ob de family."

REFERENCE:—The above information was received from Chas. Baker, who is the brother of Dayse Baker, principal of the colored Douglass School in Farmington, Missouri. Thus these facts are concerned with their mother, Mrs. Jane Baker, an Ex-Slave, who died at the age of 103.

MARY A. BELL

> Interview with Mary A. Bell,
> St. Louis, Missouri.
> (Written by Grace E. White.)

She Loves Army Men

The subject of this sketch is Mary A. Bell, 85 years old, living in a 4-room frame cottage at 1321 Argus Street, St. Louis County, Missouri.

Mary Bell has a very light complexion, light brown eyes, mixed gray hair, very long and straight. She has fine features. She is quite bent, and shows her years, but is cheerful. She is living in the same yard with her daughter who is married and lives next door with her family, Mrs. Virginia Miller and six children. Her story follows:

"I was born in Missouri, May 1, 1852 and owned by an old maid named Miss Kitty Diggs. I had two sisters and three brothers. One of my brothers was killed in de Civil War, and one died here in St. Louis in 1919. His name was Spot. My other brother, four years younger than I, died in October, 1925 in Colorado Springs.

"Slavery was a mighty hard life. Kitty Diggs hired me out to a Presbyterian minister when I was seven years old, to take care of three children.

"I nursed in dat family one year. Den Miss Diggs hired me out to a baker named Henry Tillman to nurse three children. I nursed there two years. Neither family was nice to me. De preacher had a big farm. I was only seven years old so dey put me on a pony at meal time to ride out to de field and call de hands to dinner. After the meals were finished, I helped in de kitchen, gathered the eggs, and kept plenty busy. My father was owned by de Lewis family out in the country, but Miss Diggs owned my mother and all her children. I never attended school until I came to St. Louis. When Abraham Lincoln was assassinated I had never been to school. Dat same year I attended school at Benton Barracks and went about six or seven months with de soldiers. There was no Negro school in St. Louis at dat time. The next school I attended was St. Paul Chapel, 11th and Green Streets. I went dere about six months. De next place I went to school was 18th and Warren. I went there about two years. My next school was 23rd and Morgan, now Delmar Boulevard, in a store building. I went dere between two and three years. I was very apt and learned fast. My father at de time I was going from school to school, was a nurse in Benton Barracks and my mother taken in washing and ironing. I had to help her in de home with de laundry.

"I married at de age of twenty-two and was de mother of seven children, but only have two now living, my daughter dat lives next door and in de same yard with me, and a son in the Philippine Islands. I have eight grandchildren and four great-grandchildren.

"I so often think of de hard times my parents had in dere slave days, more than I feel my own hard times, because my father was not allowed to come to see my mother but two nights a week. Dat was Wednesday and Saturday. So often he came home all bloody from beatings his old nigger overseer would give him. My mother would take those bloody clothes off of him, bathe de sore places and grease them good and wash and iron his clothes, so he could go back clean.

"But once he came home bloody after a beating he did not deserve and he run away. He scared my mother most to death because he had run away, and she done all in her power to persuade him to go back. He said he would die first, so he hid three days and three nights, under houses and in the woods, looking for a chance to cross the line but de patrollers were so hot on his trail he couldn't make it. He could see de riders hunting him, but dey didn't see him. After three days and three nights he was so weak and hungry, he came out and gave himself up to a nigger trader dat he knew, and begged de nigger trader to buy him from his owner, Mr. Lewis, because Marse Lewis was so mean to him, and de nigger trader knew how valuable he was to his owner. De nigger trader promised him he would try to make a deal with his owner for him, because de nigger trader wanted him. So when dey brought father back to his owner and asked to buy him, Mr. Lewis said dere wasn't a plantation owner with money enough to pay him for Spot. Dat was my father's name, so of course that put my father back in de hands of Marse Lewis. Lewis owned a large tobacco plantation and my father was de head man on dat plantation. He cured all de tobacco, as it was brought in from the field, made all the twists and plugs of tobacco. His owner's son taught him to read, and dat made his owner so mad, because my father read de emancipation for freedom to de other slaves, and it made dem so happy, dey could not work well, and dey got so no one could manage dem, when dey found out dey were to be freed in such a short time.

"Father told his owner after he found out he wouldn't sell him, dat if he whipped him again, he would run away again, and keep on running away until he made de free state land. So de nigger trader begged my father not to run away from Marse Lewis, because if he did Lewis would be a ruined man, because he did not have another man who could manage de workers as father did. So the owner knew freedom was about to be declared and my father would have de privilege of leaving whether his owner liked it or not. So Lewis knew my father knew it as well as he did, so he sat down and talked with my father about the future and promised my father if he would stay with him and ship his tobacco for him and look after all of his business on his plantation after freedom was declared, he would give him a nice house and lot for his family right on his plantation. And he had such influence over de other slaves he wanted him to convince de others dat it would be better to stay with their former owner and work for him for their living dan take a chance on strangers they did not know and who did not know dem. He pleaded so hard with my father, dat father told him all right to get rid of him. But Lewis had been so mean to father, dat down in father's heart he felt Lewis did not have a spot of good in him. No place for a black man.

"So father stayed just six months after dat promise and taken eleven of de best slaves on de plantation, and went to Kansas City and all of dem joined the U.S. Army. Dey enlisted de very night dey got to Kansas City and de very next morning de Pattie owners were dere on de trail after dem to take dem back home, but de officers said dey were now enlisted U.S. Soldiers and not slaves and could not be touched.

"In de county where I was raised de white people went to church in de morning and de slaves went in de afternoon. I was converted at the age of fourteen, and married in 1882. My husband died May 27, 1896 and I have been a widow every since. I do get a pension now, I never started buying dis little old 4-room frame dwelling until I was sixty-four years old and paid for it in full in six years and six months.

"I am a member of St. Peter's A.M.E. Church in North St. Louis. I told you my father's name was Spot, but that was his nickname in slavery. His full name was Spottwood Rice and my son's full name is William A. Bell. He is enlisted in de army in de Philippine Islands. I love army men, my father, brother, husband and son were all army men. I love a man who will fight for his rights, and any person that wants to be something."

United States. Work Projects Administration

WILLIAM BLACK

Interview with William Black,
Hannibal, Missouri.

He's Quit Having Birthdays

William Black of 919 South Arch Street, Hannibal, Missouri, is one of the few ex-slaves living in Marion County. He is now about eighty-five years old, and has lived his entire life in Marion, Monroe, and Ralls Counties. In chatting about his life and experiences he says:

"My mother and father come from Virginia. I don't know how old I is, but I have had one birthday and the rest is anniversaries. I think I is about eighty-five. I was born in slavery and when I was eight years old was bonded out to Sam Briggs of New London. Mr. Briggs was a good master and I didn't have a whole lot to do. My job was to take his children to school and go after dem of an evening. In the mean time I just piddled around in de fields.

"In de evening when de work was done we would sit 'round and play marbles and sing songs. We made our songs up as we went along. Sometimes dere would be a corn shuckin' and dat is when we had a good time, but we always shucked a lot of dat corn.

"I did not go to school any and today I do not even have de sense of writing at all. Unless some one guides my hand I cannot make a mark. I wish I wasn't so old now so I could go to school and learn how to read and write.

"I 'member one day when de master was gone, us darkies thought we would have a party. I guess de master knowed we was going to have one, 'cause dat night, when we was all having a good time, my sister said to me, 'Bill, over dere is old master Sam.' He had dressed up to look like us and see what we was up to. Master Sam didn't do anything to us dat time 'cause he had too good a time hisself.

"At the age of thirteen my sister was bonded out to some man who was awful mean, she was a bad girl, too. After we were freed she told me all about her old master. She said, 'One Christmas my master was drunk and I went to wish him a merry Christmas and get some candy. He hit at me and I ducked and run 'round de house so fast I burnt de grass 'round dat house and I know dere ain't no grass growing dere yet.'

"When we was freed our master didn't give us nothing, but some clothes and five dollars. He told us we could stay if we wanted to, but we was so glad to be free dat we all left him. He was a good man though.

"Durin' de war we could not leave de master's house to go to de neighbors without a pass. If we didn't have a pass de paddyrollers would get us and kill us or take us away.

"After de freedom come we could vote, but some of us never done it. To dis day I ain't never voted. De government has been as good to us as dey could. I get ten dollars a month and think I should have more, but I know dey is giving us all dey can and some day dey will give us ex-slaves more.

"I am glad dat we have our churches and schools. We don't have no business being with de good white people. Dey is cultured and we is not, but some day we will be as good and dey will be glad to have us 'round dem more. Just 'cause we is black is no sign that we ain't good niggers.

"I don't like de way de younger generation is doin'. As my neighbors say, 'the devil is gettin' dem and it won't be long 'fore he will come and get dem all.' When I was young we didn't act like dey do now-a-days. We didn't get drunk and stay dat way and kill each other. De good Lord is going to do something to all of dem, mark my word.

"I can't 'member some of the songs we sung, but when we was freed we sang 'Master's Body is Molding in the Grave', and I know some of dem is."

William Black lives by himself in a house owned by his daughter. He is unable to do any kind of manual labor and has not done any kind of work for about five years. He is active in religious affairs and attends church regularly. He is one of the few persons living in Marion County who raises tobacco. His garden plot, five by ten feet, is close to his house.

United States. Work Projects Administration

GEORGE BOLLINGER

Interview with George Bollinger,
Cape Girardeau, Missouri.

He Saw Many "Hants"

George Bollinger is a typical, old-time Negro who lives in Cape Girardeau. In his younger days he was big and powerful and even now at the age of 84 he is above the average in build. He owns his home and his is the last colored family to remain in this neighborhood which is rapidly being built up with modern homes.

George has little education, unlike his wife who is much younger and uses fairly good English. He sits on his porch and thoroughly enjoys talking of the long ago with those who appreciate listening to his story.

"Benton Hill?" he said. "Sure, it's hanted. I seen things and heard things there lots of times. Good gosh amighty! One night we was driving through dere and we heard something dat sound like a woman just a screaming. Old man Ousbery was with me and he wanted to stop and see what it was but I says, 'No you don't. Drive on. You don't know what dat might be.' Another time we's driving by there, and dey was a great big mule just standing cross de road and he just wouldn't move. I says, 'Just drive on and he'll get out of de way.' But he didn't. When we gets to him, he just parts right in de middle and half stands on one side and half on de other. We didn't look 'round. No, mo'—we just made dat hoss go.

"I don't know what makes dem hants round there—lessen it's de gold what's buried dere. And you know de spirits always come back fer gold. Sure dey's money buried dere. Didn't you all know dat? Lots of folks is dug there, but dey ain't never found it. Why dey is holes 'round dere where men's been digging for dat gold.

"Dey was one man had a-what you call it? A 'vinin' rod. That points to where things is hid. But he didn't find it neither. And then out by de Maberry place, close to Gordonville—who-e-e—I's sure enough seen things out dere lots of times. You know where dat clump of peach trees is at de corner of de fence? Dey always seems to come from right there. I worked out there for a long time. We'd get out to work early, sometimes 'twasn't good and day.

"One morning I's coming along there, on a hoss I was, and I met a hossman. He looks funny to me and when he asks me something I says, 'Git on. I ain't talking to you!' But he says, 'Wait, I wants to talk to you!' As I says, he looks funny to me and I pulls out my pistol. I always carries my gun, and I think if he makes a pass at me I'll git him. But I goes on without looking back. Now just dat one man is all I seen, but when I gets past, dey is lots of talking like dey is six or eight men. But I didn't look back.

"One morning I'd got out there real early, too early to go into de field and I thinks I'll rest awhile under de tree. I had my eyes shut for a while when something bothered me. When I opened up my eyes there was a lot a strange hosses standing 'round me in a ring. I jumped up and hollered, 'git out'. Dey turned and ran and dey run right off a steep bank on the other side of de field."

"Did you see them down there?" he was asked.

"Cose I never, nobody else never neither, dey wasn't dere, dat's why," he answered.

"Lord, when I thinks of de way we used to work. Out in de field before day and work till plumb dark. My boss would say, 'George take two men, or maybe three men, and git dat field plowed, or dat woods patch cleared'. And he knowed if he tell me, de work would be done.

"And I worked at anything. One time I steamboated for eight years. But what do dese young folks know 'bout work? Nuthin'! Look at dat grandson of mine, just crossed de porch—why he's fourteen and he can't even use a ax. Too young? Go on with you!

"I tells you dese young folks just don't know how to work. Dey has too much studying up here (pointing to his head and making motions like wheels going round.) When I's his age I's working at anything I could find. I worked on a farm and on a steamboat, I carried cross ties—just anything where I could earn money. And I saved money, too. When we bought dis house I had $2,400 saved up. And men was stronger in dem days and had better health.

"Dese young folks want too easy living. And dey ain't brung up to show respect to old folks like we is. If I goes down de walk and a bunch young folks is coming along, I knows I's got to step out of de way—'cause dey won't give any. And if some little ones on roller skates is coming down de sidewalk—you better git off or dey'll run right into you.

"I was tellin' you 'bout Miss Katie coming to see me, wasn't I? Well just last week her boy come to see me. He's maybe 25 or 30 year old. Somebody told him 'bout me and he come here and he sit right dar on de porch fer a hour and talk with me. He was a fine young man, he was."

GEORGE BOLLINGER

Interview with George Bollinger
[TR: by Mollie E. Smith].

NOTE: George Bollinger and his family live in a nice one-and-one-half story house, which they own. They have always been industrious people and their home is nicely kept. George is 84 years old and seems to enjoy life. He was glad to talk over "old times", especially after he recognized me, (The "Me" being Mollie E. Smith) and recalled that he used to work in my grandfather's Tan Yard. George Bollinger is living at 320 N. Spriggs St., Cape Girardeau, Missouri.

"We lived out on de edge o' Bollinger County. 'Ole Massa's' name was 'Dal Bollinger'. 'Ole Missus,' we always called, "Aunt Polly". Den day wuz young 'Massa Dave,' and young 'Missie Katie'.

"My Pappy's name wuz 'Bollinger' 'en my mammy wuz 'Temple'. My pappy wuz a smart man. He cud read and write. I don't know whar he learned it. An' he had de power, my daddy did. He cud break a 'Hoodoo' spell, an' he cud tell things dat happened wen he diden see it—If one a' de folks went to town he cud tell 'em jes everything dey don dere.

"Dey wuz 'bout 20, mebby 25, slaves on de place, 'en we all lived in a big, old log house. My mammy wus a good cook 'en she cud spin en weave. She made all de clothes we wore. Us chilluns never wore no pants—jes sumpin like a long shirt made o' homespun. We didden know nuthin' 'bout learnin'. Dey wuz a church, but we didden go much, 'en we never had no kind 'er gatherin's. Dey wouldn' let de cullered folks congregate—no, shu, why, even de man over at de store wouldn't let mo' dan two cullud folks come in at a time.

"I didden even know what money wuz. Massa' had a chest 'bout three feet long—up in a little attic. It wuz jes' full o' gold 'en silver money—no 'greenbacks'. It wuz covered over wif rugs, 'en I never know'd what wuz in dere—we used to go up der to play sumtimes on rainy days, an Aunt Polly'd holler, 'Ef you don' cum down fum dere de ghosts 'ul git ye'. I never seed inside de chest 'till dey bury it—dat wuz in war-time. Dey put a big hand spike under it 'en de men carry it down by de sugar grove de udder side o' de graveyard. I cud go, right now 'en show you de very spot dey bury it. De bes' times we-ens had wuz going fishing, an' man! did we like to fish. Allus we had Saturday afternoon off, 'lessen it wer wheat harvest 'er sumthin' special like. 'En Sunday's we allus fished all day long.

"One time day wuz two hundred sojers cum to our place—dey wuz Southerners, an' dey wuz nearly starved. Massa tole 'em dey cud kill dat big steer. Dey shoots him 'en 'fore he drops dey wuz on him; skinnin' him. By dat time udders had a fire built 'en de men pull out dey knives 'en dey cut off hunks; dey puts 'em on a stick 'en hol's 'em ovar de fire a few minutes—didden give 'em time to cook thru fore dey et it. Dat ole steer didden last long. 'En 'Massa' had ten cribs 'er corn. He tole' em to —— dey selves. 'Bout dat time a dispatch came, dat de "Yankees" wuz commin'. Dey went up to meet 'em, 'an dey had a battle over at Patton. Long 'bout midnight sum of 'em came back, wounded. Aunt Polly helped 'em, but she begged 'em not to stay dere, or de "Yankees" cum in, burn de house down.

"Aunt Polly 'en mammy allus know'd whut to do when a body wuz ailin'. Dey allus had a bag o' yarbs hangin' under de porch. When de sojers wuz commin' we allus hid de hosses. Massa' had lots ob 'em, 'en Missie —— had de pudttiest black mare. It's name wuz 'Kate'. Des one time de hosses musta skered 'er sumpin—de sojers foun' 'em, an' here dey com ridin' up past de house wid every on of our hosses.

"A sojer wuz ridin' 'Black Kate'. Wen 'Missie Katie' see dat—she holler, and she ran an' grab hol' de bridles, on han' on each side 'er his haid. De sojer put spurs to de mare, but she hung on jes a cryin'. I kin jes see her now; de mare a rarin' and 'Missie —— hangin on a-cryin'. She hung on till dey reach de creek. Den she lose her grip, but she sho' did cry.

"One night we had a big corn shuckin'. We shucked 'till way late in de nite: den sum de white men stay all nite. Day wuz a pile 'er shucks higher'en dat door. Nex' mornin' a bunch o' "Yankees" cum by. As dey wuz comin' thru' de yard, dey see one man runnin' to hide behin' de barn. Dey say; "Halt", but de man keep runnin'; so dey fire—de bullet thru' his had and he stop. Den dey say: "If day's one man, dey's more a hiddin.' Dey looks roun', den de haid man say: 'Men ride thru' dat pile 'er shucks 'en —— in dey hair. Den de sojers asks 'em things 'en iff'n de answers didden seem good; dey hit 'em over de haid wid dere guns. I wuz standin' right here, an' I saw 'Ole Massa' git hit on de haid once, den anudder time:

an' he fell. I sho' thot he wuz daid, but warn't. Aunt Polly fix him up atter de sojers wuz gone, but de bushwackers got him.

"Dey must a heerd about de chest o' money he had buried. Dey try to make him tell; but he wouldn't. Den dey put 'er rope 'roun' his neck an' pulls him up. Den dey lets him down: but he wouldn' tell no how—so dey finished him.

"Yes, de' nigger buyers ust'a cum roun' our place. It was sight to see! Dere 'ud be mebbe five 'or six men a'ridin' fine hosses an a-drivin' a whole flock 'er slaves along de rode; jes' like stock, all chained togedder.

"On time dere wuz Pete Smith, 'Ole Tom Johnson, an' Fred an' Sam Daughery; all niggar buyers—dey wuz at our place an' dey wud all sit dar, an' us slaves had to stan' up in front o' em, an' dey'd bid on us. I 'members I wuz full chested an' dey laid a stick across my chest to see how straight I cud stan'. 'Ole Pete' Smith wuz gonna' buy me; but my young folks begged 'Massa' not to sell me, 'cause we'd all played togedder—so he didden' sell me.

"But dey wuz gonna buy my 'pappy' an take him way off, but, my 'pappy' was smart. He had made baskets at night an' sold 'em when he cud, 'en saved de money—dat night he goes to de fireplace an' lifts up a stone; an' out o' de hole he pulls out a bag a' money an' he runs away. I ain't never seed my 'pappy' since. Las' I hurd a' him he was in 'Indiana.' When Mista Lincoln made his Proclamation (dat wuz 'fore de war wuz over), young Massa' Dave set us free. He gave us a yoke of oxen an' a wagon full o' everythin' we needed. Der wuz a feather bed 'en quilts an' meat an' purvisions—an' he sent us into de Cape—an we been livin' roun' here ever since.

"All my white folks is daid 'cept 'Missie Kattie', an' do you know, some year back: she cum to see me. Yessir; her car druv up, right der, to de sidewalk, an' she made all her grandchillun get out an' shake han's wif me. She sho' wuz a fine woman!

"'Ku Klux?' Yes, dey wuz aroun' sometime', but dey didden bother ef you mind your own bizness. But de darkies better not congregate; 'caus' day shore take 'em out an' flag' em. If dey ketch you at a neighbor's house atter dar, you shore better have a pass fum yo' 'Massa.'"

United States. Work Projects Administration

ANNIE BRIDGES

Interview with Annie Bridges, age 81, Farmington, Missouri.

"I's born on March 6, 1855; on Wolf Crick, in St. Francois County. My muthuh, Clausa McFarland Bridges, wuz borned on Wolf Crick too, but mah fauthar, Jerry Bridges, kum from Californie. William McFarland wuz our boss, and he had a lotta' slaves. Us liv'd in a log cabin, with two rooms. Yep, there wuz a floor an' we had a bed, but hit hadn't no mattress; jus' roped an' cord'd. Holes wuz in de side ob de bed, soo's de ropes cud go thru'. We all wore 'jeans' an' wrap'd an' ole sack 'round our legs; most time we went barefoot. We al's used catnip tea ta cure mos' ever'thing. Our boss wuz purty good ta us, but we larned dat ole M.P. Cayce, he wuz a slaveholder, wud beat 'Hunter' Cayce, an' ole 'nigger' man, every Monday mornin' 'til his back bled. Den he tuk salt an' put hit in de gashes. My brudders war, Alvin, Jerry, Rubin, Louis, an' Nat. Ma sista' Mary, she went to Rolla an' married. Me an' ma bruvver Jerry air de only ones a-livin'.

"I married Overdie Southerland wen I wuz 26 years ole. Abe Koen married us, but we are not a-livin' togeth'r now. I never had no childr'n by him. Ma furst job wuz with Dr. Jim Braham fur one year, an' nine months. I got $2.50 a week. I did all de housework thar.

"After de war wuz over my muthuh went to Pilot Knob to wurk in a hotel. Me, an' my muthuh went hup on Pilot

Knob, berry huntin', one day, an' we seen de leg ob a man an' his ankle bone wuz stickin' in his shoe. Thar warn't any flesh on de leg. Hit wuz near de ole Fort (Fort Davidson)." (Note: This must have been a portion of a soldier, from the Battle of Pilot Knob!)

"Ma muthuh tole' me dat dey used ta sell de little childr'n away fum de breasts ob der muthuh's. Ma muthuh plow'd in de fiel' an' wud leave her baby layin' at one end ob de fiel', while she plow'd clear ta de odder end an' kum back. She know'd a man who had a child by one ob his slaves an' den sole de chil' as a slave. Wasn't dat turrible, sellin' his own son?

"De young folks calls us 'ole fogies', but we knew how ta act, an' lots ob de young-un's don't know dat now. When I wuz growin' hup we had company an' would hav' ta wait 'til de ol' folks wuz thru' eatin' 'fore we cud eat. Sum' ob my muthuh's friens' kum one day with their 'redique'; ([TR: reticule] bags which held knitting and sewing, and were tied with a draw-string, at the top.) "They war eatin' an' I wuz sittin' on a ladder dat led hup to de attic. I come down de ladder and wuz sittin' near de bottom an' dese grown people's was eatin', den dey lean back ta rest a-while, den eat a little more, an' res' a-while. I had ta sit dare an' watch dem. After a-while I says: 'My time now'. Well, jus' for dat, my muthuh give me one ob de worse whippin's dat I ever had. Sometimes I had ta stan' in de closet, or stan' on de floor an' hol' one foot, when I wuz punished.

"Ma muthuh's stepfather wuz poisen'd in whiskey. His name wuz 'Charlie Gipson'. Onc't a man held hup a bottle an' said: 'I'm drinkin' de poisen off'. But he wuz puttin' de pois'n in. After dat, Charlie Gipson drank de whiskey out ob de bottle an' in nine months he wuz daid.

"Simon cud call de snakes an' dey wud kum frum all directions. He wud tak' de skins ob dese snakes an' put dem on de roof ob de shed, an' den when dey wuz dry, he wud mak' powder out ob dem an' 'hoodoo' people.

"We all went tuh a pahty one time an' Scot Cole's sistah et a big apple thar. After a little while, she died. So's ma muthuh tole us to not eat anythin' dat people give you; hit might be poisen'd.

"I'se been tole dat if people dies satisfied, dey don' kum bak, but if dey don' dies satisfied, dey kum back. But I never seed nothin'."

(One of the religious songs used to be):

> "Jesus in his chariot rides
> He had three white horses side by side
> When Jesus reached the mountain top
> He spoke one word, the chariot stop
> He's the lily of the valley, O my Lord."

(Following, is a 'Love Song' she sang; which she learned as a girl when attending play-parties):

> "I'm wandering down to Graybrook Town,
> Where the drums and fifes are beating
> The Americans have gained the day
> And the British are retreating.
>
> My pretty little pink,
> I used to think that you and I would marry,
> But since you told me so many faults
> I care nothing about you.

I'll take my knapsack on my back
My rifle on my shoulder
I'll open up a ring and choose a couple in
To relieve the broken hearted."

(Following is a song she learned as a child):
"I'll tune up my fiddle
I'll rosin my bow
I'll make myself welcome
Wherever I go

Rye whiskey, rye whiskey,
Ain't no friend of mine,
He killed my old daddy
And he injured my mind."

(Following is a song she learned as a child):
"Rain, rain, rain all around
Ain't goin' rain no more
And what did the blackbird say to the crow?
You bring rain, and I'll bring snow

Rain, rain, rain all around
Ain't goin' a-rain no more
Old Hawk and buzzard went to roost
The hawk came back with a loosened tooth.

Rain, rain, rain all around
Ain't goin' a-rain no more
I had an old hat and it had a crown,
Look like a duck's nest sittin' on the ground.

Rain, rain, rain all around,
Ain't goin' a-rain no more."

(Following is a speech she gave as a small child) [HR: Not ex-slave]:

"I love the cheerful summertime,
With all the birds and flowers.
I love the gentle flowing streams,
I love the evening breeze,
I love to go to school.

To read, write and spell
I love my teacher's smile again
And get my lessons well."

(Following is a speech given as a child) [HR: not ex-slave—white version]:

"Hear the children gayly shout
Half past four, school is out
Merry, merry, playful girls and boys
Thinking of games and toys
Slates, sleds, dolls and books
Oh how happy each one looks
'Now for snowballs', Harry cried
And to hit his sister tried
Sister Flora full of fun
With her little hand making one
At her brother Harry threw
Swift it flew and hit his nose
'Have I hurt you brother dear?'
Asked his sister running near
'No indeed', said he
'This is only sport for me.'"

(Following is a familiar prayer when she was a child) [HR: not ex-slave]:

"Savior, tender shepherd hear me

Bless the little lambs tonight
Through the darkness be they nearest
Watch my sleep 'til morning light
Bless the friends I love so well
Take me when I die to heaven
Happy there with thee to dwell."

(Following is a very familiar song:)
"'Dear mother,' said a little fish
'Pray, is this naughty fly
I am very hungry and I wish
You would let me go and try.'

'Sweet innocence', the mother cried,
And started from her nook,
'The hurried fly is but to hide
The sharpness of the hook'.

So he thought he'd venture out
To see if it was true
Around about the hook he played
With many a long look.

'Dear me', to himself he said
'I'm sure it's not a hook'
So as he fainter, fainter grew
With hallowed voice, he cried,
'If I had minded you
I would not then have died'."

Following are some old riddles, they may be of no value.

Riddle—'I rode over the bridge, and yet I walked.'
Answer—'Yet I' was the name of the dog

with me.

Riddle—'Big at the bottom
Little at the top,
Something in the middle
Goes flippity flop.'
Answer—Churn.

Riddle—'Way down yonder in the meadow is a little red heifer.
Give'r her some hay she will eat it.
Give'r her some water she will die.'
Answer—Fire.

Riddle—'I went over Hefil Steeple
Then I met a heap of people
Some were k-nick
Some were k-nack
Some were the color of brown tobacco
They were neither men, women, nor children.'
Answer—Bees.

(Note:—Annie Bridges is quite a character. When giving her speeches and singing her songs she dramatizes them while walking across the room. She is hard of hearing and can be heard for quite a distance. She receives an old-age pension. She is considered by many, a sort of nuisance around town, since she is always begging for something. Some are afraid of her.)

(Following is a song of Abraham Lincoln she sang):
"If it hadn't been for Uncle Abraham

What would we a'done?

Been down in de cotton field,
Pickin' in de sun."

BETTY BROWN

Interview with Betty Brown,
Cape Girardeau Co., Missouri.

"In de ole days we live in Arkansas, in Greene County. My mammy wuz Mary-Ann Millan, an' we belong to 'Massa' John Nutt, an' 'Miss' Nancy.'

"Our white folks live in a big double house, wid a open hall between. It wuz built of hewed logs an' had a big po'ch on de wes' side. De house stood on Cash rivuh, at the crossroads of three roads; one road go tuh Pocahontas, one tuh Jonesburg, an' one tuh Pie-Hatten (Powhatan).

"Now whut fo' you wanna' know all dem things? Air ye tryin' to raise de daid? Some o' 'em, ah don' wanna see no mo', an' some o' 'em ah wants to stay whar dey is. Pore mammy! Ah shore had one sweet muthuh, an' ah wants huh to stay at rest.

"De wuz jus' us one family o' cullud folks on de place. You see, 'Miss' Nancy' hired us fum her fathuh, 'Ole Massa Hanover. Jes' mah mammy an' huh chillern. She had five, 'fore de war wuz ovuh. Our daddy; he wuz an Irishman, name Millan, an' he had de bigges' still in all Arkansas. Yes'm, he had a white wife, an' five chillern at home, but mah mammy say he like huh an' she like him. You say ah don' look half white? Maybe I's fadin'.

"We live in a little ole log house, it wuz so low a big

feller had to stoop to git in. Our folks wus mighty good tuh us, an' we stayed dar wid 'um after we's freed.

"Ah don' rightly know how old ah is, but de priest writ' it all down fo' me, when ah's gittin' mah pension. Sho' ah's a Catholic. Is they anything else? Fo' fifteen year ah tended de Catholic church, swept an' dusted, an' cleaned, but ah's too ole fo' dat now, an' ah's po'ly in mah back, cain't git 'round like dat no mo'.

"We lived de ole-time way of livin', mammy done de cookin an' we had plenty good things to eat. Mammy made all de clothes, spinnin', an' weavin' an' sewin'. Ah larned to spin when ah wuz too little tuh reach de broach, an' ah could hep her thread de loom. An' mammy wuz a shoe-maker, she'd make moccasins for all o' us.

"Two o' the Nutt boys made shoes too, heavy, big ones dey wuz; but dey kep' our feet warm in winter.

"An' dey had a tan hand. Ah uste wade barefooted in dem pits an' work wid dem hides, but ah wouldn't wanna do it now.

"Dey wuz a grove o' post-oak timber, 'bout five, or six acres, all cleaned out; an' in der, dey raised bear cubs. Why, dey raised 'em tuh eat. Lawd! dat's good eatin'. Jes' gimme s' bear meat an' den let me go tuh sleep! M-m-m!

"They wuz fruit trees planted all 'long de road, planted jes' like fence-posts for 'bout a mile, an' all de fruit dat fell in de road de hogs got, we'ens could go get any of it, any time, an' travelers, 'long de road, was a'way's welcome ter hep dey selves. 'Massa' nevuh planted no shade trees. Iffen trees wuz planted dey had to be fruit trees. 'Ceptin' de holly bush, he like dat 'cause it's green in winter.

"They wuz some flowers 'round de house. Snowballs, batchelor-buttons, old-maids; jes' such old-fashion ones, no roses, n'er nuthin' like dat.

"Massa' raise some cotton, but 'Ole Massa' Hanover had sech a big cotton patch yuh couldn't look across it. An' dey all kind'a fowls yu'd find any where's, guinie's, ducks, n' geese, n' turkey's, n' peafowl's, an' lotsa chicken's a' 'cose.

"My mamma could hunt good ez any man. Us'tuh be a coup'la pedluh men come 'round wuth they packs. My mammy'd a'ways have a pile o' hides tuh trade with 'em fer calico prints n' trinkets, n' sech-like, but mos'ly fo' calico prints. She'd have coon hides n' deer n' mink, n' beavers, lawd! I kin still hear dem beavers splashin' 'round dat dam. Dis time 'er marning' dey's a'way's shore busy. An' folks in cities goes tuh pawks now to see sech animal. Hun! Ah seen all 'em things ah wants tuh see.

"Good Lawd! We didden' know whut church wuz n'er school nuther, an' the whites nevuh nuther. Dey wuz a couple o' men us'ta come by, an' hole a camp meetin'. Dey'd build a big arbuh, with branches o' leaves over de top, an' build benches; dey'd come aftuh crops wuz laid by, an' preach 'til cotton wuz openin'. Ah never know'd whut sect dey belong to, n'er whar dey go, n'er what dey come fum 'nuther.

"Yes'm, we seed sojers, an' we seed lot's o' 'em. Dah wuz de 'blue-coats'; some o' de folks call'em Bluebelly

Yank's, dey had fine blue coats an' the brass buttons all ovuh the front o' 'em shinin' like stahs. Dey call us little cullud folks', 'cubs', an' dey burn down Jonesburg. Yes'm we seed Jonesburg down in ashes. Dem 'blue-coats' wuz devils, but de 'gray-coats' wuz wusser. Dey turn over our bee-gums an' dey kill our steers, an' carry off our provisions, an' whut dey couldn't carry off dey ruint. Den dey go roun' killin' all de cullud men an' bayanettin' de chillern.

"No, dat wuzzen' de 'gray-coats' doin' de killin', dat wuz 'bushwackers' an' 'Ku Klux'ers', dey sho' wuz bad. Dey shot my little sistuh in back of her neck an' day shot me in de laig. See dat scar, dat whar dey shoot me. An' dey kill my gran'fathuh; dey sho' did.

"Gran'fathuh's name wuz 'Jim Hanover'. 'Ole Massa Hanover', he wuz a lawyer, an' he educated mah gran'fathuh tuh be a overseuh. He lived wid' 'Massa Hanover' for long time. He wuz a good man, mah gran'fathuh wuz, an' he wuz smart too, an' when de war surrenduh, dey make him Mayor of Pie-hatten, an' he made a good mayor too; people all said so, an' dey wuz gonna 'lect him fo' foe mo' year, an' de 'Ku Klux'ers said dey wuzzen' gonna have no 'nigguh' mayor. So dey tuk him out an' killed him. Dey wuz awful times. Now you know dat wuzzen right an' who's de curse fo' such things gonna rest on?

"Ah disemembuh jes' when we come tuh Missouri, but it wuz when 'Hayes'[1], an' 'Wheeler' wuz 'lected President. Down in Arkansas dey say dey gonna make us all vote Democrat. My step-daddy say he die 'fore he vote Democrat.

[¹] *HR: Rutherford B. Hayes, 19th president, 1877-81.*

"Der wuz two white men say dey'd get us to Cape Girda. Dey had two covered wagons, an' dey wuz forty-eight o' us cullud folks. We put our belongin's in de wagon. Dey wuz a coupl'a ole gramma's rode in de wagons, an' some little feller's, but de rest of us walk ever step o' de way. An' it rained on us ever' step o' de way. At night we'd lay down to sleep unduh de wagon so tired we nevuh even know'd it wuz rainin'.

"When we got to St. Francis Rivuh dey ferried us across on a big flat, an' had a rope tied across da rivuh to pull us ovuh. But we had to ford White Watuh, an Castuh rivuh, an' Niggerwool swamp. When we'd come to de rivuh de white man 'ud say: 'Ack like sojers'. De hosses 'ud swim across, pullin' de wagon, some o' de big folks 'ud grab hole' de feed box an' de rest 'ud each grab roun' de one in front an' dat way we fords de rivuhs, wid strings a' folk hangin' out behin' de wagons.

"Hoo-doos', ghosts's er signs? No mam! Ah don' believe in none of dat. Now you is tryin' to call up de devil. But wait! Ah kin tell you one sign dat ah knows is true. If de dog jes' lays outside de do' sleepin' an' has his haid inside de do', you's gonna git a new member in de family befo' de year is out. An' jes' de othuh way roun'. Ef de dog lays sleepin' inside de do' an' has his haid hangin' out, you's gwine a lose a 'membuh o' yuh family fo' de end a' de yeah.

"Dey wuz sumpin' funny happen when ma little girl die sometime ago. She wuz a sweet chile. She wuz stayin' wuth Miss' English on Henderson Ave., an' she lost her mind. Ah don' know whut's a matter wuth her, but ah brung her home to take keer o' her, but she don' get no bettuh. One day she's standin', lookin' out de front do' an' she holler: 'Heah dey's comin' aftuh me'. Ah don' know what she see, but she run to de back room an' stan' right dere.

"Her daddy an' me look at huh an' dar wuz a big ball o' fire hangin' ovuh her haid. We picked huh up, an' put huh to bed. We sent fo' de doctah an' fo' de priest, an' we got de nurse 'at we had when she fust took sick. I nevuh knowed whut wuz de mattuh with her. De priest wouldn't tell me, de doctuh wouldn't tell me, an' ah guess de nurse was ez green about it ez ah wuz. Some folks tell me she wuz conjured. Mah po' little girl".

STEVE BROWN

Interview with Steve Brown,
Cape Girardeau, Mo.

"Mista Joe Medley and his wife, Miss Addie was my young master and mistress. Old master John Medley done brung us from Kentucky when he moved from there to Cape County. I was jest a baby den. I never knowed nothin' 'bout my daddy.

"De white folks had a big log-house. It was an awful big house, with a big porch on de north side. They was some cedar trees in de yard and some fruit trees. Dey was a big log barn and split rail fences all around. Us little fellers had to help carry in de wood, and help do de feeding. Dey had lots of hosses, cows, and pigs.

"Dey was a separate house for de spinning and weaving. Cose all our clothes and shoes too, was made on de place. Massa was mighty good to his cullud folks. He never 'lowed none of 'em to be sold and I don't recollect ever seeing anyone getting whupped. No, we never had no gatherin's nor schools, nor nuthing of the kind.

"Massa had a fine big carriage and one Sunday he'd take all de white folks to church and de next Sunday, he put de cullud folks in de carriage and send dem to church. Dat's how come us to be Catholics. We come all de way to Cape, to St. Vincent's Church, down by de river. We lived away off dere in de backwoods and we didn't see much of sojers—jes' a few scattered ones come by after de skirmish at de Cape. When de war ended, we moved to de Cape and work on de college farm.

"When I's little de mostest fun we had was going fishing—we spent most of our time down dar by de branch and I guess de big folks was glad to have us out of de way."

Steve Brown lives at the end of Elm Street, Cape Girardeau.

RICHARD BRUNER

**Interview with Richard Bruner,
Negro preacher, Nelson, Missouri.**

The subject of this sketch, Richard Bruner, is one of the oldest negroes in Saline County. He claims to be ninety-seven years old and lives in the little town of Nelson.

His humble dwelling, a gray and weathered frame building of about four rooms and two porches, sets in a square of yard thick with blue grass, old fashioned flowers like holly hocks, flowering pinks and marigolds making bright spots of color. Heavily laden fruit trees, apples, peaches, plums and pears shade every part of the plot. A splendid walnut tree towers over the smaller fruit trees, the house and the porch, while at the side of the house a garden spot contains a fine variety of vegetables.

As the writer approached, the old man was seated on a cot on the little porch. The wall back of him was hung with all kinds of tools, a saw, a hammer, bits of wire, a piece of rope, part of a bridle, and a wing, apparently from a big gray goose. His long curling, gray hair is neatly parted and brushed and he wears a mustache and short beard or chin whiskers, an unusual thing among negroes in this part of the country. His skin is a light brown color and his eyes bright with his second eyesight which enables him to look on the world without glasses.

Back of the house and down the hill, is a well equipped

slaughter house, where for many years this old man has taken care of the butchering of the meat for his white friends and neighbors. He is too old now to take charge of this work, but the house and equipment is still in good repair.

This aged Negro has been for many years a highly respected preacher of the gospel. His own account of his life and adventures follows:

"Yes'm I remembers before de war, I remember being a water-boy to de field hands before I were big enough to work in de fields. I hoed tobaccer when I was about so high, (measuring with his hands about three and one half feet from the floor).

"Yes'm dey thrashed me once, made me hug a tree and whip me, I had a terrible temper, I'm part Choctaw Indian. We went to de white folks church on Sundays, when we went to camp meeting we all went to de mourners' bench together. De mourners' bench stretch clear across de front of de Arbor; de whites and de blacks, we all just fell down at de mourners' bench and got religion at de same place. Ole Marsa let us joine whichever church we wanted, either de Methodist or Baptist.

"No, I never went to no school, de colonel's daughter larnt me to write my name, that was after de wah. No'm, dey didn't care if we had dances and frolics. We had de dances down at de quarters and de white folks would come down and look on. Whenever us niggas on one plantation got obstreperous, white folks hawns dey blowed. When de neighbors heard dat hawn here dey come to help make dat obstreperous nigga behave. Dey blowed de hawn to call de neighbors if anybody died or were sick."

In response to the question as to where he joined the Federal Army, Bruner replied:

"Well you see I was a runaway nigga; I run away when I was about grown and went to Kansas. When de war broke out I joined de 18th United States Colored Infantry, under Capt. Lucas. I fit three years in de army. My old Marsa's two boys just older than me fit for de south. Dey was mighty good boys, I liked dem fine."

United States. Work Projects Administration

ROBERT BRYANT

Interview with Robert Bryant,
Herculaneum, Missouri.

Slave Married 4 Times

"I was born out by Caledonia and is 75 years old. My mother came from another family. My old master bought her from another man. She died when I was about eight years old and my father died about forty years ago. His name was George Bryant but he went by de name of Brock. I was livin' in Pilot Knob when Price's raid come through. De government gave de old man a team to make it to St. Louis. Me and my mother and my brother who was deaf and dumb went with dem but de soldiers captured us and de old man jumped off de mule and high tailed it to de woods. My mother got out of de wagon and took my brother to de woods too. De soldier rid up to de wagon and said, 'Little boy, you don't need to be afraid, I'm after your father.'

"I started to get out of de wagon and fell down under de mule and dere I was on de ground. I got up and made for de woods and got in a hole where de hogs was a-wallerin'. I had on a dress and was standin' in de mud up to my knees. I got lost out in de woods for three days. I just laid around and slept behind a log at night and durin' de day I played in dat mud-hole. If I see'd somebody comin' in de woods I would go and hide.

"A colored lady found me after three days and called

me and took me along. I stayed with her three weeks before my mother found me. I like to eat up everything dey had when I first got something to eat after bein' in de woods so long. We went from one place to another and along about two o'clock in de night you would hear something hit de house like hail. Den we had to come out of dere and hit for de woods. We would go to another house 'bout eight or nine miles away and I'll be switched if dere would not be hail fallin' on dat house about two o'clock in de mornin'. It was them bushwhackers again. We kept runnin' for about three weeks. We would go to peoples' houses for food and some of dem would give us enough food to eat for two or three days.

"I'll show you now how my mother happened to find me. One night we was in a old house and we didn't dare talk loud 'cause we was afraid de soldiers would hear us. We was afraid to light a light. All at once my mother who was in one side of de room said: 'I wish I could find my little boy.' Den de lady I was with said: 'I found a little boy playin' in de hole where de hogs wallowed. Come over here and see if dis is your boy.' So my mother come over and said: 'I can't see him but I sure can tell by puttin' my hand on his head.' So she put her hand on my head and said: 'Yes, dat's sure 'nough my boy.'

"But I wouldn't go with her. I wouldn't leave dat other woman. About 2 o'clock dat night de hail began to hit de house and we had to git out. So I went with de other woman and it was about two or three days before I would go with my mother. Two or three days later we all met again and my mother said: 'Don't you know your mother.' I knowed it was my mother 'cause my brother what was deaf and dumb was with her. Den I went on with her. I would talk to my brother with signs.

"Den we went to a little place away, away from Pilot Knob. Den my mother was free and she said, 'Robert, we is all free.' I was too young to know anything 'bout it. After we was free we put in a little stuff in de ground. We had to go to de woods to get some brush and make a brush fence around de garden to keep de cattle out. We got permission from a man dat owned a farm to build our own log house. It took two or three days to build a one room house. We made up some mud with water and made it stiff enough to stick to de chinckin'. Den we cut a big hole in one end of de building and got some flat rocks and made a fireplace. We put mud on de inside and outside of de chimney. Sometimes de chimney would catch on fire and we had to run to de branch to get water and put it out. Sometimes it would catch on fire twice or three times in one night.

"We took old gunny sacks and put leaves in dem to make a bed and we slept on de floor and had a old spread and de white folks gave us some old quilts. To make a fire we got some spunk out of a log and then took two flint rocks and to-reckly it would make a spark and catch that spunk. We banked de fire at night.

"We never had no doctor. My mother would go out in de woods and get herbs and if I had de stomach ache we would put a little bit of turpentine on a piece of sugar. If I had de headache we would put a piece of brown paper and vinegar or horse radish leaves on de head. In two or three hours us kids would be out playin' and kickin' up our heels. We would go out and get some goose grass and make a little bit of tea and pour it down for de stomach ache. We would get dis black root for constipation. We used a turnip and scraped it and would bind de foot when it was frost bit.

"I'se been married four times and had children by two wifes, had eight children altogether and all are girls but two. Ain't but one living and dat is Ed McFadden what's livin' in Fredericktown, Mo. He works for Deguire at de lumber mill and has been workin' dere for about 30 years. Most of my children died young, but three girls lived to get married. I'se married three times by a preacher and once by de squire.

"I steamboated six years on de Mississippi between St. Paul and New Orleans. I got $1 a day and board, and we sure would pack dem sacks and sing dem songs. De old mate would holler at us: 'Give me a song boys'. And den we would start out. It 'peared like de work went ahead easier when we was singin'. It would take us four weeks to make de rounds before we got back to St. Louis. We hauled potatoes, sheep, wheat, corn, cattle, horses, and cotton. There was 45 of us altogether. I never got hit but one time on de boat. De mate with knucks on hit at another feller for 'cause he was loafin' and hit me and knocked me and my load in de river. I couldn't swim but dey fished me back in de boat and rolled me over and over to run dat water out of me. I run on de 'Bald Eagle' and de 'Spread Eagle'. My mamma got after me to quit and when I got hit she got uneasy about me, but I would hear dat whistle blowin' my feet'd begin to itch and I could not help but go down to de old boat again. De old mate had my name 'doubled up'. It was Bob Rob.

"Den I went to wheelin' iron ore at Sulphur Springs. All day long I worked with 16 men loading barges with wheel barrows. Every time you took a load it had 800 pounds, and I'se telling you all, dat's some iron. This iron ore came from dat big hill down in Pilot Knob. We had straps over our shoulders and dey saved our hands and arms. It took about a day and a half to load a barge and we got paid by de ton. I did dat for about a year.

"I give my wife all my money and all de time she was givin' it away to another man. So dat was when I left her flat and went down to Charleston, Cairo, and Kentucky and stayed three years. I was workin' in de tobacco for three years. Dere was too much stoopin' in dat and I decided to come back to St. Louis. We only got $12 a month in de tobacco fields and worked from 4 o'clock in de morning to 8 or 9 o'clock in de night time. Dere was 9 or 10 in de tobacco field.

"Den I worked in de iron foundry in a St. Louis furnace. I carried iron and hustled in de casting hole. Dey paid pretty good and we got $1.50 to $1.75 a day. I worked up dere two years and den come to Sulphur Springs and went on de farm and got $26 a month. I got to be a trusty and dey put it in my hands. I worked here five years for old Mike Green. I was single den. I went down on John Coffman's farm in Ste. Genevieve County to work for him. Worked on his farm for 'bout 15 years and got $26 a month and board. He had a gang of 'em working for him. He had rows of cabins 'most a mile long. Dat was where I got married a second time.

"After I left dere I went down below Fredericktown and went on a farm again and stayed right dere for seven years. I lost my wife at dat place and sold my land. I paid $90 for 40 acres dere and had paid 'bout half on it. So I sold it back to de man what I bought it from for $45 and went to Bonne Terre and worked for de St. Joe Lead Co. and worked on de lead well and den went to tappin'. I got $1.60 for 12 hours. I worked dere until dey moved de works up here and den I followed de works right up here. Den I worked 'bout 30 years here doing de same kind of work with the same pay.

"When I quit workin' here it was about 13 years ago and I was about 62 years old. De company just laid me off on account of age. Den de supervisor dere got me a job as janitor at de colored school here at $7.00 a month. I've been janitor ever since. Dere is ten colored families in Herculaneum, and about 50 colored people here now but dere used to be mostly all colored but most of 'em done left. I lived here in dis house a little more dan 5 years without payin' rent. Den after my son got on the WPA dey begins to take $3.85 rent a month. We been payin' rent 'bout two years. The St. Joe Company owns all de houses here. We gets our water free. I'se been gettin' a pension about a year now.

"I shot a fellow once in de leg. It was de man who my wife was givin' my money to. I had a trial at Kimmswick before de Justice of Peace and served three months in de county jail at Hillsboro. The white folks come down and got me out and it didn't cost me a thing.

"A man has got more his own say now dan he did have. We can do more what we want to and don't have to go to de other fellow. Slavery might a done de other fellow some good but I don't think it ever done de colored people no good. Some of dem after freedom didn't know how to go out and work for demselves. Down at old John Coffman's lots of dem stayed with him right along same as if dey wasn't free. Dey didn't want to leave here 'cause dey didn't think dey could live if dey left him. But when dey got away up here in St. Louis dey know they can make a livin', without Marse John, but they got to 'go up against it.' Dependin' on somebody else is poor business. When I was workin' I depended on myself. If dey would have freed de slaves and give dem a piece of ground I think dat would been a heap better dan de way dey did. Look at de Indians! They're all livin'. I'se always been able to eat and sleep.

"I can't hardly tell about de younger generation, I can say dat if it was not for de old generation today de young ones would go up 'salt creek'. Dey don't want to work. Some of dem is pretty smart. Pride is de reason dey don't want to work. Dey dress up and strut out and have a good time. De old folks is de cause of it. Dey say, 'I don't want my boy to do dat; I don't want him to work hard'. I say, let him make out de same as us old folks did. If de colored people don't pick up and see about business dey is going to be behind. Dese young people won't go to church. You can't get dem in dere. Dat's de place dey ought to go. I'se been goin' to church since I was a boy. Colored folks did not raise me. White folks learned me to go to church. Mrs. Baker, at Cook's Settlement, would read de Bible every night at 9 o'clock and she would 'splain it to me. If she was not able, her daughter read it. We need a workhouse for de young people.

"De first time I ever cast my vote was for Garfield who got killed. It was in Kimmswick. Been votin' ever since, and vote all through dem all. I'se been talked to lots of times, tellin' me how to vote. Dey even give me a ballot and show me how to vote. I would stick dat in my pocket and vote like I pleased. I ain't never sold my vote but I'se been offered $10 for it. But I say if you is goin' to get beat, I say you is just beat. You ain't no man to go over there and cast your vote. You got to stand for your point.

"De first automobile I ever seen had buggy wheels. It made a terrible racket. Mrs. Baker told me dat people was goin' sometime to be ridin' in automobiles and in de air."

ALEX BUFFORD

> Interview with Alex Bufford,
> St. Joseph, Missouri,
> by Carl B. Boyer, St. Joseph,
> Buchanan County, Mo.

The wonderful meteoric display known as the "star shower" or "the time when the stars fell," occured in 1833. It was on the night of the 12th and 13th of November. Many ignorant persons concluded that the Judgement day had come, or that the end of the world was at hand. Negroes especially were very much frightened. A dance was in progress on a Buchanan County farm, attended exclusively by slaves from the neighborhood. When the star shower began the negroes were first made aware of the fact by a messenger who ran frantically into the cabin and shouted, "If you all wants to git to hebin, you'd better 'gin to say yo' pra'rs mighty sudden, 'cause the Lawd is a-comin' wi' de fire an' de glory an' de wuld'll be burnt up like a cracklin' 'fo mo'nin."

The dancers ran out, fell on their knees and cried for mercy. Not for many days did they recover from their fright. One old negro declared that if the world and his life were spared he would agree to break eighty pounds of hemp every day instead of fifty, as he had been accustomed to do.

The Negro was a part of the early Buchanan County family. They were black slaves and happy.

The negro Mammy had her proper place in the

scheme of things. She was no fiction of a later day novelist, but genuine, gentle, untiring, and faithful. The Negro mammy merits a prominent place in the picture an artist might paint, for on her broad shoulders was carried the generation which made the early history of Missouri fascinating and great.

When once a week came "Johnny Seldom"—as the hot biscuits made of wheat flour were called in Old Missouri—all other kinds of bread faded into nothingness. Two kinds of biscuits were typically Missourian—the large, fluffy, high biscuits—which looked like an undersized sofa pillow—and beaten biscuits, small, crisp, delicious—the grandfather of all afternoon tea refreshments. No "Po' white trash" can make beaten biscuits. Indeed, much of the finest flavor of all cookery belonged intuitively to the Negro. How the Negro cook managed to get biscuits steaming hot from the cookroom a quarter of a mile distant through the open yard to the dining room table has always been a mystery. She did it, however, and successfully.

Mr. Alex Bufford, an ex-slave, lives at 1823 Seneca street, St. Joseph, Missouri. Mr Bufford, (everyone calls him Uncle Alex) does not know how old he is, but says he does remember that he was a grown man at the time of the Civil War.

I heard about Uncle Alex from one of the ladies in the reference room at the Public Library in St. Joseph, Mo. She told me I would have to see Uncle Alex right at the noon hour or in the evening, as he would be at work during working hours. I didn't ask her what kind of work he did but I heeded her advice about seeing him at the noon hour. I arrived at his place about 11:50 A.M. As I got out of my car I happened to look up the alley. An old Negro driving a one-horse wagon was just entering it. I guessed in a minute that this was the old gentleman I wanted to see. When he approached I did not tell him at first what I wanted but started talking about the weather. I saw in a minute the old fellow was going to be interesting to talk to.

After we had commented about the weather, I told him what I wanted. Uncle Alex, "Ya sir, I'll be bery glad to tell you anything I kin recollect, but I don't remember like I used to." He said, "I don't know how ole I am, but I was a grown man at the time of de war and I guess I'se de oldest man in de city. I was born in Buchanan County and have libed here all my life. I only been out de state once in my life and dat wuz ober to Elwood seberal years ago. (Elwood, Kansas is only about 2 miles west of St. Joseph.) I'se just don't keer to go any place."

To my question about his family he replied. "Ya sir, I hab four daughters and one son libing, but da don't help dis ole man any. Until I got de ole age pension seberal months ago, I had a terbil time making a libing."

Uncle Alex and his brother who is younger than he, live together. The brother is an old man more feeble than Uncle Alex.

After the War Uncle Alex worked on the farm for the Conetts, near Faucett, Mo. in Buchanan County for several years. Then he moved to town and worked for the same people in their brickyard until just a few years ago.

The house Uncle Alex lives in now belongs to the people he worked for so long. He lives there rent free.

United States. Work Projects Administration

HARRIET CASEY

**Interview with Harriet Casey,
aged 75, Fredericktown, Missouri.
Interviewed by J. Tom Miles.**

"I've lived here 'bout 65 years. I was born in slavery on de Hill place in Farmington. My mother's name was Catherine. Father's name was George. A brother and sistah of mine was sold as slaves 'fore I was born. I nevah saw them. My father was sold away from my mother. Our home was not pleasant. The mistress was cruel. Her brother would go down in de orchard and cut de sprouts and pile 'em up under de house so as de mistress could use 'em on us. She also used a bed stick to whip with.

"One day we took de cows to pasture and on de way home I stopped to visit Mrs. Walker and she gave me a goose egg. And den when we got home de old mistress kicked me and stomped on us and broke my goose egg. Did'n mind de whipping but sure hated to break my egg.

"Our cabin was one room, one door and one fire place. Our mistress was a rich woman, and she had three husbands. She had a big square smoke house full of hog, beef, deer, all pickled away. She had 12 cows and lots of butter and a spring-house.

"To eat we had corn meal and fried meat dat had been eaten by bugs. We had some gravy and all ate 'round de pans like pigs eating slop. And we had a tin cup of sour milk to drink. Sometimes we would have gingerbread. Dis was 'bout twice a year.

"My brother dat was a slave ran off with four or five other boys and never come back. He went west and died in Honolulu. They had a 'niggerbreaker' in Farmington who would take care of de slaves who were hard to handle.

"Once it got so cold dat de chickens froze and fell out of the trees and de mistress gave each of us a chicken to eat. We had no shoes even in winter. I can't 'member having good clothes.

"One of our neighbors, Mr. McMullin, was a poor white but he had a heart and was our mistress' guardian. I was too little to do much but I would walk along de furrows and hit de oxen with a stick. My sistah come and got me after freedom and learned me de alphabet. De first thing I ever learned to read was, 'I see you Tom. Do you see me?' I worked for intelligent people and learned a great deal. After I married I wanted to learn a great deal and how to read. At de camp in Mine La Motte I went to school in a log house for 'bout two months.

"Dey would whip with a cat-o'-nine-tails and den mop de sores with salt water to make it sting. De traders would come through and buy up slaves in groups like stock. On de way south dey would have regular stopping places like pens and coops for de slaves to stay in; at each of these stoppin' places some of de slaves would be sold. My uncle's father was his master and de master sold my uncle who was his own son.

"When my mother died I did not know what a coffin was or what death was. So I went to my dead mother where she was on de cooling board and brushed my dress and said, 'Look at my pretty dress.'

"There was a tough gang called patrollers. Dey would scare de Negroes and would keep dem always afraid. De mistress would take a couple of us young ones to church but when we got home things were different.

"And I never seen so many soldiers in my life before or since than when Price come through on his raid. It was apple pickin' time and de mistress made us gather apples and pack 'em to the soldiers and we had to pack water from de spring to 'em. De mistress had pickets out in front of de house when de soldiers was in town.

"Once when de Union soldiers was in town a negro soldier come and got him a turkey off de fence. De next night a white soldier come to get a turkey and he looked all over de place and come up over de stile. Den de mistress goes out on de porch and called de dogs and said, 'Sic the rogue'. De soldier took out his pistol and laid it on de fence and waited awhile and looked. De dogs were jumping up against de fence. So de soldier shot de dog and then went off and got on his hoss again.

"One day a Union officer come up and had a saber and said he would cut off de mistress' head. De officer was a Dutchman. The mistress then ran to town for help. De soldier came right in de cabin and said, 'Me no hurt you.' De soldier went in de safe in de house and ate all he wanted and den went to bed in de house. Finally de law come and moved him out of de bed off de place. De soldiers would come at night and rout de slave women out of bed and make 'em cook de soldiers a square meal."

United States. Work Projects Administration

JOE CASEY

Interview with Joe Casey,
Festus, Missouri.

Sold Slave, Ill Luck Followed

"I did not get to see my daddy long. He served in de first of de war and come home sick and died at Cadet. I was born at Cadet. I lives here in Festus and am 90 years old. My mother was Arzella Casey and was a slave in Cadet. Tom Casey owned both my mother and father. De master had a pretty good farm and dat was where I worked when I was a boy. Mr. Casey never hit me a lick in my life. He was sure good to us. I had an uncle John and dey had to sell him 'cause dey could not do anything with him. Dey took him to Potosi before dey sold him. He did not want to be drove. Mr. Casey said if he had 100 niggers he would never sell another one. He said he never had any more good luck since he sold John. Losing his children was his bad luck.

"Before freedom we had our own house and stayed here after freedom. My master said, 'Well, Joe you are your own boss.' I said: 'How come?' He said: 'I'll help you.' Dey would not turn us out without a show. We stayed dere free and I went out in de diggin's in de tiff at Valle Mines. Some days I made $5 and den some days made $2. White folks would come and get ma and she would go to help kill hogs and clean up de lard. Dey paid her good. We must have stayed about 3 years at Casey's after de freedom and den went to Mineral Point and worked for de tiff and mineral. I married up dere and had about 13 children by 2 wives. I ain't got no wife now. Dey is both dead. My children is scattered so I don't know how many is livin'. I got a boy dat went to this last war and I think he is out west somewhere. I got two boys here. One is workin' for de factory in Crystal City. De other one knows lots about cement. I got another child in New York. They don't write to me. I can't read or write. Dere was no school for niggers dem days. I has to make a cross mark every time I do anything. I went to school one week and my mother had to clean tiff to make a livin' for dem children and get grub so I had to go to work. I had about seven sisters and brothers altogether. I done worked at everything—steamboating, cutting wheat in Harrisonville, Illinois. I was here when dis was all woods, man. Me and a saloon keeper have been here a long time, more'n 50 years I guess. I pay $5 a month rent or just what I can give 'em. My two boys lives here with me now and I get $12 pension.

"Dat's when my old master run when dem blue jackets come. Dey made me kill chickens and turkeys and cook for 'em. De lieutenant and sergeant would be right dere. De master would go out in de woods and hide and not come out till they rung de bell at de house.

"I voted since I been 21. I voted for Roosevelt twice. Some thinks he is goin' to get in again. What's the use of takin' money from a man for votin' a certain way? If I like you and you have treated me good all my life den I'll vote for you.

"I don't know what I think about de young Negroes today. Dey is all shined up and goin' 'round. If dey can read and write dey ought to know de difference between right and wrong. I don't think dey will amount to much. Some of 'em ain't got no sense. My mother would not let me stay out. Now, dat is all dey doin'. Last night de policeman put a knot on my boy's head; he was drinkin' and got into it with a coon. De young colored people is fightin' all de time. I don't get out. Just go to de store and come back home again. Dere is a house right near where dey has a big time every night. De whites and black ones was mixed up here till I stopped it. Right down in dat hollow I'll bet you'll find one-third white women livin' with black men. Most all de colored people around here is workin' in the works here at Crystal City. Dey will get up a war here if they keep on, you just watch, like they did in Illinois when dey burnt up a heap of coons. It's liable to get worse de way dey is goin' on."

United States. Work Projects Administration

LULA CHAMBERS

> Interview with Lula Chambers,
> St. Louis, Missiouri.
> (Written by Grace E. White.)

The subject of this sketch is Lula Chambers who is not certain of her age. However she knows she is past ninety and that she was born in Gallatin County, Kentucky near Virginia. She lives with a granddaughter, Genevieve Holden, 2627 Thomas Street, St. Louis.

Lying ill in a three-quarter metal bed in the front hall room of her granddaughter's 4-room brick apartment, the old lady is a very cheerful person, with an exceptionally fair complexion. Her brown hair is mixed with gray and she wears it quite long. Her room is neatly furnished.

"I was born in Gallatin County, Kentucky, more than ninety years ago, slaves didn't know dere age in them days when I come along. I do know I was born in July and my mammy's name was Patsy Lillard. I don't know nothing at all about no kind of father. Course, I had one but who he was I never knew. I ain't never even seen my mother enough to really know her, 'cause she was sold off the plantation where I was raised, when I was too young to remember her, and I just growed up in the house with the white folks dat owned me. Dere names was Dave Lillard. He owned more dan one hundred slaves. He told me dat my mother had seven children and I was de baby of 'em all and de onliest one living dat I knows anything about. They sold my mother down de river when I was too young to recollect a mother. I fared right well with my white masters. I done all de sewing in de house, wait on de table, clean up de house, knit and pick wool, and my old miss used to carry me to church with her whenever she went. She liked lots of water, and I had to bring her water to her in church. I had so much temper dey never bothered me none about nursing de children. But I did have a heap of nursing to do with de grown ups.

"I used to get a whipping now and den but nothing like de other slaves got. I used to be scared to death of those old Ku Klux folks with all dem hoods on dere heads and faces. I never will forget, I saw a real old darkey woman slave down on her knees praying to God for his help. She had a Bible in front of her. Course she couldn't read it, but she did know what it was, and she was prayin' out of her very heart, until she drawed the attention of them old Ku Klux and one of 'em just walked in her cabin and lashed her unmerciful. He made her get up off her knees and dance, old as she was. Of course de old soul couldn't dance but he just made her hop around anyhow.

"De slave owners in de county where I was raised—de well-to-do ones I mean, did not abuse de slaves like de pore trash and other slave holders did. Of course dey whipped 'em plenty when dey didn't suit. But dey kind of taken care of 'em to sell. Dey had a great slave market dere dat didn't do nothing but sell slaves, and if dey wanted a good price for dem de slave would have to be in a purty good condition. Dat's what saved dere hides. My owners had a stock farm and raised de finest stock in Kentucky. Dey didn't raise any cotton at all, but dey shore did raise fine wheat, barley and corn, just acres and acres of it. De worse lashing our slaves ever got was when dey got caught away from home without a pass. Dey got whipped hot and heavy den.

"In Arkansas many of de slave owners would tie dere slaves to a wagon and gallop 'em all over town and would dey be banged up. I saw a strange niggah come to town once and didn't know where he was going and stepped in the door of a white hotel. When he saw all white faces, he was scared most to death. He didn't even turn around he just backed out and don't you know dem white folks kilt him for stepping inside a white man's hotel by mistake, yes they did.

"I can't tell you any pleasure I had in my early days, honey, 'cause I didn't have none. If I had my studyin' cap on, and hadn't just got over dis terrible sick spell, I could think of lots of things to tell you, but I can't now. Right after de war dey sent colored teachers through de South to teach colored people and child, do you know, dem white folks just crucified most of 'em. I don't know how to read or write. Never did know. I am de mother of five children, but dey is all dead now. I have two grandchildren living, and have been in St. Louis seven years. I come here from Helena, Arkansas. My husband was a saloon keeper and a barber. He died in 1880 in Brinkley, Arkansas. I nursed and cooked in Brinkley after he died for fifteen years for one family.

"I wears glasses sometime. I have been a member of de church over fifty years. My membership is in Prince of Peace Baptist Church now and has been every since I been in St. Louis. God has been so good to me, to let me live all dese years. I just want to be ready to meet him when he is ready for me. My only trouble will be to love white folks, dey have treated my race so bad. My pastor, Rev. Fred McDonald always tells me I will have to forgive them and love dem if I wants to go to heaven. But honey, dat's goin to be a lifetime job. I don't care how long God lets me live, it will still be a hard job.

"I gets an old age pension. It is very little, but I thank God for dat. I have nothing left to do now in this world but to pray. Thank God for his goodness to me and be ready when He comes.

"Dis rheumatism serves me so bad I can't be happy much. Wish I could remember more to tell you but I can't."

The old woman is well preserved for her years.

EMMALINE COPE

**Interview with Emmaline Cope,
Joplin, Missouri.**

Emmaline Cope was born at McMinnville, Tenn., on August 20, 1848, and is now 89 years of age.

Emmaline's slave father was King Myers and her slave mother was Caroline Myers. They were both owned by one Tim Myers a wealthy and prominent planter of McMinnville.

After peace was declared at the expiration of the Civil War, Emmaline Cope was taken to Lowell, Kansas, and there afterwards, was married to John Cope. Thirty five years ago John Cope died in Kansas and Emmaline Cope then moved to Joplin with one girl child. They have lived in Joplin continuously since then.

When interviewed Mrs. Cope, slowly recovering from a paralytic stroke, seemed unable to give any details of the Civil War activities.

United States. Work Projects Administration

PETER CORN

Interview with Peter Corn,
Herculaneum, Missouri.

Peter Tells How Slavery Began

"I'se 83 years old and was born in Ste. Genevieve County and my old slave-time place was in New Tennessee about 14 miles west of de town of Ste. Genevieve. My master had only my mother, my mother's brother, and an old lady by de name of Malinda. My mother had six children but only four of us lived to be grown. Father was owned by a Mr. Aubushon right dere at Coffman. Mother come from way south in Kentucky and she was owned by a Master Calvin dere and when him and de mistress died de slaves had to be divided up among de children. Den my mother's mistress left Louisville and brought her here to Missouri. When mother come to Missouri she was only 9 years old.

"My old mistress, I can't say a hard word about her. Before I was borned she was left a widow and she treated us almost like white folks. She took care of us and raised us up. Mother died after she had six children and we was left in de care of dis old mistress. The Catholic people treated us like as if we was free. My mother and father was married by de priest and it was lawful. But dese other ones was married by de master hisself. When dey married de master could pick up any old kind of paper and call it lawfully married. An almanac or anything would do. But what was it? The colored people didn't know A from B and wasn't allowed to learn to read. If my master or mistress would see me readin' a paper dey would come up and say, 'What you know about reading a paper? Throw dat down.' Dis was done to keep us from learnin' to read anything.

"After we got free what did we do to get lawfully married to our slave-time wife? Understand good now. Den de squire came around and we had to get married all over again under de new constitution. It would cost $5. When de master first married us he would say in de ceremony something like dis:

"'Now, by God, if you ain't treatin' her right, by God, I'll take you up and whip you.' The girl's mistress would chastise her de same way. I would choose who I wanted to marry but I had to talk to my master about it. Den him and de owner of de girl I wanted would get together and talk it over.

"Dere is lots of people right today who can't tell you how de new constitution come up. In slave time, young man, we was stock, like cattle and hogs. If I killed 50 men nothin' was said about jail, but we got whipped den. Dat was your sufferin' for what you done done. Man, I never got but one whippin' from my master. I can tell you just how it come. It was done through takin' care of an old cow. Now, in dem times, son, dere was not gates like dere is now. You called dem 'slip bars', and would let down a rail fence called bars to let the cattle in. Understand, listen at it good now. Every mornin' I had to go up to de straw stack and drive de cows to de barn. To milk dem we had to drive dem down a lane to de house for de old cook woman to milk. As I drove dese cows dey all got through de gate but when de last cow come through she fell over de bottom rail and de master was standin' at de window and saw dis happen. De snow was about three feet deep. Now listen good. De old master was crippled and so here he come with a walkin' stick in one hand and a cowhide in de other.

"He said, 'By God, I'm goin' to learn you, by God, how to let down bars'. I said, 'Marster Jim, I let down every bar 'cept dat one on de bottom'. He jumped on me and got me down in dat snow till I couldn't see him at all. Every time he raised up an' come down with dat cowhide it cut through de snow and hit me. I didn't had nuthin' on 'cept an old pair of socks around my feet. You know if you was raised from birth like dis you could stand it. It come to me, I thought dat if I ever get to be a man I would pay de marster back for dat.

"And so after dat when we got free I was growin' on 13 years of age. My aunt and brothers come and got me. My old master was a shoemaker, and one day my uncle told me to take a pair of boots and take dem over to have half-soled. I taken dem over. I had not come across the old master since de time we was free until dis day. But when I went in de house de family was around dere and I forgot about payin' him back for de way he done treated me. Jim's mother who was dere said, 'Well, Peter, don't you wish you was back here livin' with us again?' I said, 'No, mam.' Den I went in de kitchin and talked to Jim's wife. She was a Republican and said, 'Wasn't dat hateful what she said about you bein' back here again?' De next time I met my old master, Mr. Galvin, was on de road. He was walkin' and could hardly drag. I was ridin' my horse and thought about gettin' down and whippin' him but when I looked at him I thought I might as well be whippin' a year old child. I let him go.

"Later on Jim got poor and one day I met him at de saloon in Staabtown. He wanted to get some leather from another store. He asked me if he could have my horse. I said rather sharp, 'No, I won't.' Den I thought and said, 'Mr. Jim, I'll go and get de leather myself.' So I got de leather and taken it to his home and set it in on de porch by his door. Den he said, 'Peter, I thank you a thousand times. Any time you need anything in de shoe line come to me.'

"Later on he was down and out and he come to his sisters. Dey could not take care of him so dey put him in de asylum in Farmington. I met him in Farmington on lots of days, and felt like payin' him back for dat whippin'. But just looked like every time, God would say, 'No, don't do dat. He will pay for dat. He will come down'. And he sure did pay for it. He died in de asylum out from Farmington. I never mentioned about dat whippin' to Jim Galvin, not a nary time.

"When I was freed I felt like I was goin' into a new world. It was de daughter of de old mistress what told me I was as free as dey was. It was dangerous around de house durin' of de war. So de old mistress broke up de old place and us boys was given to our godmother. Mary was my godmother and it was here I was told dat I was free. We was little and didn't know which way to go. My mistress said, 'Now Peter, you are free and de first chance we get we are going to send for your aunt to come and get you.' Dere were four of us brothers bein' taken care of by four sisters, when we was free. My uncle was in de army and served two years and had come home. He asked my aunt, 'Where are dose boys?' My aunt said, 'Dey is still with de white folks.' So my uncle come to get us. When he come he rid up and we was so glad to see him we run out and met him. He said, 'Boys, I've come after you.'

"We walked up to de house. Den de white folks was just as glad to see Uncle Julius as if he had been their brother. Den Uncle Julius said to my godmother, Mary, 'Well, Miss Evely, I come after Pete.' She said, 'Julius, I'm awful glad you've come to get him, I hate to give him up, but take him and take good care of him.' Julius was told de same thing by all de other godmothers of my brothers. All of dese sisters had de winter clothes for us cut out but dey wasn't made. De white women said, 'All your aunt has to do is to make dem.' We had between nine and ten miles to go to get down to my aunt's home.

"My aunt's husband was freed at least 15 years before de war started. His master died and he was freed by a will when the master went to de court house in Ste. Genevieve. Now, just listen good. Dis master willed 800 acres to his slaves who divided up de farm. Before he died, he put it down in a way dat his daughters and sons-in-laws could not break it 'cepting dey would raise several thousand dollars. De old slaves would sit down and tell us about it. De master turns in and pays de taxes up for 100 years. One of de trustees for de will was a Dr. Herdick and Henry Rozier both of Ste. Genevieve. My uncle's part was 40 acres and it was dis farm where I went when I come out from under de shelter of de white folks. De colored would sell 2 or 3 acres at a time and all dis farm is now sold. I was 13 when I got free and went to dis farm and there was my home until I was right at a grown man. De only taxes we had to pay was on household goods and stock. Every year when de personal taxes come due I would go into Ste. Genevieve to pay de taxes. As long as Dr. Herdick and Henry Rozier lived as overseers we was well protected on de farm. But Ed Rozier, a lawyer, tried to get us to pay de other kind of taxes.

"I was goin' on 20 or 21 before I left de farm. De old lady and Uncle died about de same time. Dey took de old lady to de River Aux Vases Catholic Church to bury her and I stayed with de old man and he died before dey got back from de funeral. We sold our forty acres and dere was six heirs. Den I went to work on a farm of Mr. Aubushon for $10 a month for 15 years. When I quit Aubushon I went den out in Washington County at Potosi and stayed with my two uncles out dere. I served in a iron factory dere for about two years. Sometimes I would get $5 a day. Den when de price would fall off I would get less. Den I come back to Ste. Genevieve County and worked by de day and den went to St. Louis. I worked dere from one iron factory to another and so den I quit dat.

"Den I 'run the river' three straight years from St. Louis to Cairo and Memphis, and Baton Rouge, and New Orleans. I den quit de down trade and rested up and made de northern trip from St. Louis to St. Paul. Everything had to be sent from de South out to California. Dat boat had nothin' on it 'cept eatin' things. So my aim was to get out to California to dig gold. I got defeated in dis way.

"De river got so low dat we would be tied up for 3 or 4 days before we could unload it. And we never made it to de port where we could unload it to send it to California. From dese ports you went by land with a covered wagon and oxen or mules. It would sometimes take 6 months to get to California from de time we left de river. My way would have been free because I could drive a team out to California. But I never got to go 'cause de river got so low. I quit de river work and done some farming for first one den another down in Ste. Genevieve County for a couple of years.

"Dey was just startin' up at Crystal City. Dere was lots in de paper about it. Now and den William Kimer, who was livin' in Jefferson County, wrote me to work for him. I would work for him from May to December durin' de wheat cuttin', thrashing, corn pullin' and wheat sowin'. Den dere was no more summer work, so Crystal City was just startin' up and dere was no railroad and dey got everything by boat and teams hauled de things from de river up to de plant. Sometimes there was from 50 to 60 farm teams down at de river haulin' de coal, brick, etc. for de company. Sometimes we would make $15 a day for de farmer man and he would pay me $10 a month and board. Den I went to Crystal City and worked 13 straight years. De most dat ever I got dere was five or six dollars a day. Dis would be about every three months w'en we tore down de furnace and built it back. At other times I would get about $4.50 a day. I done everything. Made mortar, carried de hod and brick and when quittin' time come you was tired. After I quit Crystal City I went down in Ste. Genevieve County and farmed and got married and had two children. My wife and one child, a little girl, is dead. I live here with my son and his wife. My son has been workin' for de St. Joe here for 12 or 13 years. I had to quit work when I lost my eye-sight.

"I was grubbin' hazel-nut bushes in dem rich bottoms in Ste. Genevieve County; and one day I was runnin' and fell down on a stob and it went through my left eye.

Dis happened about 40 years ago. De other eye was good till I was 45 and den I had de loss of both eyes and been blind ever since. I'se been gettin' a blind pension for 22 years. It is $75 every three months.

"Dere is only one colored family here dat owns their house. All de others rent from the company. I vote at every presidential election, but dat's about all I ever do vote. I been votin' for every president election since I was 21 years old. From de beginning to de end it's always the same, the Republican ticket. Dey joke me a good deal around here 'bout voting one way.

"As I look back on it, people ought never to have been slaves. Dat was the low downest thing dat ever was. De first startin' of slavery was when a white man would go over to Africa and de people over dere was ignorant and de white man would hold up a pretty red handkerchief and trade it for one of de Negro women's children. De Negroes in Africa was too ignorant to know better and dis is de way slavery started. I always said like dis, when de older ones that knowed de things, dey ought have learned de slaves their names as dey was in Africa. Lots of us don't know what our grandparents was in Africa. Slavery didn't teach you nothin' but how to work and if you didn't work your back would tell it. Slavery taught you how to lie, too. Just like your master would tell you to go over and steal dat hog. Den de other master from who I stole de hog would say, 'Peter, why I've lost a hog; did you ever see him anywhere?' I would say, 'No, suh'. Of course if I did not lie I would get a whippin'.

"De white people did not want to put us in a state to ourselves after de freedom 'cause dey couldn't do without us. De colored people done come up too high now to back 'em and dey got a better chance. De conditions now of de colored people is of course better now 'cause dey is somebody. But every day dey is tryin' to starve us out and give de white man a job on de state road. Dey do dat to keep us down. Dat's done more now dan ever before. It's been worse since Roosevelt got in dere. When Highway 61 was put in from St. Louis down to Festus de colored man had a part to do. Since Roosevelt got in dey won't even let a colored man walk down de highway."

United States. Work Projects Administration

ED CRADDOCK

Interview with Ed Craddock,
Janitor, Saline County Court House,
Marshall, Missouri.

Veteran Janitor

Marshall, Missouri has a life-long negro citizen who was born in slavery, but was too young to remember actual slave conditions. He is Ed Craddock, born a few years before the Civil War, the son of slaves owned by leading pioneer families. Craddock lived through the hard days of reconstruction. His own father was a school building janitor in Marshall in the 1870's, and Ed Craddock was apprenticed under his sire, finally, upon death of the latter, succeeding to the job, which he has held for forty-seven years. Years ago he married and reared a large family. Craddock belongs to the Methodist Church, serving as "second minute-man", which he explains is something like a secretary, and also belongs to the Colored Masonic Lodge. Craddock's brother is a practicing physician in St. Louis.

"Stories told me by my father are vivid," Craddock said in an interview. "One especially, because of its cruelty. A slave right here in Marshall angered his master, was chained to a hemp-brake on a cold night and left to freeze to death, which he did. My father said slaves had to have a pass to go places. 'Patrollers' usually went in groups of three. If they caught a slave off his plantation without a pass the patrollers often would flog them."

Craddock relates that his father suffered from chills and fever which, quinine, the only remedy known then, failed to cure. Someone advised him, next time the chill came on, to plunge into a deep and cold hole in the river. Ed says his father, out of desperation, tried the suggested cure, and it worked, in a way squaring with the modern medical theory of setting up a counterirritant in certain cases.

Craddock's mother was owned by the family of Marmadukes, one of whom was an early-day governor of Missouri.

ISABELLE DANIEL

Interview with Mrs. Eli Daniel,
Marshall, Missouri.

An aged negress answered the door when I knocked and asked if this was Isabelle, she invited me into her parlor, a tiny room with a rather good-looking brussels rug upon the floor, and panel lace curtains hung at the windows. The walls were hung with enlarged crayon pictures of Isabelle's husband and their sons and daughters; no other pictures adorn the walls. The center is the old family Bible occupying the place of honor; all the births, deaths, and marriages of the family have been carefully recorded in this book. An album holds next place and contains many old fashioned pictures of her "white folks" and friends of her younger days.

The outside of this little four room house is quite attractive, it was formerly painted white, but not much paint clings to it now; old fashioned green shutters still hang at the windows, a tiny little portico shelters the front door. There is room at one end for a small porch swing to be hung. At the other end an old weather-beaten chair affords a resting place for the caller.

The yard is entirely enclosed by a fancy wire fence, and a concrete walk leads to the porch.

This old woman lives entirely alone in this little cottage which was provided for her many years ago by the will of her old master.

She says she is 87 years old, but circumstances seem to indicate that she is at least 90; she said she was married and had a child about a year old when the war closed in 1865.

Her work as a slave was almost all in the house; she was taught to sew, and had to help make the clothes for the other slaves. She also was a nursemaid for her mistress' little children and at one time was hired out to the methodist preacher's family to take care of the children when his wife was ill.

She remembered joining the "white folks" methodist church in old Cambridge and going to church on Sundays and sitting in the Gallery, which was the place reserved for colored people in that particular place.

On Sunday morning Aunt Cindy got "happy" at the services and began to throw herself about and shout; the white folks on the seats below hurried to get out from under the edge of the balcony for fear Aunt Cindy would lose her balance and fall over the railing to the floor below.

Isabelle is a Firm Believer in "hants."

When she was a girl the adjoining plantation was owned by her master's brother-in-law, and on this plantation was the big old tobacco factory where the tobacco raised on several neighboring plantations was priced and hung. The negroes on her master's place said this factory was "hanted." None of them would go near this factory after nightfall, for "when the nights were still and the moon was full, you could hear the ting, ting, ting, of the lever all night long and voices of the slaves crying out and complaining, and you knew there wasn't anybody there at all, jest hants."

Isabelle was a mid-wife by profession after the war, and tells this as one of her experiences.

She was caring for a lady that had just had her second child; they lived in a cottage with a full basement under it.

The father was to take full care of the other child, a little boy, at night, and they were to sleep in the basement. The father and little son tried to sleep in the basement for two or three nights, but the father could not sleep. Something bothered him as if restless spirits were abroad. One morning Isabelle said she was standing by the door when she heard a voice, low and vibrant, saying, "No sleep here. Can't sleep here." No one was there but her and the mother and the two little children, so, of course, she knew it was "hants". This was proved to her satisfaction a few months later. The skeleton of a man was found under the basement floor.

United States. Work Projects Administration

HENRY DANT

Interview with Henry Dant,
Hannibal, Missouri.

Henry Says He's 105

Henry Dant, now living with his daughter on Davis Street in Hannibal, was born in slavery on the farm of Judge Daniel Kendrick, south of Monroe City in Ralls County. He is about one hundred and five years old, in possession of all his faculties and is able to move around the house. He seemed to have only hazy recollections, and it was difficult to keep him from wandering from the subject. The following is the story that he told:

"I was married and had three children when we was freed. The only slaves Mr. Kendrick had was my mother, brother, sister, and myself. Mr. Kendrick had three boys. Joe carried mail to Paris, and de other two, Bob and Jerome, was school teachers.

"We was treated fair when we behaved ourselves, but we had to be straightened out sometimes but we were not mistreated. We worked hard on de farm. I cradled wheat and plowed corn often till midnight. We often drove hogs to Palmyra and Hannibal. When dere was no crops in de fields we made brooms and baskets. My brother died and den I had to do most of de work. I was de only colored man on de place den. De Stage stopped at Mr. Kendrick's place and I had to look after de horses and mules. De mail come dere too, and dere was always a lot of people to be fed.

"Mr. Kendrick was judge of de court at New London and he was away most of de time. He was a big man in de county in dem days, and I had to go to town often. Once when I was driving to town with de ox team and wagon during de war, dere was soldiers on de road like you never did see. I tell you dem was bad times. I come back a different road because I was afraid, and I run dem oxen most of de way home. I got dere all right, but de oxen laid down on me once. De next morning one of the oxen was dead and in about a week de other one died. Dey just couldn't stand de running.

"Two of de master's boys got locked up over in New London or some place during de war. Dey come back after the war was over.

"I played a fiddle for all de weddings and parties in de neighborhood. Dey paid me fifteen or twenty cents each time and I had money in my pockets all de time.

"When we was set free dey gave us a side of meat and a bushel of meal. Dat's all we got. I went on a farm and farmed for myself, later I owned a farm in Ralls County. We raised corn and pigs and drove de pigs to Hannibal and Palmyra. When I got too old to farm I come here to live with my daughter. I get a pension now for about a year. It's not very much but it helps."

LUCY DAVIS

**Interview with Lucy Davis,
Cape Girardeau, Missouri.**

"In dem ole days we lived down near Hickman, Kentucky. We belonged to Masta' Joe Mott and Missus Mary Mott. Den dey was young Massa' James Andrew an' young Massa' Joe, an' dey wuz Missie Ophelia an' Missie Mary Rebecca.

"Dey had a nice big house, white wid big porches an' big locust trees aroun' in de yard. Dey only had us one famly o' slaves but dey wuz a good many er us.

"My Daddy wuz Henry Litener and my mammy wuz Rosanna Litener. My daddy belonged to Woodson Morris. He wuz a cousin of Massa Joe Mott an' lived a few miles away. He wuz allus allowed to visit us over Saturday night an' Sunday. Mammy done de cookin' at de big house an' Massa Joe allus said dey warn't nobody cud cook like Rose—dat's what he call her.

"We lived in a three-room log house an' we allus had plenty good eatin'. Hams, puddi near all year round chickens, en' sweet'taters an' possums too.

"Cain't tell 'bout no good times in dem days 'cause dey warn't none. We didden have no church but Ole Missus Mary usta carry mammy along to her church—ridin behind on her hoss. I guess dey wuz mos'ly right good to us all. The chillern wouldn' never let nobody whup me 'cause we all played togedder. But Ole Massa usta whup mammy when he'd git mad.

"When de war came Ole Massa didden go but he war a reg'lar ole seesesh! Young James Andrew went off to war an' ole Missus usta grieve for him. We ain't never seed no fightin' round our place but we could hear de big guns over at Columbus. When de sojers was round de neighborhood dey'd allus have me playing' round de front gate so I cud tell em when dey's comin' up de road. Den dey goes an' hides 'fore de sojers gits dar. Dey all skeer'd o' de sojers. I's skeerd too but dey say sojers won't bother little black gal. De sojers jes' came in en' ransack de house—dey finds sumthin to eat an' dey looks for money. Dey wants money! but dey don' find none. Den dey wants ter know whar's my folks—but I tells 'em I don't know. Dey jes left en' didden say whar dey wuz goin'.

"When de war wuz over Ole Massa Joe came in an' he say: 'Rose, you all ain't slaves no mo'—You is all free as I is.' Den you should a heard my mammy shout! You never heerd sich shoutin' in all yo' bahn days. An' Ole Missus she joined in de shoutin' too. She war glad 'cause now James Andrew would be comin' home.

"Old Missus Delia Reed, dat wuz Old Massa's sister, she wuz good 'bout lookin atter us wen we's ailin' but iffen we's sick dey'd git de doctor. Dey wuz jes as dutiful to us as to dere white folks.

"Dey usta talk—bout hoodoos an castin' spells en' sech like—but I guess dey warn't much to it er dey'd a cast spells on some a' de mean Massa's when dey beat um up. Still iffen dey had, mebby dey'd a beat um up worser or mebby killed em."

MARY DIVINE

Interview with Mary Divine,
St. Louis County, Missouri.

Was Nurse Maid At 4

The subject of this sketch is Mary Divine, 85 years old. She lives at 8004 Elinore Avenue, St. Louis County, Missouri, with her son and daughter-in-law.

Her home is an old fashioned 3-room slate dwelling, with an abundance of old furniture for such a small place. The little old woman was interviewed while mending the pockets in her son's trousers. Her story follows:

"I was born May 24, 1852 in Carroll County, Tennessee. My mother's name was Mary Whitehorn, 'cause she was owned by de Whitehorns in dat county. My father's name was James Farrow 'cause he was owned by de Farrows. De slaves had to carry dere owners' names, married or what not. My mother had three children. My first owner's name was George Whitehorn and his wife's was Jackie Whitehorn. When old Marse George died, we was handed down to Joseph Whitehorn in Miss Jackie's will. She knowed long before freedom we were going to be free, so she had in her will dat her darkies,—she always called us darkies—had caused dem to have all dey owned and it was no more dan right when we git free to divide up de plantation so every one of us could make a good livin' on de livin' we done made for dem, and dey still own and have plenty. She was a good old soul. She didn't want a one of us to leave, even after freedom been declared. She said she would never live to see it and she didn't neither. She died 'fore we was free, and dem chillun never did carry out her will neither.

"'Cause dey didn't give a one of us nothin', no, nothin' at all. Put us out wid just what we had on our backs, and dat was most nothin'. At 4 years old I had to nurse old man George's son, Joseph's baby, and de baby was most big as me, but I nursed it just de same, honey. Dey put me in dat family nursin' dat baby 'fore I was four 'cause dey put me dere in January and I wasn't four years old till de incoming May dat same year. I 'member dat right well. I nursed dat baby for two years, too, and it sure was crazy 'bout me. I loved it too, yes, I did. Den after two years dey sent me to work for de old man's oldest son, Jacob. Dey made me do all de cardin' and spinnin', make ropes and ply lines, two cuts a day, was my task and I stayed dere in dat family until after the Civil War was over.

"I heard my father got killed in de Civil War. I never knowed for sure, 'cause three months 'fore I was born, his owners carried him away to some other part of de country and we never seen nor heard from him no more. Mother never did know what happened him, no she didn't.

"Just 'fore war was declared I was still young and small but just de same I had to help pack brick to de moulders where dey would be building brick chimneys, and work in de field, too. I had it mighty hard in dem days, yes I did but den it wasn't hard as some others had it.

"I 'member during de war days, my old miss use to

boast 'bout her littlest darkey, done spun enough thread to clothe her whole family for de next three years to come. For two years after freedom was declared I worked from farm to farm and de promise we was going to get paid, but we never got nothin' from none of dat work but de old slave cabin to sleep in and food enough just so we could work.

"We had noboby down in dat country to make folks keep dere word and pay a nigger, so we just have to keep on travelin'. After 'bout three years later I cooked in de same county for a Bill Green. Got my board and keep and $1.00 a week. He kept me 'bout five months. Dey never did keep us long for pay. Den I went to John Carney's plantation wid my mamma. I card and spun dere for 'bout one year and some weeks. We got $1.00 a week and he was supposed to give us home made cloth to make us some clothes for our work, but he never did do it. After dat we went to work on Sub Allen's farm for $1.00 week. I took sick dere and dey had to call in a doctor. My mamma and me worked for him a long time, but we got ready to go and want our money he said, while I was sick it taken all he owed us to pay my doctor's bill so we didn't git nothin' dere, but a place to stay and we shore did work like slaves in all dem places, from sun up till sun down just like in slave days. Only difference was we didn't git a beatin' when we didn't suit. I couldn't make no money for clothes or nothing so I just up and married and had eleven children. Den my husband died. I had a child in dis last World War. He was my ninth child and got took in de last draft. I never heard of him no more. Dis one I'm living with named Ulysses Divine. He's de only child I got living I know anything about.

"I been here in St. Louis since Wilson's first administration and worked in de nut factory five years. I like to sew and do general housework. I read, write and spell a little but not enough to speak about. I know dis young generation's got a mighty fine chance if dey 'cept of it and 'preciate it. Course some do and some don't. I prefer living in town dan out here but my son bought dis spot. I can't make my own living no more, so I got to live on it. I git what de relief pretend to call help, 'tain't nuff for nothin' though. Dey claim I'll git a pension, but I never seen it yet. I'll be dead directly and I won't need it. I can't answer dem other questions 'bout what us slaves expect and voting, I don't know."

MARY DOUTHIT

Interview with wife of Charles Douthit, Farmington, Missouri.

Note:—While the interviewer was questioning Charles Douthit, Farmington, Missouri, negro, who was born in 1865, his wife standing in the door looked rather wild-eyed, and unable to stand it any longer, finally broke out with the following:—"Say! What are they gittin' all dis stuff fur anyway? I bet I know. They want ta find out how dey treated de ole slaves so's dey'll know how to treat the young 'uns when dey makes dem slaves. I bet they're goin' a try to have slaves again and dere are some people who want slavery back but de people won't stan' fur hit now. I don't know what de government wants to do but de people would have a most turrible war if dey tried to have slaves again. But ma muther who worked for John Coffman in Ste. Genevieve County, wuz well treated. She war really owned by the Missus and de Missus would not sell ma mamma. When de war wuz ober de missus gave ma muther some land an built her a beautiful home down dare. Ma muther wuz treated so good dat she stayed an worked fur de Missus til de Missus died. I was borned down in dat dare house dat de Missus built fur ma Muthuh and ma son lives dere now. I was down dere las week, an I calls hit home."

United States. Work Projects Administration

JOHN ESTELL

> Related by "Uncle" John Estell
> [Missouri], age 85.

Slavery

"The slaves had a hard time, some of them. All the work was done by hand. The slaves cradled the wheat. They raised hemp for clothes. The old master had one woman who made clothes the year round for the hands. We had to get a pass from the master to leave the place. If any of the slaves got in trouble they were taken to the whippin' post. If they had done a big crime they got 60 or 70 lashes with a whip, for a small crime they got about thirty, if their master would not pay their fine. The white folks went to singin' school then they would sing one or two songs that's all they knew. They would have big basket meetings. All the slaves had to set in the gallery when we went to church. Most everybody went on hossback. Some of the farmers were good to their men and some bad. When some farm had more slaves than was needed, he would hire them out to some body or sell them. New Year's day was always sale day or the day they would hire out for the year. When we wanted to get married we had to ask the master and the girls' mother and father. All the married man got Thursday night off to go to see their wives.

"At Christmas time we got a week off and we got Saturday afternoon off. At Christmas the old boss would fix a big bowl of eggnog for us niggers. The niggers were superstitious. They would not live in a house where a sinner had died. There was an old man and woman lived down the road from our house that fit all the time, and by that house after dark one night one saw them walkin' around in the house. None of us niggers would go by there after dark, we always rode around the place. People are lots smarter now than they was then."

SMOKY EULENBERG

Smoky Eulenberg,
Jackson, Missouri.
(Written from F.C.
in Sikeston District.)

"I was born on October 13, 1854. My master was Henry Walker and we live 'bout three mile from Jackson. De house was of logs. One of dose big double kind wid a open hall in between. Solomon Eulenberg was my father and he was a big fine looking man. My mother come fum Tennessee when she was ten year old.

"Master had nearly a hundred slaves and dey was about ten or twelve cabins in de quarters. Dey was a big feeding barn where we'd hitch up and go to work. De barn was built of big hewed logs, too.

"No'm, dey wasn't none of us ever try to run away. We had a good home and we all stayed till dey declare peace and lots of us kept on a staying 'cause we didn't know nothing else to do. But my father was industrious—he worked hard and saved his money and in a couple of year he bought a team and we moved to a little place.

"But lots of de cullud folks had it hard dem days—dey was jest turned loose and didn't know what to do. Some of de white folks was mighty good to 'em. If they'd hear of a family being hungry dey'd send food to 'em or have 'em come to dey kitchen.

"A cose mebbe it don't sound right but in some ways I often wish we's back in dem days. We had a fine place. Every year we'd kill seventy or seventy-five hogs—and had plenty of every thing. We ate our meals in our own cabin but every morning at seven, de colored house-woman went to de smoke house to cut meat for de day. Us youngsters all ganged up round her, hoping to get something. Lotsa times missus would ask us if we's hungry and bring us into de kitchen and give us what dey had left. Sometime she have de women make up pancakes for us. Us children had de chores to do—and any work dat we's able.

"We didn't have no school. A woman come and stay all year round jest to teach little Miss Lucy and she taught some of de cullud children to read and write. Missus would have a preacher come once a month to preach. I rec'lect his name was Rev. Watts. All of us would come into de big house for meeting.

"Many a time we seen soldiers pass on de road but dey never molested us none, 'cept to come in and eat everything that was cooked—and sometime have de women cook up some more. One Sunday morning a bunch of 'em come by—dey had been over to Burfordville and burned de mill. Another Sunday a bunch of Rebs come by and camped 'bout a mile from our place. Dat night de Blue Coats ran onto 'em. Dey killed about thirty. Next morning us boys went over there and what we saw didn't suit me none. Some of de cullud men helped to bury 'em.

"We had lots a good times in dem days. Us boys played marbles and ball and other games like boys will. On Saturdays from five to nine we all had off—den we'd congregate—and have singing and dancing. At Christmas and such days we'd have a big time. When dey's a wedding missus always dressed 'em and fixed 'em up. I rec'lect one time missus sold my mother and four children but it wasn't no trade. De woman's name was Mrs. Sheppard and she was a sassy old woman. She come into my mother's cabin and grabbed her and told her she going to take her home. Mother jes' pushed her out de door and said she wouldn't go—and she told missus she wouldn't go—so dey had to call it off—it was no trade."

(Smoky Eulenberg lives about three blocks northwest of the courthouse in Jackson. The house was all nice and clean, his sheets and pillows all snowy white and freshly ironed. He has been bedfast for a long time. His wife is an interesting person, but she remembers nothing of slave days.)

United States. Work Projects Administration

ANN ULRICH EVANS

Interview with Ann Ulrich Evans,
St. Louis, Missouri.

Wed For Economic Reasons

Although 94 years of living have dimmed her eyes a bit and the burdens she's packed through the years have bent her wiry frame Ann Ulrich Evans, a former slave, is still able to carry on. She lives in a rear apartment of the slum district at 1405 North Eighth Street with her daughter, Eliza Grant.

Ann declares she's had eleven children of her own and that from them have sprung so many grand children and great grand children that she's entirely lost count of them. The story of the incidents that have filled her life but have still left her able to love mankind and smile follows substantially in her own words:

"I was born March 10, 1843 on Dolphin Street, Mobile, Alabama. My mother's name was Charlotte Ulrich and my father's was Peter Pedro Ulrich. I am the mother of 11 children and we has over 100 grandchildren. Dere is so many great grandchildren and great great grandchildren we jes' quit countin' when we comes to dem. I has four generations, and dey give me a party three years ago, and so many of my off spring come der wasn't any room for half of 'em and even dat was not de beginning of de lot of 'em. I got a gang of 'em I never did see, and never will see, I don't reckon. Dey just write and tell us dey got 'em.

"My father was owned by a rich old boss named Captain Bullmay. He owned a raft of boats, and my father was a cook on one of dem boats. Mamma only raised two of her children. De Ulriches sold me when I was a girl to Dr. Odem in de same county, and I worked in his field, spun thread to make cloth, pulled fodder, put de spinning in, and after a while, I don't know how long, he swapped me off for two boys. My new owner was Gilbert Faulkner. He was a railroad section man. I worked in de field for him until we was set free. I had some good times and some bad times both. De man I married worked on the railroad for him. His name was Moses Evans. Dat was in Helena, Arkansas. My husband's been dead more dan 30 years now. I got four daughters and three sons living and a host of grand and great grand, and great great grandchildren living. Since my husband died, I just live from one child to the other and some time de grandchildren takes care of me, I havn't done no kind of work since my children got big enough to work. Dey been pretty good to me all my days.

"'Bout a year ago de government done started giving me a pension, $11 a month. It helps some, but don't very much, every thing's so high, honey. When freedom come I asked my old owner to please let me stay on wid dem, I didn't have no whar to go no how. So he just up and said, 'Ann, you can stay here if you want to, but I ain't goin' to give you nothing but your victuals and clothes enough to cover your hide, not a penny in money, do no nigger get from me.' So I up and said, 'Why boss, dey tells me dat since freedom we git a little change', and he cursed me to all de low names he could think of and drove me out like a dog. I didn't know what to do, or where to go, so I sauntered off to a nearby plantation where a colored slave kept house for her bachelor slave owner and she let me stay with her, and her boss drove me off after two days, because I kept company with a nigger who worked for a man he didn't like. I was barefooted, so I asked Moses Evans, to please buy me some shoes, my feet was so sore and I didn't have no money nor no home neither. So he said for me to wait till Saturday night and he'd buy me some shoes. Sure 'nough when Saturday night come, he buyed me some shoes, and handkerchiefs and a pretty string of beads and got an old man neighbor named Rochel to let me stay at his house. Den in a few weeks me and him got married, and I was mighty glad to marry him to git a place to stay. Yes I was. 'Cause I had said, hard times as I was having if I seed a man walking with two sticks and he wanted me for a wife I'd marry him to git a place to stay. Yes I did and I meant just dat. In all my born days I never knowed of a white man giving a black man nothing, no I ain't.

"Now child, let me tell you right here, I was always a heap more scared of dem Ku Klux dan I was of anything else. 'Cause de war was to help my folks. But dem old Ku Klux never did mean us no good. Honey, I used to make pallets on de floor after de war for my children, myself and husband to sleep on, 'cause dem Ku Klux just come all around our house at night time and shoot in de doors and windows. Dey never bothered nobody in de day time. Den some time dey come on in de house, tear up everything on de place, claim dey was looking for somebody, and tell us dey hungry 'cause dey ain't had nothin' to eat since de battle of Shiloh. Maybe twenty of 'em at a time make us cook up everything we got, and dey had false pockets made in dere shirt, and take up de skillet with de meat and hot grease piping hot and pour it every bit down de front of dem shirts inside de false pockets and drop de hot bread right down dere, behind de meat and go on.

"One night dey come to our house after my husband to kill him, and my husband had a dream dey's coming to kill him. So he had a lot of colored men friends to be at our house with guns dat night and time dey seed dem Ku Klux coming over de hill, dey started shooting just up in de air and about, and dem Ku Klux never did bother our house no more. I sure glad of dat. I'se so tired of dem devils. If it hadn't been for dat dey would have killed everyone of us dat night. I don't know how come dey was so mean to us colored folks. We never did do nothing to dem.

"Dey go to some of dem niggers' house, and dey run up de chimney corner to hide and dem low down hounds shoot 'em and kill 'em in de chimney hole. Dey was terrible. Den de next bad thing happened to us poor niggers after de war was dis. De white folks would pay niggers to lie to de rest of us niggers to git der farming done for nothing. He'd tell us come on and go with me, a man wants a gang of niggers to do some work and he pay you like money growing on trees. Well we ain't had no money and ain't use to none, so we glad to hear dat good news. We just up and bundle up and go with this lying nigger. Dey carried us by de droves to different parts of Alabama, Arkansas and Missouri. After we got to dese places, dey put us all to work all right on dem great big farms. We all light in and work like old horses, thinking now we making money and going to git some of it, but we never did git a cent. We never did git out of debt. We always git through with fine big crops and owed de white man more dan we did when we started de crop, and got to stay to pay de debt. It was awful. All over was like dat. Dem lying niggers caused all dat. Yes dey did.

"I don't know what to think of this younger generation. 'Pears to me like dey jest ain't no good. Dey is too trifling. I often times tell 'em dere chances today side of mine in my day. Dey jest say dey wouldn't take what I been through.

"But dey is just a hopeless lot, just plain no good. All I can say is as you say, some is some good but so few 'ginst de masses, take so long to find 'em, I just don't bother 'bout trying to hunt 'em out.

"I voted once in my life, but dat's been so long ago I don't 'member who it was for, or where I was living at de time. I never had no friends in politics to my knowing. All I 'member dey told me to put a cross under de elephant, and I did dat. I don't know nothin 'more 'bout it dan dat. Don't know what it meant or nothing. After all I been through, honest chile, I love everybody in de world, dose dat mistreat me and dose dat didn't. I don't hold nothing in my heart 'ginst nobody, no I don't. God going to righten each wrong some day, so I'se going to wait with love in my heart till dat day come. Den I speck I will feel plenty sorry, for what's going to happen to dem dat mistreated me and my people and all other helpless folks. 'Cause I seen white folks in my day, have 'bout as tough time in a way as black folks, and right now some of 'em fairing just 'bout like me.

"I 'member how de old slaves use to be workin' in de field singing 'Am I born to die, And Lay Dis Body Down.' And dey sing, 'Dark was de night and cold de ground, on which my lord was laid, Great drops of blood like sweat run down, in agony He prayed.' Another song was 'Way over in de promised land my Lord calls me and I must go'. And 'On Jordan's Stormy Banks I stand, and cast a wishful eye. To Canaan's fair and happy land, where my possessions lie. All o'er those wide extended plains, Shines one eternal day; There God, the son forever reigns, And scatters night away. No chilling winds, nor pois'nous breath, Can reach that healthful shore; Sickness and sorrow, pain and death, Are felt and feared no more. When shall I reach that happy place, And be forever blest? When shall I see my father's face, And in his bosom rest? I am Bound for the Promised Land.'

"I am a member of the Sanctified Church. I was a Baptist for years."

JAMES GOINGS

**Interview with James Goings,
Cape Girardeau, Missouri.**

"Teresa Cannon wuz my mammy. She belonged to old Dr. Cannon, of Jackson; when I was born. Tom Goings wuz my Daddy: He lived on a near-by plantation. Mrs. Dunn bought my mammy and me. Den 'Massa' Lige Hill got us fum her. I growed up out der near Whitewater. Dey wuz 'bout twenty slaves on de place, 'en we wuz all living pretty good—plenty to eat, an' clothes enuf. Dey wuzn't no school out dere, an' I didden know nothin' 'bout readin' 'bout writin'—mostly, I jes' done 'chores' carrin' in de wood 'en water en' sech like.

"I wuz 'bout ten years old wen de war wuz over, so I 'members well-nuf. They wuz a battle over at White water, I didden see it, but I heard de shooting and seed some o' de wounded men. De Southern soldiers had been round de place for 'bout a week. 'Massa' had a grist mill 'en he had lots o' corn. Dey wuz takin' our corn en' grindin' it for dey own use. Dey wuz killin' our hogs, an' helpin' der selves to whut we had. Den word came dat de 'Yankees' wuz comin'. 'Old George' was sent to take de horses to de woods 'en hide 'em. Back in de woods he met two neighbor boys, 'Willis' 'en 'Columbus Bain', en' dey showed him where to hide de hosses, an' de sojers never did fin' 'em. Our young 'Massa Billie' 'en de two 'Bain' boys got away—but de 'Yanks' druv de army clear to Bloomfield 'en furder.

"De dead wuz laying all long de road an' dey stayed dere, too. In dem days it wuzn't nuthin' to fin' a dead man in de woods. De 'Yankees' took 'Old Massa' 'en all de udder men in to Cape Girardeau 'en made 'um help build de forte.

"We often seed sojers on de roads, but dey didden bother us much, but de bushwackers, 'de wuz bad. One day, Bill Norman 'en his step-mother, fum White water Station, cum up to our place. She had on a print dress 'en a sunbonnet, 'en dat wuz all she had left in de world. Dey had burned up everything for 'um—dey house, dey grist mill—everything. But sumtimes de sojers got de Bushwackers—Dere wuz one fella named 'Bolen' dey got him 'en tuck him to de Cape. Dere dey hung him on a high gate-post, jest outside 'er town. My 'mammy', Teresa Cannon lived here in dis house wid us for a long time. She died nine year ago at de age of one hundred 'en fifteen."

RACHAEL GOINGS

Interview with Rachael Goings,
Cape Girardeau, Missouri.

"My full name wuz Rachael Exelina Mayberry (Mabrey) an' my mammy's name was Cynthy Minerva Jane Logan. You see I carried de name Mayberry 'cause dat wuz my masta's name. Masta' Josiah Mayberry. My mammy carried de name Logan 'cause dat wuz de famly she belonged to fo' Masta' bought her down in Buckskull, Arkansas. Masta had three sons, Dosh, his wife wuz Roberta, Alf his wife wuz Malissa and Byrd, his wife wuz Cully. In dem days we called 'em all by dere first name. We honored de ole Masta', but de younger folks, we didden call Masta' Dosh, or Masta' Byrd—or Missus Cully. It wuz jes Dosh, Byrd or Cully. I didden' know de ole Missus. Dey tole me she went crazy and kilt herself shortly after I wuz borned 'cause she thought I was white. We wuz de only slave famly Masta' had en he wuz good to us. We all liked him, all o' us but Cynthy, dat's my mammy I allus called her Cynthy till after de war wuz over. Cynthy always called him "Ole Damn"—she hated him 'cause he brought her fum Arkansas and left her twins an' dey poppy down dere. Cynthy's daddy was a full Cherrokee. She wuz always mad and had a mean look in her eye. When she got her Indian up de white folks let her alone. She usta run off to de woods till she git over it. One time she tuk me and went to de woods an' it was nigh a month fore dey found her—and I wuz nigh dead. Dey kept me at de white folks house till I got strong again. Only one time Masta' whip me. We made lots o' molasses on our place. Oh! lots of molasses en' dey wuz allus some barrels standin' upright wid bungs in close to de bottom so de 'lasses run out. One day I seed one o' de men fix him some sweetened tobaccy. He had his tobaccy in a box about so big, en he push de bung des way, en dat way—den down, den up den he hol' it jes loose enough so de 'lasses trickle out over his tobaccy. I watched him an thought I'd fix me some, too. I got my box fixed en' I pushed at de bung, I pushed dis way, en dat way like I seed him do when all at once dat bung flew out en' dat lasses flew all over de place. De barrel was full en' it cum out so fast I couldn't git de bung back in. I tried till I wuz wadin' in 'lasses to my knees. Den I run call Masta' and tell him a bung dun bust out. He say how you do dat? I tell him I jes knock again' 'en it flew out. Den he seed my box and he knowed how I done it. Den he laid me on de floor an' he put his foot on my haid. He took his switch and he gave me one good out. Den he kept beatin on de floor. I guess dat wuz to make de others think he wuz giving me a big beatin'. But I didden want that big foot on my haid no more.

"De big house stood facing de road. It wuz built like lots o' houses wuz in dem days, de kitchen and dinin' room on one side. Masta's room on de udder with a big open hallway between. Across de front was a big porch. We called it a gallery. Across de road, back a piece ways wuz our cabin. Cynthy did all de cookin, an she wuz a good cook. We allus had plenty good things to eat. De white folks would sit down en eat, en when dey's through we'd sit down at de same table. I 'members de first shoes I ever had. One of de men had got em fo' his little girl, en' dey was too small. So he giv' 'em to my step-daddy for me. Dey uz too big but I wore em en wuz proud of em. They wuz so big fo' me, they went dis way en' dat way en' den de heels went all crooked. I wore 'em till 'bout de time de first snow came den I guess I thought I'd wore 'em long enuf an' I throwed em away. My step daddy whipped me for dat and made me wear 'em all winter.

"I must a been 'bout eight year old when de war start. Fust I knowed, one day Masta said to me. "Child go out to de gate an see if anyone comin." I went to de gate like he tole me an' dere was men comin down de road. Whew! I never seed so many men in all my life. I went back en' tole him. He didden' say nuthin' but lit out the back way across the fields an we didden see him again fo' some time.

"After that we saw lots o' sojers—dey'd stop at our place but dey never bother nuthin. Masta told us allus to have plenty cookin' an bakin' ready when de sojers came. Cynthy'd have de kitchen cupboard piled full o' lightbread and cakes and pies—sometime dey's Rebel sojers an sometimes dey's Republicans—We called de Northerns Republicans. We cud allus tell 'em. The Rebels wore brown coats and the Northerners wore blue suits wid pretty gold pieces on dey shoulders. My! but dey wuz pretty.

"Masta' ud come home once en awhile—an den one day he come home—I can see him yet a-sittin by de kitchen stove. De stove sat back in de big fireplace far enuf so de pipe go up de flue but not too far so you could look in de oven. Dere sat de Masta lookin' like he had sumthin' to tell mammy but was skeered to. She had her mad up that day—I jes foun' a hen's nest an' wuz runnin' in to tell her. I hollered "Cynthy, Cynthy"—Masta' put up his hand en say, slow like—"Stop chile! You mustin' call her Cynthy no more. The war is over and you no more slaves. Now you must call her mammy". But dat all de difference it made—we kep' on livin dere just de same, till Masta' died two year atter de war.

"One day a mule kicked him on de laig what wuz hurt in de war. It got so bad de doctor couldn' do nuthin for it. Masta' wud holler wid pain—It wuz in de fall of de year. One day I came in and sed, "Masta' you know dat big yellow apple tree? It's bloomin again, en it's got little green apples on it." He looked at me an sez—'Chile, youre lyin". I sez, "No Masta I ain't." He say "If you're lyin' to me, I'll get up and lick you again", so I runs and gets him a branch wid flowers on, and little green apples, an when he sees it, he cries. He knows he's gonna die 'cause de tree is bloomin out of season. But I didden know it. I says "Masta' if dem apples gits ripe, we'll have good eatins''cause de big yellow mealy ones wen dey fall, dey bust wide open."

"Masta' died en if I'd a know'd what I know now I could have saved him. I'd a took young elder leaves en boiled em to make a tea—den I'd a poured dat in de sore en it ud a got well.

"Masta' musta had hundreds a acres—'cause he give each o' his boys a big farm—en dey was his dotter Caroline, by his fust wife—I forgit 'bout her—he give her a farm, too—Dis wuz down in Stoddard County, near Advance. Shortly after dat Dosh died, en de rest sold out en' went to Texas.

"We seed Masta' lots a times after he died. I sez it wuz

Masta' 'cause it looked like him. One day I was standin lookin thru de bars o' de gate wen I seen out in de road de largest dog I ever seed in all my life. He wuz standin' der lookin' at me. I says to my brother, 'Look! he's got thick sandy red hair like Masta's, en he's got a nose like Masta's, en he's got eyes like Masta's, an he sho' do look like Masta'—Den I run back onto de gallery where de adder folks is. Dat dog stan' dere lookin at us, de big brush on his tail jes a wavin', den he reach thru de gate wid one paw, en onlatch it, and walked right in. The gate went shut agin but it didden make no noise. Den he cum up de walk en go rite across de gallery in front of us. He jump over de side fence, en run across de field, en go inter de woods. We know'd it wuz Masta', jes cum to look aroun, en it git so he'd cum every day 'bout noon, jes when Masta' always cum in fo' dinner. We ain't never seed him cum outer de graveyard, but he always com frum dat way. En one day I wuz playing in de doorway of our cabin an I looked across to de big house, and dere sat Masta' in his big chair on de gallery. I called Mammy en she says—'If you're lyin', I'll whup you.' But she cum en look, en she seed him too, he had his white shirt-sleeve rolled up to his elbow and his red flannel undershirt sleeve down to his wrist jes like he uster wear it. Der he sat en while we wus lookin he got up en walked off around the house.

"I 'members one evenin' 'bout dusk I wuz commin thru de cotton patch, an' I run plum into a man crawlin' along—Dat wuz durin' de war, en der he wuz crawlin' on his hands en knees. He had de biggest hands I ever seed on a human, an his feet wasn't ever touchin de groun'—dey wuz jes floppin' one over de udder, dis way. An his face!— I've seed false faces but dis wuz de worst I ever seed— dere wuz big red en white stripes all across his face. He rared up an looked at me like a dog rare on his haunches, and jes' dat way he wuz taller dan I wuz. I didden stop to look again' but I lit out en run through dat cotton patch. Lawd ha' mercy! how I did run. I jes' knocked dat cotton one way er nother—en dey didden whip me for it when I tole em 'bout it nuther. Nex' mornin' we went down der to look, en we seed de tracks where his knees had made—thru de cotton patch, cross the road, en enter de woods. But no body else never did see him. I often studied, wuz he natchel, or jes a ghost.

"When my little brother wuz borned, I 'members dat day. Mammy and I wuz working out in dis corn patch. She wuz coverin' corn, an she jes had 'bout three or four more rows to cover, den she ran to de house. Dey wuz jes one room en she tried to made de udder children go outside but dey wouldn' go, so she ran outside in de chimney corner, en soon dey heard a baby holler. Dey called me to cum quick 'cause Mammy found a baby. By de spring house stood a ole tree—en I seed it had blown down an in de branches was a big nest an de nest wuz empty. I sez—"Rite dere's where mammy found her baby—rite outer dat nest". Dey sez, "No suh! She done found it in de chimney corner, 'cause we heard it dere." No, mammy didden need nobody to help tend to her. Aunt Hannah Erwin was a doctor woman. She could sure cure a woman if she had child-bed fever—but my mammy didden need her."

SARAH FRANCES SHAW GRAVES

Interview with Sarah Graves,
Skidmore, Missouri.

Still Carries Scars From Lashes

"Sweet are the uses of Adversity,
"Which like a toad, ugly and venomous,
"Wears yet a Jewel in its head."

—Shakespeare.

Childhood and girlhood memories are vivid to Sarah Frances Shaw Graves, an 87 year old Negro woman whose indomitable courage and steadfast purpose overcame obstacles and made possible the ownership of the 120 acre farm near Skidmore, on R.F.D. #4, where she lives with her bachelor son, Arza Alexander Graves.

The frame house which is their home, though small, is comfortable. It is surrounded by a neatly kept yard, with flower beds and a cement walk which leads from the gate to the front door.

The visit had been arranged by telephone, and as the interviewer neared the home, Aunt Sally could be seen standing, on the front porch, eagerly watching and waiting. A "close up" showed that her immaculately washed, stiffly starched, print dress and apron were unwrinkled.

Evidently she had stood up ever since she had put them on.

Her white hair was combed back off her fore-head, and held in place by side combs. Although age has lined her hands, and put deep furrows in her brown cheeks, her unquenchable will to overcome handicaps has held her body erect and shoulders undrooped. In spite of her years, most of which were spent in gruelling labor, she is rugged and healthy, and meets the world with a smile and ready sympathetic laughter.

She was eager to begin her story, and led the way into the house, where at once the unmistakable signs of good housekeeping, cleanliness and tasteful arrangement are apparent. The home, though small, is moderately and comfortably furnished. They also enjoy the conveniences and accommodations of the rural telephone, a radio and a daily newspaper.

Her life story is one of contrasts; contrasts of thought; contrasts of culture, beneficial inventions and suffrage. Not far from her home the glistening streamlined Zephyr speeds on twin rails beside the Missouri River, near the route of the slow-moving, creaking wagons on the ox-road of the 1850's.

Sarah Frances Shaw Graves

Skidmore, Nodaway Co., Missouri.

"My name is Sarah Frances Shaw Graves, or Aunt Sally as everybody calls me. Yes'm that's a lot of name an' I come by it like this. My husband was owned by a man named Graves, and I was owned by a man named Shaw, so when we was freed we took the surnames of our masters.

"I was born March 23, 1850 in Kentucky, somewhere near Louisville. I am goin' on 88 years right now. (1937). I was brought to Missouri when I was six months old, along with my mama, who was a slave owned by a man named Shaw, who had allotted her to a man named Jimmie Graves, who came to Missouri to live with his daughter Emily Graves Crowdes. I always lived with Emily Crowdes."

The matter of allotment was confusing to the interviewer and Aunt Sally endeavored to explain.

"Yes'm. Allotted? Yes'm. I'm goin' to explain that," she replied. "You see there was slave traders in those days, jes' like you got horse and mule an' auto traders now. They bought and sold slaves and hired 'em out. Yes'm, rented 'em out. Allotted means somethin' like hired out. But the slave never got no wages. That all went to the master. The man they was allotted to paid the master."

"I never was sold. My mama was sold only once, but she was hired out many times. Yes'm when a slave was allotted, somebody made a down payment and gave a mortgage for the rest. A chattel mortgage."

A down payment!!

"Times don't change, just the merchandise.

"Allotments made a lot of grief for the slaves", Aunt Sally asserted. "We left my papa in Kentucky, 'cause he was allotted to another man. My papa never knew where my mama went, an' my mama never knew where papa went." Aunt Sally paused a moment, then went on bitterly. "They never wanted mama to know, 'cause they knowed she would never marry so long she knew where he was. Our master wanted her to marry again and raise more children to be slaves. They never wanted mama to know where papa was, an' she never did", sighed Aunt Sally.

Only those who have lost their mate, and never know the end of the tale, can understand such heart anguish.

"Mama said she would never marry again to have children," continued Aunt Sally, "so she married my step-father, Trattle Barber, 'cause he was sick an' could never be a father. He was so sick he couldn't work, so me and mama had to work hard. We lived in a kitchen, a room in a log house joined on to the master's house. My mama worked in the field, even when I was a little baby. She would lay me down on a pallet near the fence while she plowed the corn or worked in the field.

"Stepfather and mama often tended their own tobacco and grain in the moonlight. This they could sell and have the money. We could go to church which was held in the school house. Sometimes they let us play with the other children after the noon dishes were washed and there wasn't anything else to do.

"There was most always something to do. Master never allowed nobody to be idle. Mama worked in the house and the fields too. At night after she come home from the field, she had to grate corn for the family next day. We didn't have many grist mills them days, an' we would punch holes in a piece of tin, and rub the ear of corn across it and make meal for our use.

"Nowadays, when you all want a nice wool dress, all you got to do is go to the store and get it", Aunt Sally commented, when asked to tell about their clothing.

"When I was growin' up an' wanted a nice wool dress, we would shear the sheep, wash the wool, card it, spin it and weave it. If we wanted it striped, we used two threads. We would color one by using herbs or barks. Sometimes we had it carded at a mill, an' sometimes we carded it ourselves. But when we did it, the threads were short, which caused us to have to tie the thread often, makin' too many knots in the dress. I have gathered the wool off the fences where it had been caught off the sheep, an' washed it, an' used it to make mittens.

"Yes'm. I worked in the fields, and I worked hard too. Plantin' and harvestin' in those days was really work. They used oxen to break up the ground for corn, an' for plowin' it too. They hoed the corn with a hoe, and cut the stalks with a hoe and shocked 'em. They cut the grain with the cradle and bound it with their hands, and shocked it. They threshed the grain with a hickory stick. Beating it out.

"I carried water for the field hands. I've carried three big buckets of water from one field to another, from one place to another; one in each hand and one balanced on my head.

"Yes'm. Some masters was good an' some was bad. My mama's master whipped his slaves for pastime. My master was not so bad as some was to their slaves. I've had many a whippin', some I deserved, an' some I got for being blamed for doin' things the master's children did. My master whipped his slaves with a cat-o'-nine-tails. He'd say to me, 'You ain't had a curryin' down for some time. Come here!!!' Then he whipped me with the cat. The cat was made of nine strips of leather fastened onto the end of a whip. Lots of times when he hit me, the cat left nine stripes of blood on my back. Yes ma'am."

Aunt Sally brooded over the whipping memories, then under the influence of a brighter thought continued:—

"I belong to the African Methodist Episcopal Church, an' I ain't never cussed but once in my life, an' that was one time I nearly got two whippin's for somethin' I didn't do. Some of master's kin folks had a weddin', an' we walked to the church, an' somebody kicked dust on the bride's clothes, an' I got blamed but I ain't never kicked it. The master's daughter Puss, she kicked it. Ole mistress she whipped me. Yes'm, she whipped me. It was the worst whippin' I ever got. The worst whippin' in my whole life, an' I still got the marks on my body. Yes'm. I got 'em yet.

"When the master come home, he was goin' to whip me again, an' I got mad, an' told him it was a lie, an' if Puss said I kicked dust on the white folks she was a DAMNED LYIN' DEVIL. He took the switch an' gave Puss a whippin' for tellin' a lie. Yes'm. That's the only time I ever cussed in my life.

"Yes'm, an' that's about all I knows about slavery and folks ways hereabouts. I can tell you about after we was freed. When we was freed all the money my mama had was 50 cents. I never went to school till after I was freed.

I went two winters and a little more to school near Burlington Junction. I never went a full term 'cause I had to work.

"I knowed my husband all my life. He was brought here by that man Jimmie Graves, that mama was allotted to. My husband took that name. His full name was Joseph H. Graves. We had one child, a boy. His name is Arza Alexander Graves. He lives here with me. It's our farm.

"I have lived on this place ever since I was married. That was in the same year that Burlington Junction was started. We first bought 40 acres for $10.00, then two years later we bought the back 80 acres for $15.00. Things is changed. We workin' for ourself now, an' what we get is our'n, an' no more whippin's. I worked in the fields and helped pay for this land. I belong to the African Methodist Episcopal Church in Maryville."

The day her family was freed, they had 50 cents. Today these children of a transplanted race, once enslaved, have through years of steadfast courage overcome the handicap of race and poverty. They threshed grain with a hickory stick, and made their corn meal by grating the ears across a strip of tin with holes punched in it.

With all her handicaps, this Negro woman has lived to an honorable old age, is self-supporting and has the respect of her neighbors. All this she has accomplished despite the fact she was once a chattel and was frequently "curried down" with a "cat-o'-nine-tails."

AUNT SALLY

Interview with Sarah Frances Shaw Graves, R.F.D. #4, Skidmore, Missouri.

Sarah Frances Shaw Graves (Aunt Sally) whose address is R.F.D. #4 Skidmore, Missouri is eighty-seven years of age. She lives with her bachelor son on their one-hundred-twenty acre farm. The home though small is moderately furnished and she enjoys the comforts of the rural telephone and radio and daily newspapers in her home. The house is surrounded by a nice yard containing many flowers and is enclosed with an iron fence, a cement walk leading from the front gate to the house.

Aunt Sally had been informed that the reporter was intending to call on her the following day and she was eagerly awaiting the arrival of the visitor. The reporter was greatly impressed by the arrangement and cleanliness of Aunt Sally's modest home. Aunt Sally was immaculately dressed in a stiffly starched print dress and a fresh white apron. Her white hair was combed straight back off her forehead and held back with side combs. She was in a very excited talkative mood, and talked freely, and laughed heartily when the reporter explained the purpose of the interview and asked the privilege of taking her picture. Actual interview follows:

"My name is Sarah Frances Shaw Graves or Aunt Sally as everybody calls me. I am eighty-seven (87) years old and I was born March 23, 1850 in Kentucky somewhere near Louisville. I was brought to Missouri when I was six months old with my Mamma who was a slave owned by a man named Shaw who had allotted her to a man named Jimmie Graves who came to Missouri to live with his daughter. Emily Graves Crowdes. I always lived with Emily Crowdes. We left my Papa in Kentucky as he belonged to another man. My Papa never knew where my Mamma and me went and my Mama and me never knew where my Papa went. They never wanted Mama to know where my Papa was because they knew Mama would never marry as long as she knew where he was. Our Master wanted Mama to marry again and raise more children for slaves but Mama said she would never marry a man and have children so she married my step-father, Trattle Barber, because she knew he had a disease and could not be a father. He was sick and not able to work so me and Mama had to work hard. We lived in a kitchen, a room in a log house joined on to the Masters house. All I knew about that part was what they told me. The Crowdes family who we came here with, settled near Possum Walk which is near the place that is now called Burlington Jct., Missouri. We were freed in 1863 but we heard so much about slavery coming back that we stayed with the Crowdes' two years longer or until 1865 when we was sure that we was freed. When we was freed we took the same name as our Masters. We then lived about two miles north of them and worked for some of the neighbors who was poor and had children and we lived on Lowell Livengood's grandfather's place for about two years. Mamma had fifty (50¢) cents coming to her and that is all the money we had. My Mama did a washing for that money for a lady and the Mistress told her that when the lady called for her washing that the fifty cents belonged to us. This was after we was freed. I went to school near Burlington Jct., Missouri and my teacher's name was Rachel Libbey. I went to school two winters a little while, I never went a full term any time. I had to work and when the busiest time was over I would go to school when I didn't work. I knew my husband all my life. He was owned by this man Jimmie Graves who Mama was alotted to, but was brought here by the man he was alloted to, named Nicholas. My husband's full name was Joe H. Graves. We had one child, a boy, whose name is Arza Alexander Graves. I have lived on this place I am on now every since I was married, that was the same year Burlington Jct., Missouri, started. We first bought forty (40) acres and paid twenty ($20.00) dollars for that, then about two years later we bought the back eighty (80) acres and I think we paid fifteen ($15.00) dollars for that. I worked in the fields and helped pay for this land. I belong to the African Methodist Episcopal Church in Maryville, Missouri.

"When I was growing up and wanted a nice wool dress we would shear the sheep, wash the wool, card it, spin it, and weave it. If we wanted it striped we used two threads, we would color one by using herbs and barks. We sometimes had it carded at a mill and sometimes we carded it ourselves but when we did it the threads were short which caused us to have to tie the thread often making more knots in the dress. In planting corn in them days they broke up the ground, one layed off the rows, one would go along and drop the corn or grain and if they wanted to plant beans in with the corn one would go along and drop the seed. They covered it over with a hoe and they cut the stalks with the hoe and stacked up the stalks. The way they raised the corn after it came up they took one horse and went on each side of a row and in the middle of every row to plow the corn. It took three rounds on every row to get it plowed. They used oxen sometimes to plow and nearly always used oxen to plow up the ground. They cut the grain with the cradle and bound it with their hands and shocked it up. They thrashed the grain with a hickory stick by beating it out. Many times I have carried three big buckets of water from one place to another, one in each hand and one balanced on my head. My Master was not as bad as some Masters was to their slaves. One time when I had over worked my Master said, "You have not had a currying down for a long time, come over here," and he whipped me with a cat-o'-nine-tails. This cat was made of nine small pieces of leather fastened on to the end of the whip. Lots of times when they hit with the cat it left nine stripes of blood. Mama's Master whipped his slaves for past-time. I have got many whippings for being blamed for doing things the Master's children did and I was blamed for it. One time when a couple was married, me and other members of the family were walking down the road and I was very careful not to kick up any dirt and to be very nice to the couple but when we got home one of the Master's daughters told that I was mean and that I kicked up dirt so that dust would get on the lady's dress and I got the worst whipping I ever got in my life by the Mistress and I still have the marks on my body, and when the Master came I was carrying the vitales from the kitchen to the dining room which was the living and bed room and when I went in I took the bread and when I came back he was standing in the door and he told me what they told him about me and I said I did not do it and if "Puss" said I did she is a "Damned lying devil" and he dropped the switch and went and talked to his daughter and gave her a whipping for telling the untruth. That was the only time I ever swore. In a few days the bride came over visiting and told them they had the sweetest little colored girl she was so lovely and kind. We were never allowed to be idle, always doing something and my work often was choring around to say I was doing something. I have gathered the wool off the fences where it had been caught off the sheep and washed it and used it to make mittens. I never was sold and my Mama was sold only once but she was hired out many times. We slept on what they called a bed, a tick filled with straw on the bed. My Mama's Master had a child near my age and my Mama always left me at the house with the Mistress and I nursed the Mistress, Mrs. Crowdes, as well as her own child until one day the curtain, which was used as a partition around a bed on which I lay near, caught on fire and then my Mama always took me to the field with her and would lay me on a pallet near the fence while she plowed the corn or worked in the field. Stepfather and Mama often tended to their own tobacco and grain in the moonlight which they could sell and have the money. One thing we could go to church which was held in the school house. Sometimes they would let me go out and play with the other children after the noon dishes were washed and there wasn't anything else to do then. I often sewed strips of cloth together to make carpet rags, there was always something to do. Mama worked in the field and in the house too. They nearly always kept a girl in the house. We did not have many mills and sometimes we could not get to the mill and we would punch holes in a piece of tin and rub the ear of corn across it to grate it for our use. Many times Mama would work in the field all day and in the evening she would grate enough corn for the family use the next day. The Masters had stores and you had to go to that store and get your needs and when the month was up you had nothing as it took all you earned to pay your bill."

EMILY CAMSTER GREEN

> Interview with Emily Camster Green,
> Cape Girardeau, Missouri.

"My mammy wuz Celie Camster en my daddy wuz Jack McGuire. We lived out in Bollinger County an' belonged to Massa George Camster. De white folks had a big house, made o' logs, wid chinkins in 'tween en 'nen dobbed over. Us cullud folks had little cabins an' we had good livin' dar. Ole Massa an' Missus Patsy wuz mighty good to us. Eatin's? Lawd we had everthin'—not de mess we has to make out wid now.

"I fell to young Missie Janie an' wuz her maid an' when Missie Janie married Mista Bradley I went with 'em down to Cha'leston in Mississippi County.

"Missie Janie an' her Mista Bradley rode in a buggy an' I sits behind. I 'member de fust time I seed de big ribber. Dar wuz a boat on it. I ain't nebber seed a boat befo' an' I says, 'Oh! Miss Janie dat house gonna sink.' She laf at me an' say dat a boat. Pore Miss Janie—dat Mista Bradley made her believe he had a big plantation an lots o' money an when we gits dar he warn't nuthin' but a overseer on de Joe Moore place. Pore Missie Janie! she wuz so purty an' she had lotsa beaux—she coulda' married rich but she jes tuk de wrong one.

"We had good times fore we lef' de ole place, fore Ole Massa died. We usta git together in de ebenin's. Dey'd say

'I's gon'a step over to de udder cabin'—en word ud git aroun' an 'for' you knowd it dey'd be a crowd. We allus said 'jest step over' no matter how far it wuz. Den some er de women ud put in a quilt an' some ud git to cookin' an' bakin. Mmm! de lassus cakes we used to have! An' den wen de quilt wuz finished an de eatin done dey'd clean out de room an dance. Dem sho wuz good times. But I 'members de las' dance we had. Ole Massa wuz sick. We's habbin' de dance an' Aunt Mary wuz dar. She wuz a spiritualis' woman—you knows whut a spiritualis is, don' you? Well, everybody wuz dancin' an' habbin' a good time—Aunt Mary say, 'Hush! I's gonna ask is Ole Massa gonna git well.' Den she say—'If Ole Massa gonna die, rap three times.' Den in a minnit comes a loud blam! blam! blam! right across de house. Den we all cry an' go home 'cause we knows Ole Massa's gonna die!

"'Bout dat time my daddy die too an my mammy marry Levi Wilson. He belong to Nelson Ellis an' when Ole Massa Ellis's daughter married Beverly Parrot dey went to Texas an' tuk my step-daddy along. 'Cose he never 'spected to see my mammy again an' he married a young woman down dar. Atter de war, dey comes back up dar an' he seed my mammy but she says, 'Go way. I libbed wid you sebben year an' nebber had no chillun by you. Now you got a young woman an' she got chillun. You stay with her. I won't bother you none.'

"My mammy allus stayed wid Ole Missus Patsy. Ole Tom Johnson, de nigger trader tuk her two brothers an' sent um to New Orleans. He usta libe in dat big house dat wuz war de postoffice is now, an' he usta keep de slaves he buy dar at he's house till he can send um down de ribber on de boat.

"One time a slave at a neighbor farm was workin' in de feel' an when he comes in, in de ebenin's he's wife wuz gone an' de cradle wuz emty. He's Massa done sold 'em. De ole man fell down on he's knees an' he begin prayin' an he pray an' he holler 'Oh! nobody know but Jesus! Nobody know but Jesus!' An' he kep' dat up a prayin' an a hollerin like dat. His ole Massa hear him, an' it made him feel bad. De ole darky keep on a prayin' an a hollerin, 'Nobody know but Jesus.' Ole Massa keep on a hearin' it, till atter awhile, he git right down der on de flo' wid de darky an' he' fess religion.

"After Ole Massa George died, Ole Missus Patsy married Woodson Parrot and went to his place in Scott County. Dey had a nice big home der an he were a good man. When he lay dyin he wuz sick a long time an' dey wuz allus some lodge men roun' him an my mammy wuz skeered of de men. De nite he died, Ole Missus Patsy had been up wid him so much she wuz sleepin—an he call out, 'Oh! Patsy! Oh! Patsy! Oh! Patsy!' three times jes like dat. Mammy wuz skeered o' dem men an she wouldn't go in an wake Ole Missus Patsy. Den ole Massa Parrot say, 'Oh! Patsy, I ain't nebber made a prayer in my life an' here I'se dyin.' Ole Missus Patsy nebber did forgive my mammy for not wakin' her till de day she died.

"Miss Janie allus had to live on rented places. Mista Bradley warn't smart an' he didn't have nuthin but she stayed with him an' done de bes' she could.

"We seed lotsa sojers cum by durin' de war, but dey nebber bothered us much. De Ku Kluxers cum roun' sometimes but mostly to see dat darkies stay whar dey belong. When de war wuz over I wanted to stay wif Missie

Janie but my mammy cum an' got me. We worked for a German family livin on Jackson Hill.

"I cud a been a spiritualis woman if I'd had a little education. I allus had visions an' ud see thing but I nebber know'd whut dey mean. When I tell my mammy she allus say, 'Hush chile, you allus a see'in things.'

"My mammy's daid now a long time but she offen comes to see me. One night I seed her carryin a bright light. She allus comes to see me when I'se in trouble but I ain't seen her now for a long time."

LOU GRIFFIN

Interview with Mrs. Lou Griffin,
St. Louis, Missouri.

Mrs. Lou Griffin, a daughter of Minnie and William Gibson, is something over ninety years old. She does not know her exact age. She tells the writer she is one of a family of thirteen children and that her grandmother had twenty-one children. She lives with a great nephew at 2935 Easton Avenue, St. Louis. She tells her story as follows:

"People tells me not to tell nothing 'bout myself to folks like you what asks me, 'cause you ain't going to give me nothing for it nohow, but somebody somewhere pays you to gather up this stuff. So I's just gonna tell you dis much, sister. Sure 'nough I was slave born. 'Fore I was big enough to do nothing us chillun used to run about in de woods while de old folks was working on de plantation. We git stole away by white folks what wasn't our owners and sold I reckon, nobody knowed where de chillun gone nor who got 'em. We know dis much, we didn't never see 'em any more.

"We just be out in de woods picking fruit and flowers. I know this though, sister, after while, de Rebels got a heap of us. I heard 'em say dey some times get fifty dollars for some of de black folks dey sold and some big healthy ones brought one-hundred dollars. Course I don't know how much money dey brought, I just know 'bout it. We use to go to de church house. If we suited de overseer he let us go. If we didn't we got lashed plenty. Dey lash you till you was forced to pray den dey whip you like anything for prayin'. But God done stopped all that now. Dis heah old Abe Lincoln come through our town. I guess you done heard 'bout him, is you, honey? If you ain't, I'll tell you. He just come 'round to see how de Rebs do de slaves. I gets so full thinkin' how de good Lawd fix it for us. He come 'round when nobody's lookin' for him. Bye and bye he says, fight for your freedom in de Yankee army instead of standing 'round here being sold and treated like beasts.

"Ole Jeff Davis was a Rebel and he rode a fine horse. Abe Lincoln come there, wid a mule. De slaves made up a song 'bout how old Abe Lincoln got hold of Jeff Davis in de army and Abe Lincoln took and rode Jeff Davis' big fine horse and Jeff Davis had to ride de mule. Abe Lincoln was United States president and Jeff Davis was de fool. We often hear tell of dem Yankees coming to our town a long time 'fore dey get there. We know when dey reached us, 'cause dey run dem Rebs way from their own place and take 'em themselves. I been all down in Arkansas, Louisiana, Mississippi, North Carolina and everywhere, being hiked around by dem Valentines, dat's de name of my mother's owners and mine too, for that. I 'haved so I didn't git licked like some more did, yes indeed I did. De bells would ring for day, sissy, and we had to get up and start right in working, yes mam. I use to love to see 'em drill dem soldiers. Sure did. I thank God it is all over now. I ain't going to tell you no more. Like to have you stay awhile, but if you want just come back."

LOUIS HAMILTON

> Interview with Louis Hamilton,
> Fredericktown, Missouri.

Never Sold His Vote

"Is 90 years old and was born right dere in Whittenburg, Cape Girardeau County, Missouri, across de creek. We was stayin' with Greenvilles den. My father was named Nathan and my mother was Mary. She died right after de war was over. My grandmother was born in West Virginia and I had three brothers and three sisters. Dey is all dead but me. My father drove an old ox team around dere hauling coal. He fought in de war and come back and went right to work and den bought him a farm back of Whittenburg and lived dere until he died.

"De first work I done was on de farm. Den I worked at Mine la Motte, and Buck Eye. Was a tie inspector and also worked in de car shop at Madison, Illinois. On de farm I got $1 a day. In de mines I got $12 a week. In de car shop I made about 40 cents a hour. I bought dis property here with my money and have been on it for 18 years. I give $450 for dis property. I've paid $11 taxes for eight or nine years and now pay $5 a year. De master had a big farm of two or three hundred acres and had four or five slaves. Sometimes my father would take me down dere in de woods to a white picnic. After my father's first wife died he did not let us run around much. We used to fight with de white kids but had no trouble with de old folks. At Christmas time, man dey treated us with fun; eats of all kinds, dat you could pack home.

"When de war was over we moved across de creek to ourselves and my father bought 25 or 30 acres. I felt like a new man when de war was over. I stayed with my grandfather until I was 21 and got married in Perry County when I was 32. I had 4 children and dey is all dead. My wife has been dead about 14 years. I've lived 25 years in Fredericktown. De young Negroes ain't no account as compared to when I was a boy. De parents nowadays don't make dem work hard enough. Dey can sleep all day if dey want to. Some of de young Negroes around here work in de shoe factory. Some load ties.

"Once when I was a baby, my sister was sitting by de fireplace rocking me and she fell asleep and let me fall in de fireplace and I was burned on de hand. Four of my fingers was burned and have never come out straight. When I was a boy I did not know what a stove looked like. We had dese old corded beds. Dere used to be a lot of wild hogs around dere and dey would eat anything dey got hold of. We would put up ice from de Mississippi River. It was over a foot thick. We wore home-made clothes and did not buy no clothes. We wore copper-toed shoes called brogans. De first time I voted was for Teddy Roosevelt. I been voting ever since. Lots of dem have told me how to vote but I never sold my vote."

FIL HANCOCK

Interview with Fil Hancock,
Rolla, Missouri.

"Uncle" Fil Hancock

The following interview, bristling with facts and vivid recollections covering more than three quarters of a century was obtained recently by a worker employed by the Federal Writers' Project in Missouri from "Uncle" Fil Hancock, eighty-six year old Negro, living at Rolla, Missouri. The old man's story, told as nearly as possible in his own dialect runs thus:

"I was born 1851, de 28th day of February. My granny come here with her missus-Hancock—when dey brung de Cherokee Indian tribe here from middlin' Tennessee, de time dey moved de Missouri Indians back to Oklahoma, what dey called Indian Territory way back 'bout 135 or 140 years ago. Our old missus maiden name was Riggs. My old master was Scotch-Irish. A big, red faced man wid sandy hair, mostly baldheaded. Us little niggers was scairt of him and run and hid when we see him coming. He weren't 'lowed to whip us, 'cause he didn't own us. Our old missus had eleven of us and he had twenty-one niggers of his own. And our old missus wouldn't let him tech us.

"We had to mind him though. But she done de whipping. My own mammy whipped us good and proper—She used a razor strop, and shore poured it on us. She was puny and sick most all de time. Dey said she had consumption, now-days dey calls it T.B. But it was plain old consumption in dem days. I 'member, she were so sick dat she were not able to hold us an' whip us, and she made one of us little niggers push de other one up to her bed while she whipped us. We took our turns in gittin' a whipping. Poor old mammy, she loved us and wanted us to do right. We never got a whipping 'ceptin' we needed it. Old granny, my mammy's mother and old missus whipped us a little, an only wid buckbresh, jes' a little 'roun' de ankles. All us little niggers was jes' like stairsteps, one after de other. I got whipped plenty, but I needed it.

"My ol' missus Hancock named me herself—called me Filmore Taylor Hancock, after two presidents who took der seats in 1850. Ol' Colonel Hancock was our master an' he was de richest man in Greene County, Missouri, and owned more slaves than any man in Missouri. His wife, old missus was born in 1804. My own granny on my mammy's side was born in 1805. My granny was given to missus, as her own de day she was born. 'Course old missus was only a year old den. Der was thirty-two of us slaves on our old missus place, and eleven of us sprung from old granny.

"We had five young missus. My young missus names were Winnie, Elizabeth, Lucinda, Luella, and Tennessee. Dey was so rich and proud, dey wouldn't look at any body to marry. Only two of 'em ever married. Dey was fine ladies, but dey shore had me plumb spilt. Some of dem whipped me three or four times, but I 'member how dey jes' breshed me a little roun' de legs, and turn away and laugh a little. I can see now I needed more'n I got. If I told a lie I got whipped for it, and old missus poured it on if we lied.

"I and de other two gals, my sisters and a brudder of mine—well, when our mammy died, old missus took us down to her house, away from our cabin, so she could look after us. Our old granny was de white folk's cook. She helped look after us. We got to eat what de white folk did. Up to de cabins where de other niggers was, had salt meat, cabbage, 'taters, and shortnin' bread three times a day. We all had plenty vegetables we raised ourselves. Every Sunday mornin' our missus sent us up a big tray 'bout three feet long, made of sycamore—and it full of flour. Once a week we had hot biscuits. But me and Squire, my brudder and my sisses, Mary and Margot had it a little better, we had what our old missus had. I was ten years an' six months old when de war come up.

"In '61, I see General Lyons, when he passed right by our house. All de Union sojers had to pass by our house time of de war. We lived on the main wagon road from Rolla to Springfield. Well child, Lordy me! dat's funny for me to tell you how General Lyon look. It was a sight to see him with them 'purties'! And we asked old missus what dat was, them 'purties' he had on his shoulders. She says to us chillun: 'He is de general. All dem odder men got to mind him'. He was killed in dat battle of Wilson Creek. Dey kept him in an icehouse in a spring, owned by a man named Phelps. He lived west of Springfield. Dey keep General Lyon two weeks, 'fore they brung him down dis-a-way. Dey shipped him out of Rolla to Connecticut—dat's what I hear de ol folks says. Dat man Phelps was our neighbor and later he got to be governor of Missouri in 1876. Crittenden was first de Democratic governor in '73.

"Old missus called us little darkies all up—and carried us down to de wagon General Lyon's body was in, when dey was bringin' him back here. And we looked at him and asked what was de matter. Old missus said 'He was killed.' He was packed in ice in de wagon and de wagon had four mules hitched to it. I wanted to know if he was de man who had dem 'purties' on his shoulders. She said 'Yes'.

"I said, 'Did marse Bill and marse George and marse Jeff Hancock hep kill him?' She said: 'Yes'. Marse Bill, marse George an' marse Jeff was my young bosses, my old master's sons. Old missus didn't seem glad or anything, jes' looked kinda sad. We asked her would he ever fight again. She said, 'No'. I won't ever forget how General Lyon looked. He rode a kinda gray-white horse when I first see him and looked so tall and proud like.

"De rebels held Springfield from 1861 till 1862, when General Freemont come in and took it. Marmaduke and Price had de biggest armies of de southerners, Freemont come sneaking in, wrapped his wagon wheels with old blankets so dey wouldn't hear him coming, and he had a body guard of three hundred. Marmaduke and Price was den in Springfield. Freemont come 'bout daybreak, and started shooting de town up. He got de town and held it.

"Marmaduke and Price drifted 'round to de Southeast part of de State and went into Arkansas. Later dey had a three hour scrummage at Pea Ridge, Arkansas. Either 62 or 63, I kaint 'member much, I was too little and scairt to know. Being only ten or eleven years old. Dey was a man named Finis McCrae, a rebel in de Marmaduke and Price Army, in de infantry. He took sick some place in Arkansas. Dey brung him to us, we being rebels, and keep him two weeks in our up-stairs, not letting any one know he was dere. We kept him till he got better and he went back into de army and fit some more.

"I seen Marmaduke in person, when he was making his campaign for governor, down in Cuba, Missouri. All de Union sojers stopped at our house to get water. We had a runnin' stream that never did go dry. They filled their canteens there. All us chillun fussed 'bout 'em takin' our milk and butter outen de spring-house. Old missus keep all her milk and butter and cheese in dere to keep it cool. When de Union sojers come by our house to Rolla dey took so much of de water to fill dere canteens it nearly took our spring dry. Took every thing we had in de spring-house—milk, butter—everything.

"I don't 'member how dey was dressed, but dey all had on sumpin' blue. Uniforms I guess. Me and four more little darkies was one-half mile offen de big road when dey passed, and got scared and run back to old missus house and hid in de old barn loft all dat night. Old missus asked us what we did for sumpin' to eat. We told her we bent de rye down in de field and rubbed de grain out wid our hands and eat dat. She took us to de house and give us sompin' to eat. De sojers was still passing de house den.

"In time of de Civil War we wouldn't come down to Rolla, we went south to do our trading. We wasn't Union and Rolla was Union Headquarters. Old Master was getting old den, he had been a colonel in some army or other way 'fore de Civil War.

"Lincoln issued 'green backs' 'long 'bout '61 or '62, after Stephen A. Douglas goes up to Washington and tell Lincoln, after he got de 'nomination dat if he didn't get

Jeff Davis and some of de leaders and prosecute 'em, he was going to have war on his hands. Lincoln tells Douglas to go back and tell Jeff Davis to lay dem guns down, dat in 90 days he would 'low dem so much a head for dere niggers. Dat if dey would free dem dey could be paid for so much a head, by taxation. But Lincoln told dem dey would all have to come back together again same as before like dey was. You see dese folks in de south had done got $8,000,000, all dat ammunition and guns and things from England. Jeff Davis and dem leaders wouldn't give it up.

"De first issue of greenbacks was $175,000,000 and de next issue was $250,000,000. We had been told all dis and I ask old missus if she reckon we could whip dem 'blue bellied yankees'. I says: 'Dey ain't got no money'.

"We called de Union sojers—'Yankees' and our side was called de Gray or de Rebels. It's 75 years, the 10th day of August, 1937, that General Lyon was killed.

"My boss—Hancock was de biggest slave holder in Missouri when de war first come up. He settled four miles east of Springfield, Missouri. He owned close to 1200 or 1500 acres of ground. From Springfield to Strafford—east. We had 375 acres in cultivation—corn, oats, wheat, rye, and clover was our main crops.

"My daddy belonged to a man named Lou Langston. There is a railroad station named for this same Langston. What was known as the 'Gulf Road.' I took my mammy's white folk's name. They were as fine and good as anybody. The first child old missus had was a boy, Bill Hancock. The first child my old granny had (on my mammy's side) was a boy, named Joe. Old missus gave granny's boy

Joe, to her boy Bill, as a slave. You see my old missus and my old granny was born a year apart demselves.

"One time my old master Hancock, got mad at my uncle, who was a growed up nigger. Old marse wanted to whip him. He tried to make my uncle put his head twixt his (old marser's) knees. My uncle didn't offer to fight him, but twisted him roun' and roun' trying to get his head out. He gave one twist dat throwed old marse down to de ground. My uncle jumped and run and jumped over de fence. My uncle did not belong to old marse but to his son, Bill. But old marse sure got mad when my uncle run. So he sold him to a man named Dokes—a nigger trader of dat neighborhood. Dokes bought niggers and sold dem on de block in St. Louis. When Dokes took my uncle away, one of our neighbors by de name of Fisher—up near Strafford, gits on his horse and goes to Springfield and tells my young boss, Bill, dat old man Hancock had sold Joe and Jane. Jane belonged to Marse Hancock. Mister Fisher had only one colored man, and he told my young boss, Bill, dat if he would buy both them niggers back, dat he would buy Jane for his (Fisher's) colored man. He didn't have no woman for him.

"Old Dokes was on his way den to St. Louis with 'em. Bill and Fisher started out, rode and caught up with dem near what is now known as Knob View, Missouri. When dey come in sight of Dokes, Bill stopped and dropped back. Fisher goes up to de wagon, stopped Dokes and asked him what he would take for Joe and Jane. They was settin' up in the wagon handcuffed together. I think it was a thousand dollars or fifteen hundred dollars he asked for both. Den Fisher beckoned to Bill Hancock to come on. Bill come up and paid Dokes what he asked.

Dokes was to take 'em back, hisself, to dere own neighborhood.

"When marse Bill rode up, my uncle said, 'Take these handcuffs off me'. Mr. Dokes took them off. My uncle jumped out of de wagon and run up to de big mule my young boss was settin' on, he reached up an' took Bill, his marster off dat mule so quick and lay him down on de ground. He commenced to love and kiss him on side of his head. He picked him up and sat marse Bill on his mule again and said, 'I know marse Bill wasn't goin' to let me be sold.' He takes him off his mule again and lay him down two times more and keep lovin' and kissin' him, he was dat happy.

"But old marse Hancock, jes' wouldn't let Joe live on his place again, no more. He was dat mad. It made him so mad to think Joe had turn him over when he had his legs twixt his knees. But young marse Bill took Joe to Springfield and hired him out to a blacksmith by de name of Lehr. He got forty dollars a month for him. Joe stayed dere till de Civil War. Old master let Joe come to de house to see his mother, my old granny, once in a while, but never to live.

"Old man Fisher bought de colored woman from marse Bill, for his colored man, and paid him as he could. Our white folks had plenty of money to get any thing they wanted.

"I first come to Rolla in 1869 and stayed till 1870. Then dere was only one brick house in Rolla, standin' where the Edwin Long Hotel now stands. Den I left and went to Cuba and stayed dere and at Salem til' 1882. I come back to Rolla when de Crandel House was built, where de Rolla

Hospital now is located. I started a barber shop here under the Crandel House basement. I have been here and at Salem ever since 1882, Rolla my headquarters.

"If I can leave enough when I die, I want to be buried at the Union Graveyard in Greene County, Missouri, where my mammy is buried since three years before the Civil War. My daddy was buried there in 1863.

"When I was young, we didn't know nuthin' 'bout churches. Us kids never got to go no place 'less de old niggers took us. And dey wouldn't take us. De older ones had church out in de brash, under de shade trees.

"I kin 'member one of my cousins carryin' me pick-a-back, one time, three miles to church. Dey only had church in de summer time, or meeting dey called it. It was allus in de woods. We dassen't be ketched wid a book to read or to try to be educated. Course every one wasn't treated dat-a-way. Sometimes de niggers would have dancin', if de bosses or masters gave dem passes. De passes read sumpin' like dis: 'Let my nigger file pass and repass to such and such a place'.

"I 'member once, my missus bought me a pair of high top red boots. My! I was proud. In dem days, we went barefoot most all year round. But my missus tried to make us happy on Christmas. I put dem boots on and I pranced round and round jes' to hear dem squeak. I done thought dat was de purtiest noise I ever heard. I asked old missus, could I go to old Massy's house. He were our neighbor, 'bout half mile—but it were dark. Old missus said, 'Hain't you scared to go?' I say, 'No'. I went up de road, my boots squeaking and squeaking. Didn't have time to be scared—listenin' to dem boots.

"Aunt Rachel, my own aunt, lived at Massy's house. You see Masseys was dere name and dey was white folks but we say Massy's house. I wanted my old aunt to see my new boots. When I got dere I called my aunt to come see my boots. She come and say, 'Hain't you scared to come here all 'lone'. I say, 'no'. I twisted and turn, round and round so she could hear 'em squeak. But when it come time to go home, I got plum' scared. Aunt Rachel had to take me. She took me where I could see our house. My! How old missus laughed when she found I had to be brung home. She say, 'I told you, you be scared to come alone'.

"In dem days no nigger got boots till he was big and able to work for 'em. I was old missus pet and she plum' spilt me. I allus got more'n de odder niggers got. Boys had cotton shirts and de gals had cotton dresses.

"You know it's a funny thing, de white folks took everything from us niggers, even try to take our old songs and have dem on de radio. We niggers say 'De white folks take everything, dis, dat, an' t'other, but what we got is jes' natural borned to us.'

"I knocks a tamborine jes' like de Georgia niggers played a tambourine, 'fore de Civil War. Dem Georgia minstrels was taken over to England to perform 'fore de Queen Victoria, way 'fore Civil War. Folks from way up East got 'em and took 'em. Dey ain't many plays like dem no more."

"Uncle" Fil, as he was familiarly known in Rolla, played for the Folk Festival in Rolla and received so much applause, he had to be helped off the stage. He is exceedingly active. He plays the old tambourine, (he owned so many years) under and over his legs, behind his head, bouncing it and catching it, never losing the rhythm an instant.

He is tall and erect, and has a remarkable memory, especially for dates, names and places. He loves children, and usually has a pocket full of pennies for the babies. His home is a one-room hut (plain shed building) back of the Post Office on Ninth Street, Rolla, Missouri. He lives alone and has no living relatives. The people of Rolla aid him with gifts.

Uncle "Fil's" favorite old spiritual is below. He says: "Dis song, I'm a tellin' you, is de truf."

Dis Is My Buryin' Groun'

Ask my Lord for mercy,
Good Lord, gimme religion,
Good Lord, gimme me a heart to b'lieve,
Dis is de buryin' groun'.
Amen, Hallelujah. Dis is de buryin' groun'.

Tell your mother,
Tell your father,
Dis is de buryin' groun',
Tell all your neighbors,
Tell all your neighbors chillun,
Dis is de buryin' groun'.

Uncle Fil says, "Niggers jes' makes dey own verses, jes' naturally comes to us, and we make our own rhyme as we go."

One of the humorous songs, a favorite of his, goes:

You, by word, now all we go,
In fact we spoke both high and low,
In the house and out of doors,

Ebening in the baby's nose.
When I was young an' in my prime,
I'se a countin' courtin' them gals,
Most all de time.
Now I'm old and you will see,
I'm not as young as I used to be.
Now when the elephant moves aroun'
The music begins to play,
Oh, the boys aroun' dat monkey's cage
I'd better keep away.
Rock the cradle John,
Rock the cradle John,
Many a man is rockin' another man's son
When he thinks he's rockin' his own.

DAVE HARPER

Interview with Dave Harper,
Montgomery City, Missouri.

Dave Is Cardinal Fan

Dave Harper, a former slave, had just tuned in on the baseball game when the interviewer arrived for he is an ardent Cardinal fan and, although he was extremely courteous, he never missed a play in that game. He was not at all reticent about telling of his life though plainly curious to know the purpose of the interview and just a bit skeptical as to its final use. Dave, who now lives in Montgomery City, Mo., has been a gardener for years, always having the earliest and finest vegetables as well as supplying others with plants for resetting.

"I'll be glad to tell you anything I remember," Dave said in reply to the request for something of his life story. "Col. Harper was my master. We lived northwest of town (Montgomery City). I was born in Montgomery County and lived dere all my life. Col. Harper had 25 or 30 slaves; dere was lots of money wrapped up in dem."

Here Dave reflected for a moment and shook his head sadly at the amount of cash invested in humans and then continued.

"He bought me when I was six years old. I was born eighty-seven years ago next January, down on Clear

Fork, southwest of Danville, near Mineola, 'bout half mile from Capt. Callaway's grave. No'm, it don't seem like dey could have found enough dirt dere to cover his body. It sure is rocky dere. Did you ever read Nat Sharp's history? It says dat one of Capt. Callaway's men was buried down dere across de field.

"I've seen slaves go through Danville in droves like cattle. Dey was chained together and dey walked 'em to St. Louis to de nigger yard. One mother give out. De man in charge made her give her baby away, she couldn't carry it no further. Someone near Danville raised de baby.

"I was sold when I was six years old to Clark Whitesides's father to nurse Clark. My mother was sold down on de Missouri River. I'll tell you 'bout dat. De Fords moved to Danville from Virginia. Dere was several brothers in together in de nigger business. Dey brought my mother to wait on Mrs. Ford and carry her her coffee. She married and had three children. De nigger traders from Virginia run an attachment to get possession of my mother. Den on de way back he took cholera and died. De case was in court when de war come up. Mr. Ben Sharp had de money, he died and dat ended it. I was sold by Thos. J. Powell, de sheriff. Mother was to be sold. Kit Talbot bid on her and de baby. She cried so hard 'cause she wanted to live with me dat Dr. Sharp paid de bid and got her. I used to go to see her real often.

"We was fed just moderate. Dere was fifteen hands. When dey come in at noon, dey ate from de big old kettle where de old colored woman had cooked de food. De next morning after he bought me, de boss carried me to de old woman and told her to take care of me. Dat morning de kettle was full of spare ribs and de people fished dem out with sticks. I didn't see no knives or forks. When dey asked me why I didn't get something to eat, I asked 'bout dem and a table where I could eat. De overseer just cried.

"De old lady took care of de children while de mothers worked. De oldest one never went to de field. She just looked after de little ones. One overseer was colored. He was an uncle of 'Big Nig' dat works at de hotel. We was fanning out wheat and one of de children was raking out de wheat. He talked back to de overseer who struck him. Dere was a singletree under de edge of de cloth. De master picked up de singletree but didn't strike de overseer, he backed off. Col. Harper raised oodles of tobacco. Dere were 16 to 17 hundred pounds to de hogshead. He raised 15 to 20 hogsheads.

"My mother-in-law was from Memphis. One day dey went to church and de Ku Klux Klan came in and beat de people over deir heads with pistols. De people went out de doors and windows. Dey could just blow a horn and de Ku Klux Klan would come from all directions.

"I was sold for $715. When de freedom come, I said, 'Give me $715 and I'll go back.' Col. Harper just gave me a quarter to buy my dinner. After de freedom, I worked in wheat harvest all season for $.75 a day. I worked for a week and my mammy told me to bring her some bacon. When de man paid me, I spent it all for a side of bacon. I felt mighty proud to take dat to her. Bacon was $.50 a pound. I stayed at Dr. Sharp's where mother worked and done chores. Later I made rails. Dey paid me $14 a month for cutting rail timber. I was paid at de postoffice and took de money home and gave it to mammy.

"Col. Harper's wife was Gen. Price's niece and Col.

Harper was a recruiting officer for Gen. Price. Young men came dere to join de southern army. Dey could always get a horse. De women stayed dere all de time to make de suits for de soldiers. De Union soldiers tried deir best to kill Col. Harper.

"One time I saved his life. Dey was going to kill him, 'bout 75 or 100 men on horses. I warned de Colonel two hours before dey got dere. Dis is how it happened. Col. Harper gave me de first day of Christmas to go to see my mother. Us children went out in de woods playing and when we come back de yard was all cut up with horses hoofs. Dr. Sharp put me on my horse and told me to tell Col. Harper dis message, dat 'dere was so many soldiers dat you might get hurt, you can come again some other time.' I told Col. Harper and he left. I didn't see him again until I was cutting wheat.

"My mistress lived dere for some time without any menfolks 'round 'cept de slaves. Dere was a horse kept dere on purpose so I could come to town every day for de mail. After a while, my mistress and her daughter went to Jarod Harris's to stay. Den I went to Harris's every morning for de mistress orders and to Montgomery each afternoon for de mail. I took de mail to de camp at night. Dat was Bill Anderson's camp over in Callaway County. Dey moved dat camp pretty often but I found it. One time de bushwhackers came to burn de depot but Col. Harper had it full of tobacco and wheat so dey didn't burn it.

"Young Billy Mathis was a lieutenant. He used to come to see mistress almost every day and bring her messages. Once a gang of blue coats was coming down de road. He got on one of mistress' horses and she told me to go 'long and bring de horse back. We went down through de woods with de bullets whistling through de air and cutting off de limbs of de trees."

Dave had apparently studied about the voodoo doctors and their wiles for a question as to conjure doctors brought a quick response:

"We call dem 'two headed Negroes'. You know dat if he could do any tricks he would keep dem from whipping him or selling him and dey couldn't do dat or dey would have done it long time ago. Tear open a pillow and sometimes dere is a mat of feathers. Sometimes dey puts things under de door step but I don't pay no 'tention to it. Dey is some dat thinks dere is something to it.

"Mother used to tell a tale 'bout when she was a little girl. Her mother went to frolics but her father went to bed, he was always tired after his day's work. One night my mother saw a woman come to her father's bed and rub her hand over his head. It didn't wake him up. De next day he took sick and soon died. I don't believe in hoodoo doctors but it is like de blood hounds can run and tree a man but if you can't find de goods it don't count.

"I worked in de hay harvest for $.50 a day. Common domestic for shirts was $.50 a yard. It took six yards to make one shirt, dat was a week's work. We lived on chickens. My mother raised a whole camp meeting of chickens. Dere never was a better white man dan Dr. Sharp. When I married I had four head of horses and three mules. I owed for one team of horses. I took typhoid fever in August and was in bed until November. Dr. Sharp and Dr. Bodine knew something was de matter but dey didn't know what it was. When de note come due, I got on a horse and rode to Dr. Sharp's. He wanted to know what

I was doing on dat horse. I told him 'bout de note and he said, 'Hum, dat's what's been bothering you. Don't you get off dat horse! I help you den you get back home and go to bed and stay dere!' He just wrote a check for $90, I had already paid $300. After I got well, I sold a span of mules to Joe McCleary and put de check in de bank for Dr. Sharp. Dat was to pay him for de note and taking care of me dat summer and fall.

"I was in de railroad home guards during de war. We had to keep de people from tearing up de railroads. I fought Bill Anderson's men many a time. Seems sort of queer when I used to take dem de mail but we kept dem from burning de railroad bridges. I served for 'bout six months near Macon."

CLARA MCNEELY HARRELL

Interview with Clara McNeely Harrell, Cape Girardeau, Missouri.

"We libbed way off 'en de backwoods, six mile tuther side o' Jackson, near Fruitland, and Ah's feared dey ain't much Ah ken tell yuh. My ole Massa wuz John McNeely. Ah don' rightly member mah ole Missus McNeely but when she die, ole Massa marry young Missie Harries fum down tow'ds de ribber. De white folks has a fine big white house an we'ens had a little log house. Dey wuz lotsa nut trees roun' dere an in de fall o' de year we'ens usta gather lotsa nuts—hicker' nuts, walnuts, an' dey wuz hazel nuts too.

"My Mammy's name?—les' see now—dey calls her Minnie—yes dat's it, Minnie. Youh see mah mind ain't so clear but when Ah talks 'bout 'em dey kinda comes back tuh me. Mah pappy's name wuz John Mitchell and he belong to a neighbor. I'se little and didn't hab much work to do. Jes chores, like heppin' to carry in wood and sech like, but mos'ly I'se jes' playin' an' tom-boyin' aroun'.

"Ole Massa had three boys at went off to war—Dey wuz Ab, an' Bob' an' Jack. We nebber seed no fightin' roun' our way but sometime we heard de cannon fum Cape. One time dey wuz lotsa sojers cum pass our place an dey had lotsa wagons an' things. Ah ain't nebber seed so many men an' I'se plum scared to death, but dey nebber bother none.

"We had big fields o' wheat an cahn an sich, but mah mammy didden work in de fiel', she spin an she weave. Ah could spin too. Ah's fill de quills and Ah'd hep her thread de loom. De loom stood out on de big porch and Ah kin jes see her sittin dar. She'd push de thread through tuh me an' den Ah'd ketch it and pull it through an han it back tuh her.

"When de war wuz over, Ole Massa call tuh me an' he say 'Clara, you know de war is over'—an Ah say 'Whar wuz it?' Ah nebber know'd nuthin 'bout de war.

"No'm, Ah don' know nuthin 'bout ghosts an sich like, but when Ah dies Ah specks to go to Hebbin an' Lawd! Ah's gonna sit all day an' shout an' sing, and clap mah han's an' stomp mah feet! Oh! Lawd! Dat's gonna be a happy time."

Clara McNeely Harrell, probably 80 or 82 years old lives in hollow—no street number west from Washington School, Cape Girardeau, Mo.

JOE HIGGERSON

> Interview with Joe Higgerson,
> Sedalia, Missouri.
> (Written by Geo. K. Bartlett, Kansas City,
> from F.C. of Kathleen Williams.)

How Did Uncle Joe Get Home?

Living at 410 West Pettis Street, Sedalia, is Joseph Higgerson, a pensioned Negro soldier of the Civil War, who can look back through the long vista of years and visualize slave life in Missouri, when the institution of slavery was at its most thriving period.

He was born a slave on a farm near Boonville, Missouri, in 1845 if his claim of being 92 years old in the summer of 1937, is correct.

He is somewhat bent and withered and his appearance of great age is accentuated by white patriarchal whiskers below the chin, while his cheeks are clean shaven; a style much in vogue during the life time of Horace Greeley.

His home, a little, four room, frame cottage, with its tiny front porch set close against the picket fence enclosing the lot, mirrors somewhat the deterioration age has placed upon its occupant. Both house and fence are weather beaten, gray from age and lack of paint.

"Could you and would you tell about slavery days?" he was asked.

"Yes Ma'am," he courteously and smiling replied, the smile revealing big, strong teeth. "Yes, indeed. Would you all step in the house and set? I am so happy to have company."

He selected the dining room, which is also the comfortably furnished living room, as the place to "set and talk". In this room is an oak dining table, chairs and a china closet, through the glass doors of which may be seen attractively decorated dishes, some of them of very old pattern. There is also an old fashioned combination desk and book case, and a chest of drawers. The windows are adorned with curtains and drapes of good quality.

The clean condition of the interior was a revelation of a 92 year old Negro man's desire and ability to keep house, and keep it clean. He lives alone, his wife having died many years ago.

There is in the appearance of this ancient Negro with shoulders now bowed; the dark brown skin, extending across the bald head; the large nose; immense teeth; shaven cheeks below which a mat of white whiskers encircle the throat, like the ruff on a condor's neck; there is in his appearance that which stamps him at once as the living bridge between the present day's civilization and a dim past; the knowledge of which exists today in the memories of but few persons.

As he talked, strange sights, scenes and cultures were told, sometimes with words that have changed much in meaning.

As his mind pictured the scenes of those old days, this primitive blending of both Indian and Negro races, at times unconsciously reverted to the primitive sing song recitative chant of his ancestors, particularly when narrating his outstanding pleasant memories.

This is his story:

"Old man Higgerson was my mastar. We lived on a farm and dere was a big family of us. I is the only one left. The farm laid just below the Lamine and Missouri Rivers, and I can't tell exactly where it was. Everybody called us 'free niggahs'—cause Higgerson slaves was treated so good. Yes, ma'am. My mammy lived to be 80 years old—and didn't have a gray hair in her haid. She was part Black Hawk Indian,—and I show it in me too."

Then as his thoughts raced back to slavery days, the pictures of youth crowded thick and fast, and he burst forth into a half chanted description of the panorama of his memories. "I've seen hundreds of Indians pass thru the country, on foot. Boss man let' em have a shack overnight. Next mawnin dey set out on foot, and take up de road, one behind the othar. Yes, suh! Just wrapped in a blanket one behind the othar. Winter and summer, and barefoot too!"

Then he told of game and game ways.

"Yes suh! I done seen wild deer hop ovar fences, and hundreds of wild turkeys. We used to build turkey pens and dig a trench, put feed in dere and covar it ovar wid bresh and de turkeys would come to feed, and we would trap' em. Yes, ma'am, an I done seen 100 to 150 wild turkeys in a flock. I has dat! Lots of wild pigeons, too. I has seen a thousand geese flyin' over in the early mornin'.

Then I've trapped quail too, in rail pens, built ten feet square. Yes, suh!

"But listen!—slaves couldn't shoot; was a law agin it in slaves times; no slave could own or shoot a gun. We couldn't shoot game. An' dat come dis way. President Jackson say, 'Keep books and guns outa slaves' hands if you want to keep 'em slaves'."

Joe Higgerson chuckled a little with a glint of humor in his eyes and changed the subject.

"Everybody made whiskey in dem days, had little 'stilleries all over the country, made apple and peach brandy. Good too. One day I was sent to a neighbor's for brandy. I took a little taste and walked on. Den I took anoder little taste, and walked on. Den I took anoder little taste and sot down de jug. Den I took anoder little taste, and so on and so on. Pretty soon I looked up, and I nevar did know how I got to whar I'se gwin ter. Nobody ever say anything about it or tell me nuffin! I guess somebody carry me whar I'se gwin ter."

He was asked if he ever remembered seeing slaves sold at Boonville.

"Yes, ma'am!" he exclaimed. "Why down at Boonville, woman and a baby was put up to be sold, and de buyer he want de woman, but he don't want de baby, so they separated 'em, and was gettin' ready to put 'em on de boat for Noo Orleans, and ship 'em down de river, and de woman she ran back to kiss de baby goodbye, and de tradar picked up a whip and cracked it and shouts, 'A bellerin' cow will soon forget its calf'. She was sold down de river and nevar saw de baby again. Now dat was sad." He paused and then resumed.

"One tradar, name of Henry Moore, he used to handcuff all the niggahs together till time to put 'em on de boat for Noo Orleans. Dey always carried whips and they'd crack dem to see how far de darkies could jump. Yes, Suh!! Yes, Suh!!! Deed they did!!!"

This reminiscence tickled him mightily and he laughed heartily at thoughts of the capers the negroes cut when the whip cracked.

"An I remembers one boat load. Boat load got as far as Cairo, Illinois, and lots of de darkies jumped overboard and was drowned."

"Were the overseers on the plantations Negroes or whites?"

"Overseahs, white," Higgerson replied, "Overseahs white. A darky was the niggah driver. Darkies didn't ever get to go to the big house where the planter lived. De niggah driver reported to the overseah, and the overseah reported to the boss.

"Now this is the way with me," Higgerson continued. "My father, who was also my boss, he kept a store, and I went to de store to take care of de children, cause de boss done send for me. Well, one time when the wah was on, some Federal soldiers come and done scared me so bad I forgot all about de chile and run home, and de soldiers burned de bridge, you had to cross befo' you got to de store. So after dat de ole man run a boat across."

Hoping to get some idea of how Christmas was celebrated among the Negroes on the farms and plantations the aged man was asked what he remembered of Christmas, in slavery times.

"One Christmas I never goin' to forget", he replied.

"Jes before Christmas lots of people came to de store to buy and de groun' was all covered wid snow. An de man what run de store was getting ready to close up, cause it was getting dark, and close at dark a man come and wanted in and de store keeper wouldn't let him in. An it got later and later, and by an by Joseph, dats me, was sent to de store to find why de storekeeper ain't come home yet and Joseph went to de store, and looked in and saw de old man on his back, his throat cut wid de blood runnin' all over de floor and $1,400 dey knowed he had—gone. Dere was whiskey and blood runnin' all over de floor. Whiskey was cheap dem days; good whiskey, too.

"When they set the niggahs free, the boss man come out and read de papers to 'em sayin' dey was free. And I went to Boonville and joined de Union Army, November 23, 1863. I served in de 25th Corps, Second Division under General Whitsell. I was in de last battle of de war at Palmetto Ranch, Texas, on de Rio Grande, just 36 miles from de Gulf. When I was discharged from de army to go home, I thought—why I have no home, where shall I go? Den I decided to go back to Boonville. All my family was scattered.

"But I was lucky. Someone had started to build a shack, and had not finished it. I got permission to finish it and picked up building material here and dere, and made it into a home. I never been without a home since. My wife and I lived together 61 years. She is gone now."

Slave Narratives

DELIA HILL

> Interview with Delia Hill,
> St. Louis County, Missouri.
> (Written by Grace E. White,
> St. Louis, Mo.)

Smoked 'Em Upside Down

The subject of this sketch is Delia Hill, over 90 years old. She lives at 1338 Argus Street, St. Louis County, Missouri.

Delia Hill is a good natured, well preserved old lady. She is quite tall, medium in size, dark complexion and her hair is almost entirely white. She is very neat in her quaint, frame three room cottage. She shares her home with a widowed companion who appears to be well in her 50's but is able to work. Delia Hill's story follows:

"I was born in Cold Water, Mississippi more dan 90 years ago but don't know jes' how old I is. My first owner's name was Marse John Hawkins and he had a big mill. He had me and my mother with 14 other chillen, Aunt Ellen and her 8 chillen, and Aunt Tilda with all her chillen. I don't know how many Aunt Tilda had. Anyhow Marse John owned every one of us. Later on he sold me to Marse Dave Stafford, a circuit rider. I got a scar on my eye today whar de ole overseer throwed a fork at me cross de table, 'cause I went to sleep, I was so tired while fanning flies off him while he's eatin'. I had to fan flies every meal time with a fly brush. They worked me so hard, I'd just go on to sleep standin' up. Dat old overseer was a mean old devil any how. Well when old Marse come home from de circuit ridin' I told him 'bout it, and he fired dat overseer right then and told him if my eye went out, he would look him up and kill him. I never seed him anymore.

"Dey sold us niggahs so bad down dere where I come from, dat when I was little I got sold from my mother and she never found me till after de war in 1871. Was we glad to see each other? I say we was. I was raised up hard, honey. I can count de winters I ever even had shoes on my poor feet. When Marse Dave bought my mother he only bought her and 6 us chillun. He was fairly nice to niggahs, but he didn't have as big a drove of 'em as de other plantation owners, but child we could hear niggahs hollen' every night on different plantations all around us from lashings dey gittin' from dere old overseers and masters too, for dat matter.

"My owner raised mostly cotton and corn, my mother wove all de clothes we wore, she even done all de spinning. During de Civil War, my old Miss use to hide us niggahs in de woods to keep de Yankees from seein' us. Dey pass through our place and got most all our stock just de same and all dey wanted to eat besides. But dey never found a one of us. After dey pass by we all go on back home.

"Dey sent us to church reglar and de preacher say to us, any you all see anybody stealin' old Miss chickens or eggs, go straight to old Miss and tell her who 'tis and all about it. Any one steal old Marse hogs or anything belong to old Marse, go straight to him and tell him all about it. Den he ask us, what your daddy bring home to you when he come, and what he feed you chillun at night. We scared to death to tell anything 'cause, honey, if we did de niggah get a killin, and our mammy tie up our feet and hang us upside down by our feet, build a fire under us and smoke us, scare us plum to death. We swear mammy goin' to burn us up. Lord, child, dat was an awful scare. Yes, mam, it was. De old preacher told us go on work hard, tell old Miss and old Master de truth and when we die God going let us in heaven's kitchen and sit down and rest from all dis work we doin' down here.

"We believe dat den. We didn't know no better, honest we didn't, honey. Our old Miss used to tell us, I want all my niggers to always tell de truth. If dey kill you, die telling de truth. But bless your soul, our mammy done smoked 'nough of us up side down, to not tell dem white folks nothin', a lie, nor the truth. No sir'ree. Who want to get smoked up likely to burn up hanging there as not. Now ain't dat so? No, sir, tell dem white folks, dey find out anything, they jes' find out by themselves, dat's it. I never did read or write. I been married three times. My last husband I married October 31, 1901 and moved right out here in dis house November 6, 1901, been here ever since. My husband been dead now 18 years. My children all died while dey was babies. I had six children. I wear glasses sometimes, but I praise God I can see good without glasses.

"De government gives me a pension and I git along fairly middlin'. Since peace been declared I made my living doing laundry work and cooking. I nursed right smart in Memphis. My mother died in 1893 here in St. Louis. Her name was Eliza Mullin, but I never did know how old she was. She didn't neither. I am a Baptist and go to church reglar as I kin, but I suffer so hard with indigestion. I can't go no place much. Guess dat's 'bout all I can remember worth 'membering, hope it helps de book out."

LOUIS HILL

Interview with Louis Hill,
age 78, Farmington, Missouri.

"I's borned on October 13, 1858 on the southeast side of Farmington, Missouri. My muthuh, Rose Hill, was borned in Virginia. She kum ta Missouri as a girl an frum dat time on she wuz a slabe fur John Hill, our boss. She worked thar till our freedom. Our family had three boys, Peter, William, and me an two girls, Sallie and Malinda. We bunked up in a cabin with one room. All us kids ate on da flo frum da same plate an da biggest dog got da mos. We generally wore a straight slip like a nightgown an hit fastened round the neck. (In the old South boys were dressed in this fashion until about ten years old and were called "shirttail boys".) Tak dis off an we war naked.

"The ole lady, the wife ob da Boss was da devil's sister. Her name was 'Whip'. She beat da ole folks mor'n tha kids. She used tha cowhide an we got a lickin' whether we did anythin' or not. We had ta git up early an after given supper we war put ta bed an did not 'pilfer' round. We had ta go on Sunday ta the Boss' Church, tha Carmelite or Christian Church. Ma muthuh wuz no han ta tell big yarns an so I know no ghost stories. We wuz raised very sensible. Tha white folks did not help us ta read an write. I learned that after we war free. I never did go ta school. Our games was 'Wolf on tha Bridge', an 'King-Kong-

Ko.' We always had ta be doin' somethin', even if it war pickin' up kindlin'.

"I member when Price's army kum thro here in '64 or '65 on their way ta Pilot Knob. I wuz 'bout six or seben years ole. I an ma sister had bin down ta the white childr'n school ta take them dinner. We had ta bring tha basket bak an we sat down in tha corner ob da graveyard ta eat whut wuz left in da basket. Da graveyard was nex to da Fredericktown road and jus across frum our house. All at onc't I heard the mos' turrible noise an saw soldiers kum up da road. We war sure scared. We jumped up, ran cross da road, jumped over da fence an begun ta tak out fur da house. Da soldiers laughed an said somethin. One soldier on a horse kum up ta de fence, tore off da top rail, an with his horse jumped ober da fence, an took out after us, but he nebber cud catch us. We wuz sho runnin'. I wuz carryin' da basket and if I had a throwed it down we would a showed that soldier some runnin'. Da soldier turned his horse round but we went straight to da house to da Missus. She say dat dey was only havin' a good time an would not hurt us. We stood at da house an looked, an it took 'bout all afternoon fur da soldiers to pass. Thar war horses, wagons and cannons. Da soldiers durin' da war took all da Boss' horses away an he had only a yoke ob oxen lef.

"After da freedom we all had ta get out an work. We had a big family. I work'd at da lead smelter at Mine La Motte in 1872 an work'd thar fur six years. I made $2.50 a day an dat was good wages then. I batched thar. I larned ta read at Mine La Motte when a white man taught me in evenin's at da mine between shifts. Afterwards I work'd in Bonne Terre at da smelter but got lead colic an quit thar.

"I think slavery wuz a curse on human nature. I believe in nobody bein' in bondage ob no kind. Da Almighty wuz not a goin' ta let slavery las' much longer. You know whut He did about da people in Egypt."

(Note—Louis Hill lives in a very nice home. He is a quiet negro, and except for a short time, has spent his entire life in Farmington. He receives an Old Age Pension. I did not inquire about his marriage, for, from knowledge I have gained, he lives with a colored woman to whom he is not married.)

United States. Work Projects Administration

LOUIS HILL

Interview with Louis Hill,
Farmington, Missouri.

He Swapped Liquor For Lessons

How he traded liquor for lessons in reading, writing, and arithmetic is one of the interesting facts of his younger life recalled in an interview recently obtained from Louis Hill, an ex-slave, now living in Farmington, Missouri.

Louis believes that the government should have made some provision for the aid of the Negroes during the early struggle following their emancipation.

Regarding the part which he takes in politics, Louis declares that his invariable rule is to "look over de field and vote for what he thinks is de best timber."

The story of his experiences as given to the interviewer is told as closely as possible in his own words which follow:

"I was too young to know what to expect from freedom. My mother picked up and left de white folks in de night and took us kids with her. Dat was after we was free but dey wouldn't let her get away in de daytime very handy. Dey did not pay my mother anything after she was free. In dem days kids didn't question de old folks like they does now, so I didn't find out much. Dere was two sisters, two brothers and myself what left dat night with my mother. We all had some bundles, and when we left de old mistress in de dark we went to some neighbors several blocks away. We didn't have to go far away 'cause dey could not force you to go back after we was free. But my mother did go back and work for de mistress a good while but she got paid den. We stayed here for quite awhile and den went up to Valle Mines.

"I piddled around and hired out for first one and den another and did what a kid could do. When you earned any money dem days you had to give it to your mother and didn't know what she done with it. About de first work I done was for Mr. Boyer, a Frenchman, up in Valle Mines in de diggin's. I dug mineral, zinc, etc. I got 50 cents a day. He did all de diggin and I 'coached' it from de head of the drift to de shaft. I had a little car on wheels dat run on a wooden track. I reckon I worked for him 'bout two years. My mother would go out to de big dirt pile called 'scrappin' and would pick out de zinc and lead chunks and little pieces.

"Purt near every Saturday we would take de ore down to Furnace Town and get it weighed and get a check for it. Den we come back to Farmington after several years and lived with my sister's husband and worked around at a little bit of everything. I was gettin' to be a pretty good sized boy and went to Mine La Motte and worked on de furnace. My first work at dat place was at $2 a day and later on I became a 'charger' and got $2.50 a day. I stayed with dem six or seven years. After I left dere I went to Bonne Terre and got married and got mine sickness or lead colic from workin' in de furnace and had to quit. I come back to Farmington and is been here ever since.

Den I worked at sawing wood, chopping wood, and at a soda factory and beer depot and peddled ice and delivered soda and beer to Knob Lick, Syenite, Graniteville and Bonne Terre. I worked here for a long time.

"I'se had four children and two is livin. De boy is in Los Angeles, California and the girl is in Seattle, Washington. My boy is a chauffeur for an old, rich feller by de name of Clark and he has been in de same job for 16 years. He gets $100 a month, room and board. He's been wanting to quit but de old man won't let him. My son's daughter does de cooking for dis rich guy. My son is 56 years old now.

"My daughter is 54 and is married. What she does is more dan I can tell you. Her husband was a soldier in de regular army, in de 10th Cavalry, and was in de Philippines, and Cuba and so my daughter is been around some. She been away from here for about 23 or 24 years.

"I think de young Negroes need settling down and have more education and not so much good time. I didn't have much of a chance. We was turned loose barefooted and had no schools den and when dey had schools I had to work. But in Mine La Motte a Mr. McFarland would come over to our cabin and teach me readin', writin' and 'rithmetic. He was an awful drinker but was smart. I would give him a little something to drink for teachin' me. I took lessons for 'bout a year. I sure do like to read de newspapers now and can write letters. The young generation thinks too much about goin' and having a good time. A little 'task master' wouldn't hurt de young people. I wasn't in de slavery long enough for it to hurt me none. I was free when I was 5 years old. My mother, however, was worked like an old horse and de best part of her life was spent in bondage.

"I believe de government should have made some provision for de slaves when dey turned dem loose. De government could have compelled slaveholders to give slaves a little track of land, a cow and a horse and give 'em a start. De slave had made what de white man had. I actually believe de Negroes would be better off today if they had done dis. My old mistress just had oodles of land. Of course de white folks was not used to work and dere was plenty for de Negroes to do if dey wanted to work.

"I voted as soon as I got a chance. De first time I voted was in 1880. I'se had 'em try to pay me to vote but I told dem my vote was not for sale. You know you ain't dictated to unless you is 'wishy washy'. Once, a feller asked me how I voted. I said, 'Just to suit myself.' I generally look over de field and vote for what I think is de best timber. Dey is goin' to have a hot time in 1940, for dem that lives to see it. It's a free country and a man should not have to own property in order to vote. Dey ought not to oppress anyone."

RHODY HOLSELL

> Interview with "Aunt" Rhody Holsell,
> Fredericktown, Missouri.

Slaves Happy To Be Free

"Aunt" Rhody Holsell, 89 years old, of Fredericktown, is one of the interesting ex-slaves in Missouri. According to her story she was 17 years old when the Civil War ended. Her mother and father were slaves and both of them had died before the beginning of the conflict. She believes that she is part Indian as her great grandmother is believed to have been an Indian squaw.

The following is her own version of events which played a part in her life during her slave days and since that time:

"When dey turned me loose I was naked, barefoot, and didn't have nothin' to start out on. They turned us loose without a thing and we had to kinda pick ourselves up. We would go out of a Sunday and dig ginseng and let it dry for a week and sell it to de store. We would make about a dollar every Sunday dat way, and den we'd get our goods at de store. The master and all de boys was killed in de war and de mistress married some 'hostle jostle' who helped to kill the boss. I was jus' not goin' to stand dat so dis was when I left home.

"Abraham Lincoln done put a piece in de paper saying

dat all de slaves was free and if dey whipped any of de slaves after dey was set free dey would prosecute them. Me and another little old woman done some shoutin' and hollerin' when we heard 'bout de freedom. We tore up some corn down in de field. De old missus was right there on de fence but wouldn't dare touch us den. Once de mistress struck me after we was freed and I grabbed her leg and would have broke her neck. She wanted to apologize with me de way she had treated me but I would not let her. They thought it was awful dat dey could not whip de slaves any longer.

"I den worked from one farm to another. I would stay a year or two each place. Dey wanted me to stay. Dey said I was de best plow boy dey had. I would cut de old roots and dey would pop but dey paid me nothin' and dey didn't give you no clothes. We got so much in de share of de cropping but dey would not share with me so I would leave. So I come to Fredericktown to try to find my mother's people but when I got here dey done told me dey was gone to Illinois.

"I den come right out of de field and went right into the dining room. I was never turned off from any of my work. I would just work 'till I got tired and quit. Talk about bein' happy! We was sure 'nough some happy people when dey done took dat yoke offen our necks. Before I was free we had to shuck three wagon loads of corn a day. De wagon would hold 40 bushels. I'd come home and my fingers would be twisted from so much work. De oxen would slobber all over de corn before we picked it. It was cold out dere in de field an' I would wrap my feet up in my dress and wait till de wagon would drive up. I had no shoes on. Man, I don't know how I'm here today.

It just was de mercy of God that took care of me. When my mother was dying she done asked God to look over us and it must have been her prayer dat helped me to still be here.

"When my mother was sick once de doctor come and brought his wife. De wife always come with de doctor. De doctor would not allow de family to give de medicine, 'cause he said de family would give in to de sick person. De wife of de doctor would give de medicine when de doctor was asleep. I never seen de family give medicine till I come up here. De doctors always come and stay till de sick person was out of danger and de wife always come with him.

"Lord, people nowadays don't know nothing 'bout nothin'. Child, I spun backwards and forwards to de wheel till I wore my feet out till de balls of my feet was wore to de blood.

"Lots of slaves went to Illinois after freedom, but I never been out of de State. I don't go to frolics of any kind. I just come here and settled down and never rambled 'round. I've lived in dis house 55 years and have buried purty near all my family right out of dis house. I ain't never had a fuss with any of my neighbors, and I done took de bitter with de sweet. I ride in an automobile only to funerals. I ain't been on a train but once or twice and dat was 'bout 40 years ago. I'm interested in church now, can sit and listen to preachin' and singin' all day, but I sets right here while dey has all dis other excitement. It's been seventy years since I done been to Farmington to a picnic. I don't want de pension so much to roam around but to be protected in my old age and to have a few more days of peace. I don't care nothin' about clothes.

"I been votin' at that thing ever since it started. Dey would take me a free ride when votin' time comes. You can't turn around for dey wants to take you to vote. But after de voting dey won't pay no attention to me. I never did vote only a straight ticket and I always went my own way. Dey would sometimes tell me how to vote but I didn't pay them no mind. My husband did not believe in women voting and he said it would tear up de country. He said he wanted to be in heaven when de women voted. Garfield was de first president I ever voted for.

"I believe it would been better to have moved all de colored people way out west to dem selves. Abraham Lincoln wanted to do dis. It would have been better on both races and dey would not have mixed up. But de white people did not want de 'shade' taken out of de country. Many of de bosses after de freedom couldn't stand it and went in de house and got a gun and blew out his brains. If Lincoln had lived he would have separated us like dey did de Indians. We would not have been slaughtering, burning, hanging, and killin' if we had been put to ourselves, and had our own laws. Many a person is now in torment because of dis mixup. God give us a better principle and we could have had thousands of whites slaughtered but we didn't after the freedom.

"De present generation is a lost condition. If dey don't girdle their lines and pull dem up closer and ask God to help 'em and quit going to dem 'hog holes' and drinkin' it is going to be death and destruction. Dis not only is true of the Negroes but white folks, too. Mother and father think it is alright. Dese undertakers is goin' out all de time, night and day, on the highways and pickin' up de carcass of people. It's sin dat is wrong with de world.

De future of the Negro is of the past. We have some good friends among the white folks but de devil is just got so strong dat de good can't hardly stand. We have some good citizens in dis town. I can't read or write but I used to have the white lady read the funny side of the paper when I set down to eat.

"Once during de war de soldiers was around me very thick. I was coming back from carryin' de dinner out in de woods to Sam Hildebrand. I took him a table cloth, napkins and everything first class. I went down to de house and hid de basket in a hollow log and crossed de creek and dey hollered, 'Halt!' De soldiers was cussin' me like a bay steer. Dey said, 'I'll kill you right here and blow your brains out if you don't tell.' I told dem I had been up dere to water de calves so dey give me my pass and let me go on to de house. I would not tell dem nothin' 'bout Sam Hildebrand nor where he was hiding. While Sam et his meal I would stand 'round and watch in de woods. I was de oldest one on de place and I was de only one what had to carry his meals to him.

"I would get up many mornings and hear the bugler blowin'. Das when dey was callin' the pickets in. You would see de pickets come in just a-flyin' and out sent de fresh pickets on duty. I was not scared of dem. Sometimes de soldiers stayed 'round our place for two weeks and camped. Dey was about 500 and de men laid out on de ground under a government wagon and in some houses around about. Dese soldiers would go out with sabers and whack de heads off of de sheep, hogs, and calves and in about five minutes would have dat yearlin' skinned and dash it into de boilin' kettle. Den dey would take a long knife and cut off a big piece of meat with the blood runnin' out. Dey did not cook de meat done and did not put much salt on it. It sure was funny, seein' dem soldiers eatin' a big hunk of meat with de blood runnin' out. Dey always had bread but don't know where dey got it. They was so tired and wore out and their feet was sore and de infantry was almost barefooted. Dey was always dressed in blue. Sometimes we would have 30 or 40 yards of goods on de loom and dey would tear it off and send it home to their family. We was glad enough to get dem to take dis and get out. There would not be a man on de place when these 500 soldiers come. We always managed to bury dat gentleman (money). I can remember the boss took out of his chest his money, enough to fill the table, and put it in a buck skin bag and he went off with another man. I don't know what become of de money and dey was killed and there was no one left to tell de tale.

"I sure had it rough and tumble since de war. Of course I don't have a boss now. I've worked on de farm, as a dining room girl, washin', ironing, and hiring out. I would get about $9 to $10 a week. I was workin' for de railroad people den when de road was runnin' strong here. My husband he died 40 years ago and he done left me with about 15 cents, and the mortgage on dis house was about $130. I had a wagon worth about $40 and old Dr. Newberry took dat for his bill. Den I would do two or three washings before I come home and would come by de undertaker's and leave him some money on de funeral. My daughter is a grass widow and she lives here. Her ex-husband shines shoes down town, but he don't help us none. My daughter has got three children.

"I don't go to church lately. It's embarrassing to go in

this hot weather. I know where I want dem to bury me. All the old folks buried out at de old colored cemetery.

"I goes down here to de store and if I can't get de money dey waits till I can, I can get it on a credit. Dey think Aunt Rhody is one of the leadin' persons of de town. Of course I don't run all over town but go to one store. Dey have got used to me and dey know it sometimes takes an hour for me to make up my mind what I want to buy. When I go to de store they kid me and say: 'Why, Aunt Rhody, ain't you dead yet? You is goin' to outlive us all.'

"Slavery learnt me how to work and I wasn't feared of no kind of work. Most of de people around here don't know nothin' 'bout work. A little slavery would do dis young age some good and dey is goin' to get it. Dis young generation is slaughtering our people up, down in de south. Our people don't know what freedom is down there. Better not go down there and talk about freedom. My brother went down there in the south and got back so far from de river dat he never got out. I guess de exposure and the beatin' killed him. Lots of places dey votes down there, but de votes is thrown in de waste basket and dey don't count. These people can't beat up us people and jump up on a bed and close their eyes and die and expect to go to heaven.

"I ain't never heard de Bible read till I was free in Fredericktown. When we was slaves we did not have much time to get out and sin much. Dis generation is goin' to destruction. It's all on account of not mindin' their parents. Dey is just hard-headed. It's caused by de way de old folks acted and is bein' put on dis present generation. I tell 'em, you don't think dat you can walk these streets and fall dead and never said nothin' to God to move this gulf of sin and den expect to go to Heaven. I'm tryin' to serve God and fightin' all de time against de devil to keep him from knockin' me over. I'm not a person to go on with a lot of nonsense. I talk to de young people all de time around de stores and tell 'em dey is got to get up from there to make it across de river. Dey all talk about me preachin' a sermon around de stores. But de devil's already got de 'bill of sale' on dem. I'm talkin' to de Lord all de time cause my stay is going to be mighty short now."

AUNT RHODY

"Aunt Rhody" Holsell,
Fredericktown, Missouri.
Interviewed by J. Tom Miles.

"I've lived in Fredericktown ever since de war and only two or three times I've been out of hollering distance of town. I was seventeen years old when de war was over. My boss was Thos. McGee in Wayne County. My mother and father were slaves. My great-grandmother was a Indian squaw. My mother was dead four years 'fore de war and my father was dead three years.

"I sure can 'member 'bout de war. De funniest thing was some soldiers camped at our house. Man, I would pull weeds in de cotton patch, and when I got a little older I was a-carding and spinning and dat wheel was a-singing. I spun all de chain all through de Civil War and I spun all de warp. De boss treated us very good. De boss would know every row of corn we would hoe; sometimes we would break de corn off and den we got a whipping with a weed.

"De boss lost all three of his boys with their shoes on in de war, but dey did not join de army. De boss was also killed. De boss had a race horse and de soldiers found dis out an de boss tried to get de hoss out of de state to New Orleans until after de war. My brother got de race hoss down there all right. My brother got on Knight and rode clear to Cape and his closes were torn off. He get to Cape just as de boat was pulling out. Dey killed de boss when he got on another hoss an he was shot 'cause de soldiers thought he was on de race hoss. Dey killed de boss in August on Monday. De boss was going that day to Greenville to make his will.

"After de war I worked my way to Fredericktown. I started out bareheaded an barefooted. I worked from one farm to another. I worked at one farm for two years and at another for one year. These people paid me a little. It took 'bout five years 'fore I got to Fredericktown. I did anything. I cradled five acres of oats and my husband bound it. I didn't fear no kind of boss. I have ten great grand-children, and one great-great-grandchild.

"I took Sam Hildebrand's dinner to him many times and when Sam was killed in Southern Illinois dey tried to get me to go up to Farmington to identify him. But I would not do it. I told dem dat he had a mark behind his shoulder dat dey could see. I 'member once when Sam Hildebrand was shot and came to our place to have his sore washed out. I held de wash pan for old Tom McGee to wash his wound.

"De old folks had all kinds of tea to heal people. De old mistress took de 'ridicue' [TR: reticule] with her and would be gone for a week going from one sick person to another. My boss caused my mother's death. She was on a wagon of oats and was being pulled by a yoke of oxen. De wagon turned and she fell off on a sapling and it went through her skin and dey had to saw de sapling off and she had to lay with dat snag in her side till de doctor twenty miles away come. It was in August and she died with poison. Her coffin was made right out on de work bench. Dey didn't have anything in de coffin but a winding sheet scolloped nicely and a shroud for de body. It was a miracle to me when I came up here to see how dey dressed up de dead people. When I die just wrap me in a clean sheet. That was what my fore-parents had. It's better to think whar dat soul is. Two wheel carts was mostly used at funerals in those days with oxen. The driver would be walking along beside driving.

"De Boss said one man was treated mean and they could not do anything with him. The old fellow would play his gourd and de snakes would come 'round. Finally dey sent him down to New Orleans and sold him on de block.

"If you move on Saturday you won't stay long. If de boss decides about you on Tuesday or Friday these are hanging days. I can't read or write but I have a little mother sense. We have three spirits, evil spirit in de grave, another spirit which is wandering, and a spirit in heaven.

"I think slavery is good for dem dat understands it. We are all slaves now. We have a rough and tumble business. Slavery was cruel but it's about as bad now. Them days they didn't hang anybody for doing bad things. I may be wrong. I been voting ever since de mess got up. My husband said he wanted to be in heaven when de women would be messin' 'round among de men and voting. I wish we had a whole lot of Abraham Lincolns now. He did a great deed when he took de yoke off us colored people. We will get a little rest anyway."

United States. Work Projects Administration

HENRY JOHNSON

Interview with Henry Johnson,
St. Louis, Missouri.
(Written by Grace E. White.)

The subject of this sketch is Henry Johnson, over ninety years of age, living at 1526 Hanley Road, Lincoln Terrace, St. Louis, Missouri. Henry is of dark complexion and has a wealth of long white hair and feminine features.

His eyesight is good. He is in excellent health for his age. The old man admits that his main weakness is chewing tobacco. He was seated in the living room of his 4-room, old fashioned frame cottage which is poorly furnished, but clean, where he lives with his wife, at least twenty-five years younger than himself. His story follows:

"My name is Henry Johnson. I was born in Patrick County, Virginia and was raised all over de state. I was only sold twice. My father's name was Bill Alexander and my mother's name was Fannie, but I didn't know nothin' 'bout my parents till I was past eighteen years old or about that. I never knowed my real age. My owner's name was Billy Johnson in Patrick County so I always carried his name. When I was a little bit 'a fellow, I used to pack water to twenty-five and thirty men in one field, den go back to de house and bring enough water for breakfast de next morning. When I got a little bigger, I had to take a little hoe and dig weeds out of de crop. If our white boss see a little grass we overlooked he would handcuff our feet to a whipping post, den chain the slave around de stomach to de post and strap de chin over de top of de post and place your hands in front of you.

"In de start de slave has been stripped naked, and lashed, often to death. Dey would be left strapped after from twenty-five to fifty lashes every two or three hours to stand dere all night. De next day, de overseer would be back with a heavy paddle full of holes that had been dipped in boiling water and beat until de whole body was full of blisters. Den he'd take a cat-o'-nine-tails dipped in hot salt water to draw out de bruised blood and would open everyone of dem blisters with dat. If de slave did not die from dat torture, he would be unfastened from de whipping post, and made go to de field just as he was. Often times he would die shortly after. Dey did the women de same."

Here he showed the writer scars on his head and shoulders which he said were from those beatings.

"I never knowed what a shirt was until I was past twenty. When my young master went three miles to school, he rode on a horse, I had to walk along side de horse to carry his books, den go home and fetch him a hot dinner for noon and go back after him at night to carry dem books.

"My boss had eleven children. He had one hundred and twenty-five slaves on one of de plantations, two hundred on another. On all his plantations he owned better'n 1500 slaves. He was one of de richest land owners in de state of Virginia. He often told me I was born just one hour before his youngest son. I stayed with dat family until way after de war was fought.

"Dey would take a great string of slaves in de road on Sunday and make us walk to church. Buggies with de white folks in would be in front of us, in de midst of us, and all betwixt and behind us. When we got dat four or five miles we had to sit on a log in de broiling sun, while a white man preached to us. All dey evah would say would be niggers obey your masters and mistress and don't steal from 'em. And lo and behold, honey, de masters would make us slaves steal from each of the slave owners. Our master would make us surround a herd of his neighbor's cattle, round dem up at night, and make us slaves stay up all night long and kill and skin every one of dem critters, salt the skins down in layers in de master's cellar, and put de cattle piled ceilin' high in de smoke house so nobody could identify skinned cattle.

"Den when de sheriff would come around lookin' for all dem stolen critters, our boss would say, 'Sheriff, just go right on down to dem niggahs' cabins and search dem good, I know my niggers don't steal.' Course de sheriff come to our cabins and search, sure we didn't have nothin' didn't belong to us, but de boss had plenty. After de sheriff's search, we had to salt and smoke all dat stolen meat and hang it in old marse smoke house for him. Den dey tell us, don't steal. Dey raised turkeys in de 500 lots and never did give us one. So we wanted one so bad once, I put corn underneath de cabin and a turkey, a great big one, would come under our cabin to eat dat corn. One day when I got a chance I caught dat old gobbler by de neck and him and me went round and round under dat old cabin house. He was de biggest strongest bird I ever see, I was only a boy but finally I beat. I twisted his neck till he died. Den I took out up to de big house, fast as anything, to tell my old miss one of our finest turkeys dead. She said stop cryin' Henry and throw him under de hill. I was satisfied. I run back, picked dat ole bird, taken all his feathers to de river and throwed dem in. Dat night we cooked him, and didn't we eat somethin' good. I had to tell her 'bout dat missin' bird 'cause when dey check up it all had to tally so dat fixed dat.

"My old master told me when de war was being fought and the Yankees was on de way coming through Franklin County, Virginia, 'My little niggah, do you know how old you is?' I said: 'No sah, boss.' He said: 'You are seventeen years old.' I never even saw my mother and father until I was in my twenties. A white man taken me to Danville, Virginia to drive his carriage for him. After I was dere a spell a colored man kept watching me so much I got plum scared. Dis was after de war was over. Den one day, lo and behold, he jumped at me and he grabbed me and asked me where was I staying. I did not know whether to tell him or not, I was so scared. Den he said I am your father and I am goin' to take you to your mother and sisters and brothers down in Greenville, Virginia. When he got me dere, I found two sisters and four brothers. Dey was all so glad to see me dey shouted and cried and carried on so I was so scared I tried to run away, 'cause I didn't know nothin' 'bout none of them. And I thought dat white man what brought me down here ought to have saved me from all dis. I just thought a white man was my God, I didn't know no better.

"Well, when my folks finally stopped rejoicing, my mother only had two chickens. She killed and cooked dem for me. My father and brothers would go to work every day and leave me at home with my mother for over a year. They would not trust me to work, feared I would run off 'cause I didn't no nothin' 'bout them. Hadn't even heard of a mother and father. My brother and father would work all day and only get one peck of corn or one pound of meat or one quart of molasses for a whole day's work from sun up till sun down. We had to grind dat corn for our flour, and got biscuits once a year at Christmas and den only one biscuit apiece.

"After a little better'n a year after I come, the white man told my father to bring his family and move from Greenhill, Virginia to Patrick County, Virginia to his big farm, and farm dere for him and he would give him one half of all he raised for his share. We went, and did we raise a big crop. He kep' his word all right and we stayed dere till de white man died five years later. Den we went to another farm. We had cleared enough in the five years to buy us a fine pair of oxen and had money besides. So we went to another farm and went to work giving the owner of the farm one third of the crop and kep' two thirds ourselves. We stayed there two years. Then father sold de oxen and went to Sweetville, Virginia and bought $200 worth of land and stayed about five years. We made our crop with a hoe and made good. Den I left home and run about all over, learned how to play a violin and made my livin' with it for a long time.

"I quit dat and railroaded about eight years working on sections and new grading. Den went to Decatur, Alabama and worked with a land company putting down pipings about three months. I quit dat and married Anna

Johnson and come to Giles County, Tennessee. We had one son.

"I came to St. Louis from Tennessee more dan forty years ago. I got work right away at Cycle & Harris Steel Plant on 18th Street and worked dere about six months, when I got scalded almost to death on the job. I got a new nose and a new ear from dat accident. All de flesh of my right arm was off to de bone. I was in de hospital eight months from it and I got $500 out of de damage suit. I bought me a horse and wagon out of it and done light hauling, and moved out here in Lincoln Terrace and been out here ever since.

"I landscaped out here for sixteen years until I was disabled to work hard any more. I got a garden but I can't make any money from it, 'cause all de other folks out here got gardens too. I am a deacon in Mt. Zion Baptist Church right here at de corner. Rev. Thomas is my pastor.

"I only went to school three days in my whole life but a colored friend taught me how to spell out of a blue back spelling book. His name was Charlie Snowball. I was learning fine until I got burned. Den my eye sight was poor for a long time, but I see now very good. I only need glasses for to read what little I can read. I can't write at all. My grandfather was 135 years old when he died, and my father lived to be 135.

"De white people in Missouri sure have been mighty good to me since I been here. I have as nice clothes as any man in St. Louis, good clothes what I mean. All been given' to me by white people able to give somethin'. I have not had to buy a hat, shoes or suit of clothes for over twenty-five years, and got far more good clothes dan I can ever wear out till my dying day. I think these 20th century white folks dat have principle are trying to make amends to Negroes to make up for the meanness their foreparents done to us, so I try to forgive 'em all in my heart for the sake of a few good ones now. I've buried two wifes from dis very house. I am now living with my third wife and she is a mighty fine woman. We have been together about sixteen years."

HANNAH JONES

> Interview with Hannah Jones,
> St. Louis, Missouri.
> (Written by Grace E. White,
> St. Louis, Mo.)

Bred Slaves Like Stock

Hannah Jones was born in Cape Girardeau, Missouri, August 3, about 1850, the daughter of Lottie Oil and Noah Thompson. Her story follows:

"The niggers had three or four wifes before de war, as many as dey could bear chillun by. But after de war dey had to take one woman and marry her. My mother had three chillun by him and de odder wifes had three and four chillun too. Old man, Ben Oil raised my mother. He was an old bachelor but his brothers were all married.

"Ben Oil had 100 niggers. He just raised niggers on his plantation. His brother-in-law, John Cross raised niggers, too. He had 125 niggers. He had a nigger farm. His other brother-in-law we call old man English, had 100 niggers. Dey all jes' had nothin' else but niggers. Before de war broke out, Tom Oil and John Oil come up dah and taken all us niggers but eight and eight acres of land he left for Ben Oil's housekeeper. Old Marse Ben died and after dat Tom carried us all back down der to New Orleans wid him and opened up a nigger pen. Dat's a place like a stock yard where dey auction us off. De old ones was de ones dey was anxious to get shet of. We only know our ages by known' we is born in corn plantin' and cotton pickin' time. We never even knowed de days of de week.

"I had three aunts to die in all dat huddle of niggers. De doctors make us go walking every day 'cause dat was de only exercise we git. One of dem aunts dropped dead on de street while walking. De other two died in de slave pen. My grandmother was a fine seamstress. She sewed all de sewing for de white folks. Three days after her first baby was born dey made her git up and make twelve stiff-front, tucked white shirts for her old mistress' boy who be goin' off to college and she was so sick and weak, some of de stitches was crooked. Old Miss ordered de overseer to take her out and beat her 'bout it. Before he did de doctor looked at her and said 'tain't no use beatin' her she won't do you no more good. She's stone blind, but she can have chillun right on. So dey kept her for dat and she bore twelve more head of chillun after dat.

"My mother was black as a crow and her hair was so long she could sit on it. Dey brought a huddle of niggers over amongst de Indians from all over de south and Maryland and intermarried 'em wid dere own sisters, brothers, cousins, nieces and de like. De niggers didn't know for years dey was any kin. When dey want to raise certain kind a breed of chillun or certain color, dey just mixed us up to suit dat taste, and tell de nigger dis is your wife or dis is your husband and dey take each other and not know no better and raise big families to de white folks liking.

"I never can forget one Sunday morning de rebels come into Cape Girardeau. De old Miss what raised me had just killed two hogs and put 'em in de smoke house. I got up bright and early dat Sunday morning. I looked out toward de smoke house and seed two white men out dere dressed in blue clothes and dey just went in Old Miss' smoke house and help dem selves. I run right fast and told old Miss what was going on out der in her smoke house. But dere wasn't no men folks around so we couldn't help ourselves. Dey told us dey was 300 strong and just den some others come over de hill and told 'em come on, hurry up so dey climbed de hill in a hurry leaving dere. They had three gun boats and dey turned one of dem things loose up der as dey was goin' and Lawd child dat thing destroyed property for miles around.

"Some of dem rebels had ball bats, some had sticks, some riding and some walking. Dey killed three of us niggers in our camp dat morning. All de nigger men been taken away just leaving us nigger women and chillun. Dey burned down frame and log huts just de same. My mother lived to be 115 years old, two uncles lived to be 100, one sister over 60. I use glasses when I read but am blind in one eye. My husband has been dead 37 years. He was an old soldier so Uncle Sam gives me a pension.

"I had 15 head of chillun. I have now seven grandchillun and four great grandchillun. I has been in St. Louis 17 years and lives with my daughter Nancy McDonald, 2804 Dayton Street."

United States. Work Projects Administration

EMMA KNIGHT

Interview with Emma Knight,
Hannibal, Missouri.

Emma Was Really Rough

Emma Knight, living at 924 North Street, Hannibal, Missouri, was born in slavery on the farm of Will and Emily Ely, near Florida, Monroe County. The following is her story as she told it:

"We lived on a Creek near Florida. We belonged to Will Ely. He had only five slaves, my father and mother and three of us girls. I was only eight or nine years old. De Elys had eight children. Dere was Paula, Ann, Sarah, Becky, Emily, Lizzie, Will, Ike, and Frank. Lizzie was de oldest girl and I was to belong to her when she was married.

"De master of de house was better to us dan de mistress. We didn't have to work none too hard, 'cause we was so young, I guess. We cut weeds along de fences, pulled weeds in de garden and helped de mistress with de hoeing. We had to feed de stock, sheep, hogs, and calves, because de young masters wouldn't do de work. In de evenings we was made to knit a finger width and if we missed a stitch would have to pull all the yarn out and do it over. De master's girls learned us to read and write. We didn't have hardly no clothes and most of de time dey was just rags. We went barefoot until it got real cold. Our feet would crack open from de cold and bleed. We would sit down and bawl and cry because it hurt so. Mother made moccasins for our feet from old pants. Late in de fall master would go to Hannibal or Palmyra and bring us shoes and clothes. We got dem things only once a year. I had to wear de young master's overalls for underwear and linseys for a dress.

"My father was took away. My mother said he was put on a block and sold 'cause de master wanted money to buy something for de house. My mother told me she come from Virginia or down south some place. Dey brought her in a box car with lots of other colored people. Dere was several cars full, with men in one car, women in another, and de younger ones in another, and de babies in another with some of the women to care for dem. Dey brought dem to Palmyra and sold dem. Master Ely bought my mother. I don't know where my father come from.

"Mistress always told us dat if we run away somebody would catch us and kill us. We was always scared when somebody strange come. De first we knew dere was a war was when some soldiers come through. We was sure scared den. Once a man come and we thought he was a patroller but he asked for something to eat. Mother took him to de mistress. She gave him something to eat wrapped in a paper and told him to get off de place.

"Some Union soldiers come and told us that we was free like dey was and told us not to be afraid, dey wouldn't hurt us. Dey told us de war was over. De master told mother not to go away, dat if she stayed a while he would give her a couple hundred dollars. We stayed a while but she never got no money.

"We come to Hannibal in an ox wagon. We put up at de

barracks and den mother went to live with Hiram Titchner. He lived right where de postoffice is now. I hired out to Mrs. James across de street for my clothes and schooling. Mrs. James had two girls. One of dem learned me not to be such a tomboy and not to be so rough. I tell you I was a bad girl when I was young. I could climb every tree on de master's farm and my clothes was always in rags from being so rough. My mother used to whip me most every day with a broom stick and even hit me with chairs. I guess I was bad. If I had a dollar for every broom handle that was laid across my back I would have lots of money. I tell you we was raised plenty tuff dem days.

"De young folks can't stand such raising dese days. Dey just couldn't go through what we was through. The young folks now just couldn't do it at all. We never was 'lowed on the street after nine o'clock. We sure run for home when the church bell done rung on de hill at nine o'clock. Now-a-days de young folks stays out half de night and dey steal and even kill each other over triflin' things. I know it 'cause I see them do dese things. I 'spose dere parents are a lot to blame.

"I was married when I was young, less dan twenty I reckon. I had one girl but she is dead now. Her boy lives with me. I gets a pension, seven dollars a month, for about a year now. This little old shack belongs to me. I go to de Baptist Church over on Center Street when ever I can. We used to go to church on de corner 'cross from de postoffice. Dere is a big store dere now."

United States. Work Projects Administration

HARRIET LEE

Interview with Harriet Lee,
Cape Girardeau, Missouri.

"Mah mammy tole me ah wuz jes fo' year ole wen de war end, so ah don' 'member much 'bout fo' de war. Ole Massa wuz Buckner Caldwell an' ole Missus, we a'ways call Miss Coon, dat de only name ah knows huh by, jes Miss Coon. He war a fine ole man but she war a hard one. Ah wuz name aftuh young Missie Harriet.

"De white folks had a fine house, a very large house standin' high up on a bluff 'bout a mile an three quawterhs fum Cumbuhlain' Rivuh. Dat wuz in Smith County, Tennessee.

"Ah don rightly 'member 'bout how many slaves dey had, but dere war sev'ral cabins whut us cullud folks live in.

"Mah mammy and daddy wuz Sarah an Bob Tadwell. Mammy wuz raised in Vuhginyuh an' when she wuz sixteen yeah ole she wuz put on de block an' sold in Nashville.

"Mah mammy wuz a seamstress. She nevuh work in de fiel', an' she don' know nuthin' 'bout cookin', but she do fine sewin'. When dey put her on de block dey has some o' huh work dar tuh show what fine sewin' she kin do. Yuh know all de sewin war done by han' an mah mammy'd sew sometime till huh finguhs nearly drap off.

She sew de fines' tucks an' she make all dem fine tuck bosom shurts fo' de men.

"One time a man come an' wunna buy mammy an me. Miss Coon wuz gonna sell us unbeknownst to ole Massa. Ole Massa wouldn' sell none o' his people, but Miss Coon ahways try to put things ovuh on him an' he couldn' do nuthin 'bout it but go git drunk. Ole Miss Coon put de price on us a way up high—'cause mammy sech a fine seamstress an' ah wuz ahways a buxum chile, nevuh sick er nuthin. But he say dat too much an' he go on home. Aftuh while wen dey so much talk 'bout freein' de niggers Miss Coon sont him word dat she come way down on de price but he sont back word dat he got ez much sense as she got.

"We lef' thar when we wus free. My mammy ahways got work a sewin'. Ah stayed wuth one white woman fifteen year.

"Yessum de Ku Kluxes cum aroun' right smaht. De woman ah stayed wuth wouldn' 'low no foolishness roun' her place an' dey nevuh bothuh huh none, but dey beat up some o' de neighbors. One ole man dey beat till he die."

MATTIE LEE

> Interview with Mrs. Mattie Lee,
> aged 78, Fredericktown, Missouri.
> Interviewed by J. Tom Miles.

"My mother was a slave in Franklin Parish, Louisiana, 'bout 200 miles from New-Orleans. I was born in 1862. My mother's name was Caroline Head by marriage. She was born in slavery. Her home was in Mississippi first and she emigrated to Louisiana 'cause de land was worn out. I had seven brothers and sisters and all are gone but me. My mother was separated from my father two times. My mother was married three times due to being moved around. My brother's father was sent into a free state under some consideration. Bush Baker was my mother's boss. De boss had two plantations. De morning I was going to be born de overseer began to fight my mother and a colored man took a hoe and said if the man hit her again he would knock his brains out. The overseer had been at this place for four years and had not been paid. Mother was confined in de field and dey got her to de house. If Baker had been thar he would have killed de overseer. Three men came up to kill de overseer with guns for beatin' my mother and de overseer had to leave. My mother never did get over her troubles dat morning. Mrs. Baker said it would be better for mother to work in de field 'cause mother could then take better care of her children.

"Mrs. Baker was kind and tended de children when

dey was sick. Mrs. Baker took us to Texas during de war 'cause she was afraid the Union soldiers would take her slaves away from her. After peace was declared de soldiers came and told de white people dat de slaves was free. But we never did leave Mrs. Baker's place. After de war was over Mrs. Baker took us back to Louisiana. We traveled with a team of oxen and three teams of mules with wagons. Some of Mrs. Baker's slaves staid in Texas and never did come back from Texas. Dis was in 1865.

"I can 'member de home place. De county road went close to de front gate. Mrs. Eliza Baker had a beautiful yard and after de war she would have us come and stay in de yard to be protected from de jay-hawkers. De high water would come past de fence and we would play in de water. One time a jay-hawker come and git one of de children in a skiff and den we yelled and de mastah come out with his pistol and hit de jay-hawker over de head. So de jay-hawker turned de child over again. So we did not play down in de water no more.

"De mistress had a long table out in de front yard under de smokehouse shed and here all us children had our food. It was good food. Mrs. Baker had a fig nursery in de front yard and we would go and pick washtubs of figs. Some were dried and others were put up. Mrs. Baker had a plantation of 1,800 acres. On week ends we would dance and they would always be getting married. We had a colored man on de place who could read and he did de marrying. De only school I ever went to was to a night school here fer a short time. Dey would tell me a story 'bout 'de bear an de Grand-ma' an 'bout 'little Riden' Hood'. Dey use to tell us some awful yarns. Dey would kill over 100 head of hogs every year and cure it, and I can't get used to buyed meat today. Mrs. Baker would take anyone in de wagon to church dat wanted to go. My aunt went to church but would not be baptized.

"I 'member when de Ku Klux Klan started out when dey would dress up in white and dey had a noise like 'O-O' 'O-O'. But we were not 'fraid of dem 'cause we knew dey would be killed if dey come on de place. I think a lot of Abe Lincoln. I have often thought how hard it was to give up his life, fer de United States. But Christ died for to save de world and Lincoln died to save de United States. And Lincoln died more Christ like den any other man dat ever lived.

"Dere was an old colored man on de place and he would drive Jeff Davis 'round and would keep Davis in his house and feed him. This was when Jeff Davis was a boy, and a orphan. Jeff Davis gave dis colored man, Montgomery, a lot of land. It's a good thing dat slavery is over. Anything wants a privilege outside and not in a coop. Slaves could not be natural when they was dis way. Everybody wants to do somethin' with demselves.

"I staid in Louisiana till 1875 and got mad and left and went to Madison Parish, Louisiana. It was not de white people dat made me leave here but it was my father. Den I went to Vicksburg for seven months, den to St. Louis on a mail boat. It cost me $8.50 to come from Vicksburg to St. Louis. I found work in St. Louis in a little while. Never did have to worry 'bout where I was going to sleep. I left Madison Parish 'cause we had a flood when de levee broke.

"I came to St. Louis in 1883 and did all kinds of house work. I got a dollar a day. Den I came to Fredericktown 'cause I wanted to own a home. You were never sure dat you could have a sure claim to land in St. Louis. It was a 'quick Claim'. We lived one mile above Fredericktown and had seven or eight acres. I married in Fredericktown and have no children. My husband has been dead since 1908. I made my way fine by washin' and ironing an made $18 a week since my husband died. I paid $985 for dis house."

WES LEE

Interview with Wes Lee, Cape Girardeau, Missouri.

"My mastuh's name was Peter Burns and we lived out in Cape County, close to the Houck place. My daddy's name was Charles Lee. Mammy's name was 'Lizabeth, and old mastuh bought her from de Catholic priests. Old mastuh had a big white frame house and it had lots of trees 'round it. There was a saw-mill jes' across de road.

"I was just a little feller during de war, but I can remember dat when de Rebel sojers come by our place old mastuh had de table set for 'em, and treat 'em fine—'cause he's a rebel—den when de 'Yankees' come along he give dem de bes' he had, and treat 'em fine 'cause he's a 'Yankee'. Old Jedge Ranney live on de next place and he and old mastuh was good friends—but he was such a hot southerner he couldn't stand old mastuh to act like dat. In a way I guess old mastuh was right for none of de sojers never bother nuthin' on de place.

"One time de blue-coats was coming by de jedge's place. De jedge had lots of turkeys and dey was roosting up in de trees. I don't think de sojers was bothering nuthin', but something must've skeered dem turkeys for dey commenced making a awful racket. Den de jedge, he come out, ask what dey doing to his turkeys—and he raise a big fuss. So den de sojers druv' into de barn—dey was a great big barn with a drive through de middle. Dey jes' drove in de wagons, loaded 'em with corn and hay—and dey caught some chickens and dey take all de jedge's best hosses. De jedge jes' stand there and watch 'em. He can't do nuthing 'cause de more he say de more dey takes. But dey never bother old mastuh's place none—'cause he make friends with both sides.

"One time de Rebel sojers was there. Old mastuh had de table all set with everything fine to eat. And de Rebels was jes' getting ready to eat when we hear de big guns from de forts, at de Cape, and word come dat de Yanks was coming. I can jes' see dem Rebel sojers yet—how dey rolled out of there. Most of 'em was a-wearin' coonskin caps with de tail a-hangin' down. And how dey did go! Dat was de time Mahmaduke was a-tryin' to take de Cape. I hear de Yanks overtook him about Allenville and had a skirmish there.

"No'm I don't much believe in ghosts and de like—and yet one time out there by Benton Hill—you know dey always say Benton Hill's ha'nted—well I was comin' along there one evening 'bout dark—and from across de road come two men—dey was dressed in kind of white suits and had big, floppy hats on. Dey didn't say nothing and cross de road, right in front of me—with dey heads hanging down. When I gets a little past 'em I thinks—wonder where dey's going? So I looks back and sees 'em start up dat hill and then jest plum disappear. I studies 'bout that, and next morning when I goes back, I goes to look and see where de tracks go. De clay on dat hillside were so soft if you'd put your hand down it would leave a track, but dey warn't a sign of a track whar I seed dem men walk up dar and disappear. After dat I always carry me a lantern when I goes by dar, at night, and when folks tells me 'bout spirits dey seen I don't never tell 'em I don't believe 'em."

United States. Work Projects Administration

PERRY MCGEE

Interview with Perry McGee,
Festus, Missouri.

Perry Is Right At 87

"I was born near Fayette, Missouri, not far from New Florence on September 2, 1850. Dat makes me right at 87 years old. My father's name was Stephen Estol and Mother's was Agnes Swiney. My grandfather's name was Albert McGee and he was borned in Virginia. He was a carpenter. My grandmother's name was Emily and she was a slave in Glasgow, Howard County, Missouri. I was born just three miles northwest of Glasgow. My boss den is now a banker in Kansas City. His name is James Alwald Swiney. Once he was a preacher in St. Louis and I saw him preachin' dere once. He seen me going along de street one day. I never would have knowed him, only he said: 'Hey boy, where you from? Where did you hail from?' I said: 'I hails from Howard County.' He said: 'Come in.'

"I went in and stayed dere mighty near all day and ate dinner with dem. He come out on de porch and told me not to call him master but to call him Mr. Swiney. We talked all evening and he told me to be a good boy and to be truthful.

"You know Abraham Lincoln offered $300 a head before de war for all de slaves but de people would not sell any more dan you would cut your shade tree down in your yard. So dey elected Jefferson Davis President. A man by de name of Grigsby was a slave buyer. It was like you would want a hog or cow and dey would put slaves on de block and 'cry them off'. You have got to make profit on de deal. A good strong man would sell for $300 and some for $100. A house slave was worth more dan a field slave.

"Dey wouldn't sell my mother. De old mistress would not allow my mother to be sold. I had only one sister and two brothers. One brother died when I was a baby. De Rebel soldiers taken me. I was a waiter. When Price's raid come they took me off de farm. After dey left Pilot Knob dey come up through Missouri and fired on Glasgow and only 900 militia and regular soldiers could not fight 90,000 rebels. So dese 900 ran and blew up de powder magazine and it sounded just like thunder and looked like a black cloud. De rebels went on across de river and said dey was going to make de niggers smell hell. De soldier said, 'Hey, little nigger, we want you to go with us and wait on de Captain.' I was light as a feather almost and dey boosted me up on a horse behind one of de soldiers and took me to Glasgow to a eatin' place. Dey had hard tack made without any salt or any shortnin' about em. There was plenty springs up there. I had to clean off de horse, and played marbles and turned handsprings and dey had me for a monkey. I could walk on my hands. Lots of times dey would chip in and pay me a little. When I left and was free I had $18 in nickels and dimes and had only one piece as big as a quarter. I was as 'fraid of a Union soldier as of a rattle snake. Horace Swiney come to town and begged de soldiers to let me come back so he brought me back on his horse. I was in Glasgow about three days.

"One day young Swiney come out and told us we was free and for us to call him Mr. Swiney and not master. Dere was only one colored family who left the farm here of 800 acres. All de rest of us stayed right dere. He had about 70 slaves. De old man made a talk and said dey was plenty of land dere and we could all stay and work as we had been. After de freedom dey paid me 10 cents a day or $3 a month and board. Man, I done everything. I carried water on my head. See! my head is flat and I ain't got no sense. I had to carry water in 'piggins', something like a well bucket with one handle so you could catch it with one hand and set it up on your head. Dese buckets was made out of wood on de place dere by a good carpenter. De piggins would hold 2 gallons of water.

"I've had 12 children and I was married 55 years when my wife died. I only got 6 children livin' now, 4 boys and 2 girls. One of my girls, Alice, is a teacher in de college in St. Louis. She went to four colleges, at Champaign, Illinois; Lincoln University, Jefferson City; University of Chicago and at Honolulu University where she is dis summer. She has been teaching about 5 or 6 years. She teaches geography and mathematics. I went naked, barefooted, and hungry and send my daughter to school. She went to grade school right here in Festus. Alice is 42 now and she wants to marry and have four children. Bessie is my other daughter, and she has taught school for 18 years. She is a graduate of Lincoln University and taught at Cape Girardeau 4 years, at Lost Creek in Washington County 2 years, in Festus for 6 years, and in Appleton, Missouri, too. Bessie is married now and she don't have any children. I stays right here with her.

"My son, Granville McGee, lives in St. Paul, Minnesota, and works on de Northern Pacific Railroad and is a waiter between Chicago and Seattle. He's been with dem 17 years. His is a six day run and he has 6 children. Another son, W.C. McGee, lives in Lansing, Michigan. He is a Democrat. When de Democrats is in power I is a Democrat and when de Republicans is in power I'se a Republican. Dat's de way it generally goes. My son up in Lansing is editor of the Lansing Eye Opener, and has been editor for several years. He is another one who had a pretty good education and is a graduate of Lincoln University, too. He was a porter for a railroad before he was a editor. You got to have a pretty fair education to be a porter now. My oldest son, 61, lives in Rockford, Illinois. He was born in Crystal City and when he was here he was an inspector in de sand mines. He is a furnace man over at Rockford in a glass factory. He has been working for de glass company ever since he was big enough to walk. He is married and has one child. My son, Oscar, is a railroader and lives in St. Louis and is a porter on a train what runs between St. Louis and down in Mexico. He is married and has no children and never will have none. His wife had a accident.

"After I was free I come to St. Louis and done a little of everything and worked for my step-father and worked harder for him dan for my master. I sawed wood and drove a cart. We had a coal and wood yard. I did not get paid but could eat. I worked for him until one day I met my father's sister on de street and she asked me some questions on Morgan Street in St. Louis.

"Den I went with Uncle Jim McGee to live and he took me down to Greenville, Mississippi and picked cotton and worked as a porter at de hotel dere. I got $12 a month and board. I didn't stay down dere very long and come back to St. Louis and worked at Billing's Bank dat was a saloon and was paid $18 a month and made extra about $25 on tips. I worked for him for about two years plumb 'till I come down in Jefferson County. I worked 30 years over in the plate glass factory in Crystal City and had to quit dere on account of my eyes. I was firing in de furnace. I sometimes made $4 a day and board at de factory. Den I worked for 27 years for de Festus Mercantile Company and done a little bit of everything. I gets $11 a month now as an old age pension.

"I was 21 or 2 when I first voted. My first vote was for U.S. Grant for President at Hematite, Missouri. My last vote was for F.D. Roosevelt. Lots of dem wanted to pay me to vote a certain way but I never paid any attention to dem. I'm a Democrat now. I don't think a man ought to be allowed to vote unless dey know what dey doin'.

"I'se went to school only three days in my life. De missus learned me my A, B, C's and all de rest I learned myself. I paid $1.50 a month to go to night school in St. Louis for three months and learned to read and spell, but I just can't write. If I had de chance dat de young folks have now I would go as high as you could go. I can talk some German 'cause I worked for a Dutchman once. De young generation of colored people ain't goin' to amount to nothin'. Dey don't want to work, but one out of a thousand might do something. Dey all think dey know too much and don't want to learn no more. My other boys will never know what my son knows. De young ones don't appreciate their advantages. Booker T. Washington had a hard time. We will never have no more like him. Some of de slave holders treated de slaves better than dey is today. De young generation is about at their best now.

Dey think too much about their pleasure. Dey don't have enough work to do. I used to work 16 hours a day. Now dey is got it down to 6 hours a day. I think it was good for some of de colored people to be slaves.

"I think it would be better if some of the ones now were slaves and it would teach dem to work. My young mistress treated me good and I went with her right behind a horse called Andrew. She thought a heap of me and I thought a heap of her.

"Dere ain't but two classes of people, good and bad, and dey been tryin' to separate de black people from de white people but de line has already been cut. Colored women is havin' white children. I think dat is wrong. Dey ought not to mix dem up, but I ain't goin' to try to separate 'em. Dat is de reason I voted for de Lincoln Bill. If people do wrong let 'em be punished accordin' to law no matter what color.

"Slavery hurt de men who owned de slaves. De Negro was only de shade tree. De master would set back in de shade and tell de Negro what to do. I hear so many say, 'I'm free!' But there is only one person who is free and he or she is de one dat God has set free. God set forth in de heart of Abraham Lincoln dat every man should earn his bread by de sweat of his brow. Man is his own free agent. De masters measured out bad measure and dey got worser in de end dan de slaves.

"What is ruinin' dis country is de love for money. God is goin' to rule dis world."

JOHN MCGUIRE

Interview with John McGuire,
Herculaneum, Missouri.

Bondage Was Great Burden

"I was born in Valle Mines in the northern part of St. Francois County. My mother's name was Sophie McGuire. She was a slave of Henry Bisch and my father was named Philip McGuire and was owned by John McGuire. I lives here in Herculaneum and am 74 years old. My father worked in de mines and my mother worked in and around de house and cooked. She was more of a house girl. I had three brothers and seven sisters. All my sisters is dead 'cept two. One of dem lives in De Soto and de other in St. Louis. One of my brothers lives at Crystal City and one has worked for over 20 years for de St. Joe Company here at Herculaneum.

"I'se heard my mother and father talk about what a hard time dey had when dey was set free and went to housekeeping. First dey moved in a house dat was already built and den dey built a log cabin. My father dug de zinc and lead ore to make a living at Valle Mines. He would get so much a ton and would sometimes make $2 a day and den sometimes he would not make anything. I lived at Valle Mines till I come of age and den moved to St. Louis where I worked for 30 years. I worked in a boiler room, in de steel works, and drove a team. I hauled sand, cinders, lumber, dirt, etc. I got about $1.50 a day when I worked in

St. Louis. I was married for about 35 years and my wife is dead and didn't have any children. When I left St. Louis I worked in de mines at Fletcher and den came over here and have been 'scalawaggin' around since I been here.

"I 'membered how my mother used to tell about an old colored man who ground her scissors and he ground dem on both sides and dey would not cut anything. Dat sure made her mad. I used to have to turn de old grindstone for my father to get his ax sharp. He like to wore me out. I feel like I growed up with more freedom now since we has no slavery. I believe if de colored people had never been brought to dis country dey would be further developed dan dey is this way. Our people has been under bondage in dis country for over 200 years. Being in de bondage has been a great hardship on our race. Dis condition might have some effect today with some people. Dey might say, 'Well, dis fellow will amount to nothin'' 'cause his parents was slaves.'

"I can read and write and went to school in Valle Mines at night and paid for it. It cost $1 a month and I went a part of two terms. I learned to read and write from my father. My father's master would not allow him to have any books, but de master's son would steal a book and when dey was in de mines working I had some free time. My father and de master's son would go off in one side of de mine and dere learn to read and write.

"In some ways I think de young generation is much better off dan I am or was. But, on de other hand, it seems to me like dey is more rude but as de younger ones grows up maybe dey will be better. De younger generation has a greater opportunity, but dey is behind in doing things against the law. You all knows such like as stealing, killin', robbing and swindling is going on now more dan when I was a boy. We have some mighty rude colored children. Dere is several reasons for dis rudeness. It's caused by letting children go as dey wants to go. De parents gets so dey feels dat their child is too good to correct. Another reason is a whole lot de breeding of de children. I think dat since slavery de Negro would have been better off if he had been put on a reservation to hisself. It would have come more natural to civilize de Negro dat way dan de way it is now. Dere is a lot of white men get Negro women and a lot of white women get Negro men. Dat would never have happened if de races had been separated. I'se been down in Southeast Missouri and de colored race is treated pretty bad down dere."

United States. Work Projects Administration

ELIZA MADISON

> Interview with Eliza Madison,
> aged 75, Fredericktown, Missouri.
> Interviewed by J. Tom Miles.

"I was born in Stoddard County, Missouri. My mother belonged to John Sitzes and my father belonged to Lark Abernathy. I can jes remember how afraid us chillun was of de soldiers. De boss had a big plantation and raised everything dey ate and wore. We had a cabin dat joined on to the house. My mother was jus' like a man and worked in de fiel' and made rails. My aunt wove. I picked up chips. My mother was the type dat they had to treat good. De master had eight children. There was a white school of three months. I did not go to school.

"After de war was over we all worked for twenty-five cents a day but didn't get paid in money but in food. Mother was sold twice, and my father was sold away from my mother. I don't 'member anything 'bout my father. I was 'bout four years old when de war ended. 'Bout all we did on Sunday was to dig ginseng and fish. One of de slaves would go out to a dance and get in in de mornin' and he would get a whippin'.

"After de war some Ku Klux come through our place and de white folks said they could tell who dey were by de walk. After de war was over de soldiers were going to take some of de colored women south, so we hid under de stairway. De soldiers fought to get de slaves to go and my mother had a scar on her shoulder dat dey made. De soldiers took some of de slaves south and sold them somewhar' and we never heard from them again.

"Black root was a purgative medicine as well as goose grease. For whooping-cough dey would use honey and alum.

"At Christmas we'd get candy or a new dress. On one Christmas old Christine or Santa Clause would wrap up in a blanket and this is how we got our presents. Down thar de hickory nuts grew big and it was a funny thing when we found out dat old Christine was giving us our own hickory nuts.

"I can't 'member 'bout any hoodoo business but once a Negro man borrowed a pair of boots from another man and when he returned them thar was a snake's tooth sticking up through de sole of one of de boots."

DRUCILLA AND RICHARD MARTIN

An Interview with Drucilla Martin, age 102, and Richard Martin, age 92, Poplar Bluff, Missouri.

"I 'se half Indian and I look it too, and if I wo' gold rings in my ears and nose I would look just like my mammy did 'cause she was full blooded Indian. I don' know what kind, but she was big and tall and had black hair, she could sit on it and it was as coa'se as a mule's tail. She carried a tom-hawk and eve'y one stepped to one side when they met her on the turn-pike. She wus from Giles County, Tennessee. Giles County, Hear Me! And her name was 'Eirar-Lu Ellen'. My father's name was Spencer Johnson, don't guess I seed much ob him 'cause mammy and him wasn't married.

"We stayed on, for Mars Pinter, (Mr. Pointer), from the time I 'member 'till the war closed, and we wus free; and you had better never let Mars hear you call us slaves. He'd not stand for it; hear me! We didn't farm, 'xactly; Mars Pinter owned the iron works and most of his people worked in there. Best I 'member we did raise our eats and that wus all 'cause the nearest trading post wus Nashville, Tennessee, and that wus a long way, them days.

"I had nine brothers and sisters, and they wus: Monroe Henderson; he wus the House servant, Jefferson, Ida, Felia, Laura, Izora, and I don' 'member the other two; guess they died when they wus babies, but all we was named the same names as Mars Pinter kids; and we played with them, hear me! we played with them.

"Then when I wus big 'nuf I wus put to cardin' wool and cotton, we wusn't paid no money for our work we didn' need none; we had ever'thin' we needed, and plenty of good stuff to eat, and good warm cloths to ware.

"Them 'nigger' boys wus so proud to 'long to Mars Pinter that they would break up white rocks and scatter them on the turn-pike, and make nice, white shiny walks for Misses. When the carriage was ordered out for a drive, first mammy walk out with a white cloth, rub it over the carriage—huh; better not find a speck of dirt on the carriage.

"Mammy allus taught all her white and dark children, when interin' the presence of elders, to make your' 'obedience', (bow), and then, sit quiet.

"Men, them days wore long hair too, but sometime they cut it off, if it got too long and hot. They would turn a milk crock down over their haid and even it off some.

"We didn' know nothin' much about the war, we didn't want to leave Marse, and that wus all the difference it made us. I do 'member 'Ol' Jeff Davis, come to 'Marse' and say: 'Gib me them niggers and I will carry them down to Fort Pillow and hide them in the cave until this is over'; then 'Marse' run them off, and said: 'better not put any of my people in a cave, they worked for me and made all my money: I gwine to do right by these people.'

"Where we lived we never heard tell of a 'form school,

never needed nothin' lake that; didn't know what one wus.

"One thing I does 'member well, and would like to know if anyone else was there and 'members it. I went with my 'Missie Pinter' to see them hang John Brown, he was a 'Whig'; they brought him from the Culpeper County Court House, in Virginia, and hung him to a beechwood tree, at Harper's Ferry; on the bank of the James River. Now they sing 'Hung him to a sour apple tree', but that ain't right. I saw it and I know.

"I said a while ago we wusn't paid no money, but I did know what it wus 'cause 'Marse' never put lock or key on his cellar-door, and he kept food and his money in small barrels down there and we could play wif it and never once did anyone try and take any of it.

"I learned to iron too, and there wus two women stood there ironing every day, they sho' could make them purty lace 'broidery underskirts stand alone.

"My mammy was in full charge of the house, and all the 'Marse' children, and when they pass her, she say: 'Lif yo' dress', then if'n she see little spot dirt or wrinkle, make dem take off all de clothes and change. Den she say 'Take off you shoe', smell their feet, Huh! She call 'Lisa, bring that foot tub', then she would wash and dry their feet and put on clean stockings. Mammy wus clean as a new pin.

"When I got any size to notice I wus dum-confounded to hear my mammy talk up to the white boys comin' to court 'Missie Pinter's' girls. Mammy meet them at de door and say: 'What you want?' They say: 'I come to call on Mis ——'. She say, 'What you got makes you think got right to call on my fine daughter? What you own? Can you hire her work done? Do you think my daughter is gwin' to marry any' por' white trash, and have to work hard all her life?' Then if'n he couldn' give a good account for himsef, mammy would swing her tom-hawk and yell: 'Be-gone, don' come back'. 'Nother thing a young man had better not come courtin' in his shirt sleeve, better have on his coat or mammy would 'back' in he haid.

"Then after the war wus over, and we wus free, it wusn't hard to find work. I wus allus honest and religious, 'longed to the Southern Babtist Church. I got work among the rich white people and traveled with them. Then I worked as laundress in the U.S. Marine Hospital, in St. Louis, for seven years; when George Washington was President. I worked on the 'Chas. P. Shoto' steamboat as chamber-maid, and made lots of trips to Florida. I was maid for Mrs. Busch, in St. Louis, and they wus powerful rich, they made that beer up there.

"Richard says, he wus bawn May 8, 1845, on the corner of Beale and Main Streets, Memphis, Tenn. And I wus bawn May 8, 1835, in Giles County, Tenn. We neither one had much bad treatment but we is glad slavery is over."

RICHARD AND DRUCILLA MARTIN

Interview with Richard and Drucilla Martin,
Poplar Bluff, Missouri.

Called on and talked to Richard and Drucilla Martin, old time negroes, who were slaves. They talked fluently, really enjoying talking about the 'good days' as they put it, as they say their master was good to them.

Richard is rather short and wears a beard, which is snow white. He claims to be something better than ninety years old, he says about ninety-four or five, and Drucilla is ten years older than Richard.

About four or five years ago their home which they owned was destroyed by fire, and having no insurance, they have since been living in a poor substitute for a house made of pieces of tin, wood, and old boxes, built under the branches of a tree.

Richard was in a hurry to go to town and see if their old age pension checks had come yet and invited us to come back some other time.

Drucilla said she was the slave of John Pointer. Her mother who was part Indian wore a ring in her nose and carried a tomahawk, had ten children, and mothered the ten children of her master's wife. Drucilla does not remember much about her father, as he was the slave of another family.

Although Drucilla does not have any education, she can quote verse after verse from the Bible. She told some gruesome stories of how some of the masters treated their slaves. She said there never was a book printed that really told how some, or in fact the majority of the slaves were beaten and abused. To most masters they were not any more than stock. She said some of the young girls were beaten until they would die. Some of the little colored babies that were born out in the field or on the road were left to starve or be eaten up by the hogs.

Drucilla said some times their master would rent them out to other white men to work them if he didn't have anything for them to do. Some masters would put their feed out in troughs for them just as they were feeding cattle. Some would give them cotton seed to eat. She said they would go home and cry and tell their master how they were treated and their master would tell them they wouldn't have to go work for any one that did them like that.

In 1865 when the slaves were freed, Drucilla said she felt all out in the world as if she did not have a place to go and their master was afraid to let them stay with him even though they begged to stay, as it was then against the law. She was sent to St. Louis to do servant work, for a white family, that was very wealthy, and she stayed with them for twenty years. Drucilla has been married twice, and is the mother of ten children, but knows of only one daughter, or rather, she was the last one she has heard from out of the three that she thinks are still living, and that was fifty years ago.

Drucilla and Richard Martin

Drucilla Martin was a slave in Giles County, Tennessee; Richard Martin was a slave in Memphis, Tennessee.

The aged old couple are going to receive $8.00 apiece per month old age pension, and a check for $80.00 back pay. When worker asked Drucilla what she was going to do with her pension money, she said she was going to build a little house, "As Mammy is tired living in that shack".

When we got up to leave, the old Negro mammy ran out and fell down and kissed our feet. There were two workers stumbling along trying to get down the rocky path that leaves the little shack, with their eyes full of tears, and the muscles of their throats tightened, until they could only wave back, as the feeble voice was heard to ring out over the hill, "Honey chiles come back to see mammy some more, and she'll give yo all somethin' out of her garden."

HATTIE MATTHEWS

> Interview with Mrs. Hattie Matthews,
> aged 58, Farmington, Missouri.

"Ma mathuh wuz Louisiana Anthony an she married an liv'd in Libertyville, Missouri, in St. Francois County. She are dead now, but ud be 'bout 78 if she war livin'. She wuz born into slavery. Ma grandmuther wuz Harriet Smith, an she wuz born in 'bout 1820 an she war 'bout 40 years ole wen de War begun. She wuz a slabe near New Madrid, Missouri, an died wen she wuz 'bout 90 yars ole. Ma grandmuthuh had 14 childr'n an wen de war ended, her master, Shap Phillips, tak one ob her girls named Phebe an put her on a hoss an took her away with him an we neber heard from her agin. We think she wuz taken south ta work fur som'body. When ma grandmuthuh got free she an my grandfather, who worked fur another master, bought a small farm near Knob Lick, in St. Francois County, Missouri. Dey bilt dem a house an bought only 20 acres at a time an finally had 120 acres.

"I used to lay wake nights a-lis'nen ta stories dat muthuh an grandmuthuh ud tell about slabery days. I know a lot ob stories but hab furgot many ob dem. My, how she cud tell 'bout dose times, an dey ware true too. Wen ma grandmuthuh got married dey jus jumped ober a broomstick an dey ware consider'd man an wife. Dis ware de custom den. De master ud hole de broomstick. I ask grandmuthuh wat she ud a-done had she fall'n ober de broomstick. She say, 'Well I didn't fall, but jump'd clear ober hit.' I member dis 'cause hit seemed so funny. Brogan shoes war wore then. Dey war ob rough leather and de shoes had brass toes. All de clos wuz wove an de only fancy clos ma grandmuthuh had ware giv'n ta her by de Missus.

"Shap Phillips had a good many slabes an grandmuthuh wuz de cook. She wuz very strong an cook'd in kettles bigg'r dan dey habe now. Whenever a negro slabe had a baby she had ta work rite on. If she work'd in de fiel she ud take de baby long and lay hit down in de rail fence corn'r in de sun. De baby had on only a slip. De master ud ride his hoss in de fiel an had a horse whip dat wuz platted, an he ud cut de slabes with dis whip wen de slabes slack'd hup. If de babies cried de muthuh had ta get de master's permishun fore she cud pick up their baby.

"De scraps from de white folk's table war all thrown into a kettle. Ma muthuh ud stan clos by an she ud grab in de kettle with both han's an eat whateber she got. Den, after all de grown slabes did dis, dey wud call 'Pot liquor time' an de childr'n ud run to de kettle an drink wat wuz in de bott'm ob de kettle. Dis wus generally de juice or water frum greens. Sometime de childr'n got a piece ob cornbread. Dis wuz all de childr'n got ta eat an of course dey war always hungry.

"De master had a polly-parrot an dese parrots ud be plac'd ta hear an watch wat de slabes did. Dey war not always seen by de slabes an wen de master wuz away de parrots wud member wat had happ'n'd an report it. One of de slabes wuz bakin' bread an she tok a pan full ob biscuits an hid it under de cushion of de chair. De ole Missus come in an wuz sick an she started ta sit down in de chair.

De parrot wuz sittin' up dar an say, 'Missi bissi burn you.' The Missus lifted up de cushion an foun de pan o bread. She wuz sick and couldn't whip de slabe so she wuz goin' to habe de master do it wen he came in. De slabe wuz mad so she tok de parrot an wrung its neck and threw it out hind de house thinkin' she had kil'd de parrot.

"De Missus had to go out dare fur somethin' an de parrot say, 'Poor polly, layin' in de sun.' De master den really beat de slabe wen he came in. Ma grandmuthuh knew de lady dat dis happ'n'd to in New Madrid. Ma grandmuthuh got whipp'd only onc't an de master wuz sorry 'cause she fought back. She wuz strong an a good work'r. Ma grandmuthuh wuz up fur sale on de block once an dey offer'd several thousand dollars fur her but she wuz a good worker an she wuz not sold. Wen de rebel soldiers come de slabes ud hide but wen de Union soldiers com de slabes ud run to dem.

"Wen de master had company he ud tak meat skins an grease de mouths ob all de slabe childr'n. Den wen de company cam de master ud call' all de slabe children in an say, 'You little rascals have been eating!' He wanted to create de impression dat he wuz feedin his slabes better dan de other masters round dare.

"Grandmuthuh said dey had lots ob hoodoo business. I ask her why dey didn't hoodoo de white folks ta get dem out ob de way. She said de negroes couldn't hoodoo de white peoples 'cause dey had strait hair. It wuz somethin' 'bout de oil in de hair. White folks habe ta wash dere hair ta get de oil out, but negroes habe ta put oil in deir hair. But de slabes sure could hoodoo each other. Somebody who wanted ta hoodoo somebody else wud tak snakes an frogs an pulverize um an put de stuff in a bottle. Dey den dug a hole in de groun under de step an buried de bottle in de hole. When de person (for whom the hoodoo was intended) took a step ober dis spot dey wud habe pains in deir legs. Ma grandmuthuh cud see de snakes come up inside deir legs an dey had to cut a hole in deir legs ta let de snakes out. Sometimes dey ud get a person ta take de snakes an frogs from a person, and den de person who put de hoodoo under de step or porch ud lose deir charm and die. Ma grandmuther say she saw many a frog an snake come out ob a person's mouth. De slabes were turrible ta each other. All such as dis went on in de dose days. This here hoodoo business still goes on down in Mississippi. I'm shure glad I don't live down thar. Ma cousin got into an argument with a negro girl down thar an they couldn't settle hit. So she (my cousin) wrote to somebody who wrote back an tole ma cousin all 'bout this here other girl such as her amount of insurance, etc."

LETHA TAYLOR MEEKS

Interview with Letha Taylor Meeks,
Smelterville, Missouri.

"My full name is Letha Taylor Meeks, an' I'se bahn down in Panola County, Mississippi close to da Tallahatchie Ribbah. Mah fathuh an' mothuh wuz Andy and Susan Tayluh. We belonged to Ole Massa Billie Welborn an' our Misses wuz Ole Miss' Cloe.

"Dey had a fine big house, we call it de mansion. Dey had po'ches an' galleries bof. Der wuz trees all aroun', pine trees an' cedahs, an' oak trees. An' de yawd wuz full a flower bushes.—big snowballs an' lilacs, an' rows of flags, an honeysuckle vines, wid de mockin' birds an' doves a singin' roun'—an dey wuz jay birds too. An der wuz big vegitable gahdens an fruit trees. In de sto' room in de fall der wuz a'ways bags full er dried apples an' peaches, an' pumpkin an cahn, strings o' onions a hanging up, an heaps o turnips an' sweet 'taters, an bins fulla 'taters. An' they wuz lotsa cabbages an' collards in shelters in de gahden.

"Miss' Cloe dress mighty fine. She wear calico prints roun' home, but when she dress up she wear silks an' satins' with hoop skirts an a rare-back hat tied unduh her chin.

"When de white folks go tuh church at Fredonia us cullud folks go too but we sits up in de gallery. We didden hab no school but sometime de preacher an his wife 'ud come to stay wid de white folks an dey'd a'ways hab classes fo' us chillern. One time dey stayed dar nearly a yeah.

"Us chillern usta play hide an seek, honey on de bee ball, frog in de meadow, an' eberthing playable. Ah learned tuh spin an ah'd fill quills till ah had a whole basket full an' I'd wind de broches. Mah mothaw hepped with de weavin. Dey made all our clothes—'member one time dey made sech fine gray homespun for de men's pants. Ole Mothuh Ret was seamstress for de white folks—we called her Mothuh Ret—her name was Henrietta. De looms an' spinning wheels was in a big room down in de basement. Dere wuz a big fireplace in de room.

"Mothuh helped wuth de cookin, too. An ah'd help her on cleanin' days. Our folks shore had fine funicher an' things, an' de fines' silver an candles all ovah de house. We made de candles; put a string in de mold, den po' de grease in—Dere was fine candles for company.

"'For de sojers came all de silver an' fine things wuz hid. Dey had two basements—de big one unduh de whole house n'en a small one in back—unduh de small one wuz a cellah, an in dat cellar dey hide all de things—barrels o' taters, sacks o' dried fruits an vegetables, de meats an' lawd, en puvisions—an de silver till dey had it full up—den dey puts back de puncheon boahds—an' fills in wuth dirt jes like it warn't nuthin unduh there.

"Dey had two sons go off tuh war. Columbus came back when de wah wuz ovah but Wallace died wid measles. When he leave to go tuh war, he tell me he gwine tuh come back, wid Lincoln's head on a stick but de Lawd sent him back wid his head in a coffin. Dey had all us cullud folks come through de house to see young Massa lyin dar in de big front room in his coffin.

"Dey was mo dan a hundred slaves. Dey wus three cabins close to de mansion an our fambly lived dar. In de quawters dey wuz 'bout fifty cabins but dat wuz 'bout five mile fum us—over on de udduh place. Young Massa Willyum live in de big house ovah der. He didden go tuh wah an one time de sojers come an' look for him. Dey cain't fin' him so dey burn de house down 'cause dey think he's in dar—but dey nebber bothuh our place.

"Fust time ah ebber seed de Yankees, it wuz one Saturday—I went out tuh let de calves into de grove. When ah look down de road an ah see one man come roun de cornuh, den anudduh—den mo—till ah see it de whole ahmy comin—Den ah's skeered an ah runs back to de house ahollerin', 'De Yankees is comin'.' Dey comes on up de road an into de yawd an' one man grab me an' he say 'Is you de little gal what run to tell um to hide 'cause we's comin'?' Ah tells um I'se de little gal whut run but ah never tells nobody to hide. I is sho' skeered. He hol's me while de mens look aroun' but dey don' tarry long.

"De nex' day, dat wuz Sunday, Ole Forrest come by wid his Rebel sojers—an' dey stole Massa's fine mules. Massa had a fine pair o' matched mules, dey wuz iron gray an' he druv dem to de carriage. Well, early nex' mornin' de feeder, he wuz Henry Nance, he come to our cabin an asks my fathuh is he seed Gains and Fox—dat's de mules. My fathuh say no dey mus' be out in de grove, but he say no, he hunt an' he call an' he whistle fo' em but he can't start 'um no place. Dey hunt some mo' den say dey better go tell Massa. After a little Massa say 'Henry an' Andy, you don' need tuh go to do fiel' dis mornin'.' Dey knows whut dat mean an' dey jes sit dar. Den Massa go out to de dogwood thicket an' he cut a bundle o' switches, all he cud carry. He take de men out to de bahn lot, has 'em take off dey shirts an' he wears out all dose switches. Den he say iffen dose mules not in de lot nex' Monday mawnin' de gonna git double de dose. Massa think dey sell de mules to de sojers an' pocket de money. But by nex' Monday mawnin' my fathuh an' Henry Nance is in Memphis—dey runned away.

"An' de nex' time de Yankee sojers cum through dar, Ole' Uncle 'Lias tuk Massa's fine carriage an' two mules an' him an' three women escaped to Memphis.

"When de war is ovah Massa call us all up an' tell us we's free. He say to my mathuh 'Now Sook',—her name's Susan but dey all call her Sook—he say 'Now Sook, you is free as I is'—but we stay dar jes de same. An' Massa he writ to Memphis fo' mah fathuh tuh come back, but he don' come so Massa go tuh Memphis tuh git him. Massa's got a eatin' cancer an he want my fathuh tuh come back. My fathuh wuz a'ways kind of a fohman. Massa'd tell him whut he wanted dis group o' men to do, an' whut he wanted dat group tuh do, an mah fathuh saw they don it. So when Massa goes fo' him he comes back.

"In Memphis he tells Massa he knows whar one o' his hosses is whut wuz stolen. Massa tells him kin he swear to it, he kin have it. So mah fathuh goes to de law 'bout dat hoss—Dey asks him can he 'dentify it—an' he say it got a white star on its face an' a white stockin on lef' hin' foot. So he git de hoss.

"I'se married 63 years ago—got de license outa

Sardis. 'Bout twenty year ago ah went back dar tuh visit—tuk some o' my chillern an' showed 'em de chuch dere at Fredonia whar we usta 'tend service.

"Dey war mos'ly perty good to us down dah—'cose we nevah cud go nowhars 'thout a pass or we'd git whupped. Dey had a doctor woman to take care o'us iffen we's sick. Her name's Miss Ellen—An' dey's good an' careful 'bout womens when dey's gonna have a baby. She wuz jes given light work to do, 'cause dey wanted big healthy famblies.

"One time dey wuz Ku Klux come to de do. Ah nebber seed em 'cause ah run an' crawl unner de bed, but ah heerd um say, 'Please gi' me some water, I ain't had a drink since de battle o' Shiloh.'

"Ole Jeff Davis sho' made it hawd fo' de cullud folks but wid Abe Lincoln an' de grace ob de Lawd we's all free now."

United States. Work Projects Administration

WYLIE MILLER

**Interview with Wylie Miller,
Cape Girardeau Co., Missouri.**

"I'se gonna be 83 cum nex' Nobember. Mah mammy's name wuz Easter. We belong to Ole Massa Henry Miller so we goes by de name o' Miller. Mah daddy's name wuz Israel an he belong to a neighbor name Brown so he go by de name o' Brown. Ole Missus name wuz 'Frohnie an dey had three boys whut went off tuh war. Dey live in a two-story frame house—dat down close to Bloomfiel'.

"De fust time we ever seed sojers, dey wuz a big crowd o' 'em cum up to our place. When us chillern seed 'em we crawl unner de house—white and black, all o' us. De Blue Coats look unner dere an' dey say, 'Come out o' der, you, or we kill all o' you'. We's sure scared but we crawls out. Dey didden hurt us none, but dey 'rests Ole Boss. Dey takes him up stairs an' acks him things. I spects dey didden do him no harm but dey keeps him locked up.

"Dey wuz a feller hangin' roun' dere named Bolen, Nas' Bolen—he wuz a bush-wacker and we seed dem Blue coats chase 'em across a ten acre fiel' but dey didden catch 'em. Den dey take all de bes' meat in de smoke house—we sho' did hate to stan' dere an' see 'em cut down all dem good hams. An dey had de women folks inside a cookin' fo' 'em, an a bakin bread. An' de sojers wuz all roun' de bahn an de gran'ries feedin our cahn to dey hosses. When de sojers lef', my mammy an' a feller name Nash Miller escape an' go off wid de sojers.

"Den one time de Seeseshes, under Marmaduke, come through dar on dey way to Cape. De Blue Coats was camped at Round Pond an dar de Rebel sojers run into 'em an' dar's whar they had de big battle. De Rebels nebber bother us none nuther 'cept jes for gin.

"When de war was ober, Ole Massa call us all up to de fron' porch and tell us now de war is ober an we is free, but it don' make much diffrence. We stays dar jes de same for few year. Ole Massa wuz allus good to his cullud folks, but fo' a spell he had a overseer. He wuz a Denmarker an' his name wuz Martindale an' he wuz tuff.

"I 'members one night de Ku Kluxers came—dey wants a drink o' water. One man say 'Gimme some water. I ain't had no drink sence de battle of Shiloh.' I had to carry water for him 'bout ez fur as fum here to cross de street and dat man drink five big buckets full an say he want mo'. My young Massa Wes, he step up, an' tell um to leave here an he say 'Wylie, don't you carry no mo water.' Dey don' wanta go—dey had on white gowns button' up de front wid black buttons an' masks on dey faces.

"Young Wes, he had a pistol. He call it a Remington an' he jes es soon shoot 'em as to say 'Hodey-do!' So he tell 'em again, 'Git out fum here, I know you.' Den dey goes but dey say to me, 'Boy, we don' wanna ketch you out at night'—an' didden."

LEWIS MUNDY

*Interview with Lewis Mundy,
Hannibal, Missouri.*

Men Growing Weaker And Wiser

Lewis Mundy, now living on West Center Street, Hannibal, Missouri, was born in slavery on the farm of John Wright, five miles north of La Belle, Lewis County, Missouri. He has lived in Hannibal more than thirty years, and has a wide acquaintance among both whites and colored people. The following is his story of his life.

"Mr. Wright had eleven slaves, my mother and ten of us children. Mr. Wright had eight children. My father was owned by Billy Graves, whose farm was joined to de master's farm. I don't know where he come from, but mother was brought here by de Wrights from Virginia. Our master and mistress was good to us, but of course my own mother had to whip me often. She used a whip made from twisted buckbrush twigs and did it sting!

"I worked in de fields most generally. When I was small I rode one of de oxen and harrowed de fields. When I was about ten or eleven I plowed with oxen. I'se plowed many times with a moldboard plow with an iron share on it.

"We never wanted for clothes very bad. We wore long shirts dat reached to de knees until we was twelve or fourteen years old. Dem wool shirts sure was warm. We had one pair of shoes a year. Many times I done went after de cows barefoot when dere was more dan a foot of snow on de ground. It didn't seem to hurt me. I was toughened to it.

"After we was freed mother stayed with master for about a year, den she moved over toward Newark and worked out till she got straightened out so she could keep house for herself. I stayed dere for a while longer until I got work on a farm at fifty cents a day. After a while dey paid me seventy-five cents a day. We didn't get nothin' from our master after de war. I 'member de Bowans, though, give dere slaves eighty acres of land.

"I 'members dere was a Ku Klux Klan in de county, but dey never bothered me none. I tended to my own business and never bothered nobody. I never was arrested in my life and I never gives de policemen no trouble.

"I got married when I was about twenty and settled in Jetto in Knox County and worked on a farm. We had two children. One of dem died years ago, and I am living here with my other daughter. After a while we moved to Palmyra. I worked 'round on farms until about 1903, den we moved here to Hannibal. I worked in de Burlington shops for seventeen years, till dey told me I was too old to work any more. I is getting a pension now for more dan a year. Dat sure 'nough helps a lot.

"I has voted ever since I was old enough. Dey used to tell me how to vote. I always belonged to de Baptist Church and belongs to de Helping Hand Baptist now. My mistress belonged to de old time Christian Church and I used to drive her to church with a bay mare she had.

"We used to sing, 'I Am Bound for the Promised Land', and 'Heart (Hark) From The Tombs Mournful Sound', My mother used to sing, 'You All Ought To Have Been There,' 'Roll, Jordan, Roll', and 'Do, Lord, Do Remember Me.' Dey don't sing them old songs no more.

"Mankind: De young folks now days ain't like we used to be. Why, in Monticello dey used to have a log jail, but now dey is got one made of stone and iron. Dey just can't hold 'em no more. I guess it's right dat dis world is growing weaker and wiser. But de young folks has a better chance. Look at de big fine schools dey has now. Dey ought to get along better dan dey do."

United States. Work Projects Administration

MALINDA MURPHY

> Interview with Malinda Murphy,
> Farmington, Missouri.
> Sent in by J. Tom Miles,
> Farmington, Mo.

"I was born right here and was about four years old at de time of de war. We was owned by the Hills at Farmington. My mother plowed in the fields, and hauled wood in de snow. We had no shoes and made tracks of blood in de snow. Us little tots had to go all over de field and pick up feathers. De mistress would go along with a stick and say, 'Here is another feather to pick up.'

"When de soldiers came we had a good meal. De soldiers had on blue coats, and when dey came we would be switching off de flies with a long pole with paper on the end. De soldiers would then say 'We don' need that, come on and eat with us.'

"We wore linsey dresses and all slept together and were bound to keep warm. When de war was over we was free to go but de only thing we had was a few rags. So we walked to Valle Mines, twenty-four miles north in Jefferson County. We walked it twice 'cause we would carry a few rags a little piece and den go back after de rest.

"At Valle Mines we could make a little money digging ore and selling it to de store. De mines were on de surface and mother dug in de mines. After we had gone to Valle Mines, Overton Hill, de son of de Hills, came up dere and asked mother where she had hid de money and silver during de war. She told him but after three weeks he came back in a buggy and took mother with him to de plantation and she showed Overton where to dig close to a cedar tree to find de money and silver."

MARGARET NICKENS

> Interview with Margaret Nickens,
> Hannibal, Missouri.

"Mag" Preaches Thrift

Margaret Nickens, now living at 1644 Broadway, Hannibal, Missouri, was born in slavery on the farm of Pleasant McCann about six miles from Paris in Monroe County, Missouri. She was a daughter of George Morrison and wife, slaves of Pleasant McCann. The following is her story as she told it:

"Mr. McCann was a rich slave holder. His daughter, Georgia Ann, was married to a Mr. Dawson and lived in Liberty, Clay County. When I was 'bout eight years old de Dawsons come back to Paris to visit. Dey had two children den so dey took me as a nurse for de children. Mr. Dawson didn't believe in slaves and he didn't own none. My mistress had only one slave to do de cooking and she took me for to be de nurse.

"De baggage and slaves and other things dey hauled in a covered wagon and de white folks rode in a rockaway. When we was fixing to leave, dere was lots of people standing 'round. My mother had to stand dere like I wasn't hers and all she could say was, 'Be a good girl, Margaret.'

"When we was at Liberty de first soldiers we seen was

General Price's men and later we seen lots of Union soldiers.

"De day dat de slaves was freed Mr. Dawson told me dat I was as free as he was and dat he brought me here and he would take me back if I wanted to go. I said, 'If I still have a mother and father I wants to go to dem.'

"When we got back to Paris my mistress Georgia Ann said, 'Oh, that black good-for-nothing lazy gal, I should have left her at Liberty, but Mr. Dawson would bring her.' I didn't like her 'cause she wasn't very good to me and now I don't want to meet my mistress in either hell or heaven.

"I was about eleven years old den. We moved from dere to Palmyra. My father split rails and built fences (they didn't have wire fence in those days), and shucked corn and worked on farms or whatever kind of job he could get to do. My father didn't get no land nor money like some of de folks did. Most of de white folks was good to de slaves and didn't whip dem unless dey was sure 'nough bad.

"My father come from Virginia and my mother from Kentucky when dey was little. Dey never seen dere parents no more. Dey watched for a long time among de colored people and asked who dey was when dey thought some body looked like dere parents, but never could find dem. Dey was so small when dey left, dey didn't even remember dere names.

"I have been working for de Col. Dan Dulany and de Mahan families here in Hannibal for three generations, more'n sixty years. I'm not working nowhere now since Mr. Mahan died about two years ago.

"I am saving my money, what little I has, but de younger folks now days don't save anything. Dey just want a good time. I tell dem to save for a rainy day even if it's only an umbrella, because it will rain some day."

Margaret Nickens is called "Mag" by her friends. She is about eighty-five years old and lives alone in a home that she owns. She reared and educated one daughter who taught school over a period of forty years in the Negro public school in Hannibal. The daughter died eight years ago.

United States. Work Projects Administration

ELIZA OVERTON

> Eliza Overton, age 88.
> Interviews with Maggie Kennedy,
> John Franks, and Emma Body,
> Farmington, Missouri.

Note: Since Eliza Overton, an ex-slave, is now with her daughter, Mrs. Mamie Robinson, in Detroit, the following information was gained from interviews with Mrs. Overton's children now living in Farmington. They are: Mrs. Maggie Kennedy, age 66; John Franks, age 56; and Mrs. Emma Body, age 71. The oldest of the three children can recall life during these days and the others recall stories told them by their parents.

"Our muthuh, Eliza, was born a slave in 1849, on da farm of her boss, Mr. Madden in New Tennessee, Ste. Genevieve County, Missouri. Eliza's muthuh wuz also a slave. Muthuh wuz sol' with our grandmuthuh to John Coffman of near Coffman, Missouri, in Ste. Genevieve County. Mr. Coffman had thousands of acres. He had three plantations an' one wuz at Libertyville, Missouri. He had 'bout two hundred slaves. The negroes war tak'n frum one plantashun ta the other, and our grandmuthuh work'd at all three places. 'Ole man Coffman' wuz a mean ole slave hol'er. He war afraid of his slaves an' had some one else ta do da whippin'. They war rougher on ma aunt Eleanor, cause she war stubborn. They wud punish de slaves severely fur 'membrance. They whoop'd with a rawhide whop an' trace chains. Wilson Harris wuz whooped at a tree onc't an' when dey got thro' he say he wud fight. They whop him some mor' 'til he was weak an' bleedin'. The other slaves had to grease his shirt ta take it off his back ta keep frum tearin' off de flesh. We can go down thar now and pick out trees whar the slaves war tied an' whipp'd. The trees died on de side whar de slaves war tied. There are three trees on de Coffman farm that I seen dead on one side, an' sum' war in the yard. Thar is one clos' to the Houck Railroad Station thar.

"When John Coffman was sick he say he wuz goin' ta ride 'Jap', a roan hoss, into heaban. So he ask us ta take good care of 'Jap'. I know Coffman didn't go ta heaban 'cause he died an' lef' 'Jap' here.

"Mr. Coffman had a whole row of slave cabins. Our cabins war small an' we had a corded bed, trundle bed ta slip unda' the big bed ta save room, home made split bottom chairs, tin plates, wood'n boxes, an' a fireplace. John Coffman gave us a 'lowance of food. We had hogsheads an' jowls. Many tha time we ran short on food so's one night muthuh went out to whar the hogs war. Mr. Coffman had so many hogs he didn't know how many he had. She had da water hot an' the hogs war a long ways from Mr. Coffman's house. So she hit a hog in da head with the ax an' kill'd it. Afta' killin' it she went to the cabin ta get the water an' when she kum' bak one of the other slaves hed stole de dead hog. So she hit another one in de head an' after fixin' it hid the hog under de puncheon floor of the cab'n. This was done offen. Mr. Coffman use ta kill 'bout one hundred hogs at one time an' den put dem in de smoke-house. Ma muthuh ud get the key to the smoke-house an' load up an' carry some meat home.

"Ma Aunt Comfort tole de white boy ta thro' a knife at

ma muthuh. The boy hit ma muthuh jus' 'bove de eye an' den grandmuthuh whop'd Aunt Comfort fur tellin' the white boy to do this.

"In ever cab'n thar war fiddles an' on Sunday we could have a good time. One of de games we wud play out in frunt of the cab'n was 'Swing-Ole Liza Single'. This here game wuz play'd by havin' two rows line up an' a man wud dance up or down the line an' swing each one. We wud all sing an' pat our han's an' feet ta keep time for the dance.

"Thar wuz some preachin' goin' on in the cab'ns an' out under the arbors on Saturday nights an' Sunday. The preacher wuz a slave too. Two songs that we 'member they sung war: 'We'll Bow Around the Altar—Whil'st My Lord Answers Prayer', and 'Git in the Chariot and Ride Right-Along'.

"Our fauthur wuz also a slave of a Mr. Patterson but he wus treat'd well. When Mr. Patterson died our fauther was will'd ta Mr. Patterson's daughter. Our fauthur, Jacob Franks, wuz a trusted negro an' a teamster who drove frum Ste. Genevieve ta the plantashun. He used ta swim the river 'Aux Vases with his team. He'ud bring bak things frum Ste. Genevieve that war hard ta git. Salt wuz hard ta git at this time.

"Our muthuh, Eliza, married Jacobs Franks wen she wuz 16 years ole jus' after she wuz free. She wuz always rather puny an' wuz worth very little as a slave. Onc't she was sold with three others an' brot' only $50. Our muthuh has 5 children livin', 19 great grandchildren, and two great grandchildren, Paul Evans, 6, and Andres,

3. Our fauthur died 43 years ago an' our muthuh married a Mr. Overton an' he is also dead now.

"A Mr. Jones bought our aunt an' tok' her ta Shelby County, Missouri. Our aunt had two children by Mr. Jones. One of 'em wuz so white dat Mr. Jones couldn't sell him fur a slave.

"When de slaves war freed, we war tole ta go anywhar we pleas'd. For'nately muthuh married at onc't, but others did not care ta leave thar way of livin' 'cause they had no money, no homes, and did not know how ta do thar own work. But Jim Blackwell, who had been a slave fur John Coffman, saved up a lot of food in his cab'n an' then when he was freed, he went out in da woods an' built him a home of his own. He cut down de trees an' made his cab'n thar an' liv'd.

"I hear a woman stan' up an' say we would be bettah off today in slavery. I say,'Why?' She say: 'You would hab ta look aftah nothin' of your welfare.' 'If that's what she wuz talkin' 'bout', I said, 'ma fauthuh wuz ten years ole fore he put on a pair of pants. He had ta wear wooden shoes an' a tow shirt.' I wud not liv' twenty-four hours, bein' a slave now. I wud' not habe stood it with ma temper."

DELICIA ANN WILEY PATTERSON

Interview with Delicia Patterson,
St. Louis, Missouri.

Delicia Had Some Temper

The subject of this sketch is Delicia Ann Wiley Patterson, better known as Lucinda Patterson, 92 years of age and lives in a 3 room kitchenette apartment at 2847 Delmar Boulevard, apartment 103.

The old woman is a very neat little brown skinned, white haired person. She lives alone in her neatly furnished snug little quarters. When the writer introduced herself and asked for an interview, Lucinda seemed rather peeved and she said:

"I'm hot, and mad because the landlord sent the paper hanger here and started to clean up my apartment, then come and taken him away before he finished, because I am old.

"I got plenty temper and I been sick, and when I get mad I get sick all over again. I turned off the radio, 'cause I don't want nobody talkin' to me and I don't want to talk to nobody, I've told my history enough. I don't want to tell it no more anyhow, and especially today the way I feel."

But she seemed too good a subject to let go on with

a merely perturbed mood, so I visited with her until she was in good humor, and very willingly gave me the following story:

"I was born in Boonville, Missouri, January 2, 1845. My mother's name was Maria and my father's was Jack Wiley. Mother had five children but raised only two of us. I was owned by Charles Mitchell until I was 15 years old. They were fairly nice to all of their slaves and they had several of us. I only got whipped once in the whole 15 years there, and that was because I was working in the garden with one of my owner's daughters and I pulled up something that she did not want pulled up, so she up and slapped me for it.

"I got so mad at her, I taken up a hoe and run her all the way in the big house, and of course I got whipped for that. I did not even have to sleep in the cabins. I slept on a pallet in the bedroom with old marse's children. I was a pet anywhere I worked, because I was always very neat and clean, and a good worker.

"When I was 15 years old, I was brought to the courthouse, put up on the auction block to be sold. Old Judge Miller from my county was there. I knew him well because he was one of the wealthiest slave owners in the county, and the meanest one. He was so cruel all the slaves and many owners hated him because of it. He saw me on the block for sale, and he knew I was a good worker so when he bid for me, I spoke right out on the auction block and told him: 'Old Judge Miller don't you bid for me, 'cause if you do, I would not live on your plantation, I will take a knife and cut my own throat from ear to ear before I would be owned by you.'

"So he stepped back and let someone else bid for me. My own father knew I was to be for sale, so he brought his owner to the sale for him to buy me, so we could be together. But when father's owner heard what I said to Judge Miller, he told my father he would not buy me, because I was sassy, and he never owned a sassy niggah and did not want one that was sassy. That broke my father's heart, but I couldn't help that. Another nigger trader standing right beside my father's owner said, I wouldn't own a nigger that didn't have some spunk. So I was sold to a Southern Englishman named Thomas B. Steele for $1500. He had an old slave he had in his home for years as their housekeeper, and his wife did not like her, and he had to sell her to keep peace at home so he put me in his buggy and taken me home to his wife and told her, 'I bought you another girl, Susianna, but I don't want you to lay the weight of your finger on her when she disobeys. Let me know and I will punish her myself.'

"I lived in that family until after the Civil War was over. Mr. Steele's wife's people had a big family and they visited the Steeles a great deal. Mr. Tom didn't like them because they were Yankees and the Steeles were Union. So one time Mr. Tom was going away on a trip and he knew when he was gone, his wife would have all of her folks in the home visiting, and that was against his wishes. He told me to keep tab on every time her relatives come to the house and how long they stayed, and tell him when he come back home, and that he would leave orders in the home to let me work in the field, so I would not have to bother with that great big family. When he left all his wife's folks come right down on our plantation, so I had to work in the house for them so hard, I did not have time to even look at the field.

"When old boss come home I told him, I had not worked in the field and why. Him and his wife had a big fight about that, and she hated me for a long time, and said, the idea of her husband taking a nigger's word to hers and mistreat her on account of it. But he did not let her bother me about nothing, so I stayed on with them until one day, while I had a fly brush in my hand fanning flies while they ate, she told him something I done she didn't like. Just to please her, he taken the fly brush out of my hand and just tapped me with it. It didn't hurt me a bit, but it made me so mad I just went straight to the kitchen, left all the dishes, put on my sunbonnet and run away. I stayed two weeks. He sent everybody he thought knew where I was after me, and told them to tell me if I would only come on back home, no one would ever bother me anymore. I hid in the woods that whole two weeks and was not afraid. I would be afraid out in those woods now, but I wasn't then. At night I would come up to some of the slave cabins who were my friends and eat and stay all night. So I went back home after my 2 weeks off as a runaway nigger and no one ever bothered me any more either. I came to St. Louis with them, during the Civil War.

"When freedom was declared Mr. Steele told me that I was as free as he was. He said I could leave them if I please, or could stay, that they wanted me and would be glad to have me if I would stay and his wife said, course she is our nigger. She is as much our nigger now as she was the day you bought her 2 years ago and paid $1500 for her. That made me mad so I left right then. Since she was so smart. Her husband told her, now Sue you might as well face it. There are no more slaves and won't ever be any more, regardless of how much we paid for them. So just quiet yourself down, she don't have to stay here if she don't want to, but till this day some of their children come to visit me, but they never give me anything ever.

"I hired myself out to a family named Miller's at $3.00 a week, and lived on the place. I had a baby about 3 years old. I married before the war and when my baby was 2 weeks old they taken my husband in the army. He died in the army. I worked for the Millers about 11 months. One day Mrs. Miller misplaced her silver thimble and she accused me of stealing it. She did not tell me that but she told the white nurse girl, and the nurse told me. I got so mad at her for that, 'cause I never stole anything in my whole life and never been accused of stealing, so I quit. They begged me to stay and offered to raise my salary, I told them I would not work for anyone who felt I would steal. The very next day she found her thimble in the nursery where she remembered she put it herself, but forgot about it at the time. She thought it was lost.

"I don't know what the ex-slaves expected, but I do know they didn't get anything. After the war we just wandered from place to place, working for food and a place to stay. Now and then we got a little money, but a very little. I only voted once in my life and that was when working for Mr. Gerhart. He was a real estate dealer and he taken me to the polls and showed me how to vote for a Republican president. It has been so long ago I don't even remember who the president was, but I do know he got elected. I think the time will soon be when people won't be looked on as regards to whether you are black or white, but all on the same equality. I may not live to see it but it is on the way. Many don't believe it, but I know it.

"My father's owner's children use to take my father in their basement and teach him to read in a blue back spelling book. I never got any education. My English is good because I boarded all the first Negro school teachers and Negro principals St. Louis ever had for years. Charlie Brown, the late Hutchinson Inge, Clarice Hubbard, Wm. Turner and Chas. Newton, the old pioneer Negro teachers had their meals in my home. I had a lovely home, and have lived well in my time right here in St. Louis. I am a member of Central Baptist Church and been there for years. I think this young generation should advance much faster than they do. Their advantages are very good, but they don't seem to be appreciative of them. If I would of had their chance in my day, I really would make good use of it and improve every moment of my life.

"Charlie Brown started me to attending night school, but I couldn't keep my mind on my studies, I was always thinking of home and my business. I was afraid the girl that helped would forget to grind the coffee for breakfast or fail to put everything on the table for breakfast next morning. Many of the teachers had a great ways to go and had to have an early start, and I could not afford to be using the time in the morning doing the things that should be done at night. I always believed in doing things as they should be done, on time.

"That's why my services were valuable, any place I worked, whether as a slave or free, and I still stand by that idea. I have done laundry work so satisfactory that I got $5.00 for doing up one white dress, 50¢ each for embroidery skirts and 25¢ a piece for vests. I never did work for nothing but wealthy white people."

MARILDA PETHY

Interview with Marilda Pethy,
Montgomery City, Missouri.

Sold At 6 Weeks Old

Marilda Pethy, a former slave now living in Montgomery City, Mo., is a coal black woman with distinctly negroid features. Her voice and manner of speaking are vividly reminiscent of the negro of the "Old South". She lives with her daughter, Polly, and numerous grandchildren whom she tries to rule with an iron hand. This does not work so well with the younger generation which largely disregards the irate old woman. All this lends quite an air of belligerency to the tumble-down building that houses them.

Polly and Marilda sat in the shade of a mulberry tree where the former was ostensibly doing her washing not far from the big iron kettle where she heated her water.

"Yas'sum, I sure remembers dem days", Marilda replied as the questioning began. "Why, I seen people handcuffed together and driv 'long de Williamsburg road like cattle. Dey was bought to be took south. I had two brothers and two sisters sold and we never did see dem no more. I was born in 1857, April first, on a farm two miles south of Williamsburg, on a farm dat belonged to William Hayes. My mother was Louisa Hayes from Memphis. She never seen her mother or father and didn't know her name, so she just went by de white folks' name.

You know dat's how dey done in dem days with names. She never had no brothers or sisters here. She was sold when she was six weeks old. Father, he belonged to Billy Martin and he was Sam Martin. He run off to de war 'cause he was tired of bein' whipped and slashed. So he jes' run off and joined de army.

"I was sold with mother when I was six weeks old. We went back to see de old place after we was free. Dat place has been sold and torn down. It had a tall white double log house. Dere was three cabins, it was a large place. De John Bain place, dey calls it de Jeff Jones place, ten miles north of Williamsburg, had de same kind of a house but dey had just two cabins. De Bain place was not so large but dey had a right smart of land.

"We done right well. Dey give us cornbread and buttermilk in a tin can. We crumbled de cornbread up in de buttermilk and dat's all we ever had to eat. Yas'sum, we generally had 'nough. Well, on Sunday mornings we had biscuits made out of dis stuff dat dey feed cows—shorts, dat's it. We had biscuits made out of shorts and sorghum. Dey was plenty of it. We had meat once in a while. Dey was dead oodles of prairie chickens and patridges den but de wild pigeons was hard to kill. We never did get none of dat meat. Christmas never meant no more to us dan any other day. Dey give mother sorghum and shorts to make gingersnaps.

"Dey had a big back log in de fireplace and a forestick and we put de wood in between. It was my job to take care of de dog irons. Dey was kept shinin' with grease. De missus would say, "Marilda, grease de dog irons!' I had to grease dem all over, too. I taken care of de children. Mother done everything. Dey had two cooks but both of dem done all kinds of work. Mother was de regular cook for Mrs. Hayes.

"Old Miss sold de other four children end sent 'em south. Mother and me brought $1,200. When I was nine or ten years old I was put up on de block to be sold. I 'member dat just as well. Hit was just a piece cut out of a log and stood on end. Dey was offered $600 but my mistress cried so much dat master did not sell me. Freedom come soon after dat.

"I often wish dat some of de younger race had lived through dat time. Dey wouldn't have been so sassy and impudent as dey is now. De older people'd have done something 'bout it, too." (Marilda's tone and facial expression left no doubt as to what the older people would have done.)

"Dey was a battle on Freeman up on Grand Prairie. Dat's northwest of Williamsburg, up where de Mattocks and Harrisons lived. It was right where de Ridgeways and de Jones's lived. Dey was fightin' in de evening and dey fit all night. I took de baby upstairs on de porch and listened to de fighting. 'Rally once again, boys, rally once again!' Boom! Boom! Bang! Bang! Boom!" (Marilda was equal to at least one army.)

"Dey walked in blood for miles! Dey took de best horses dat old master had. 'Bout 500 soldiers come to de house and ordered supper. Dere was a tall log smokehouse and dey went right up to de tip-top and got de hams. De middlin's and de shoulders was lower but dey got de hams. De women worked all night and dey got through cooking 'bout daylight. What did dey cook? Why, dey fried ham, made biscuits, and fried eggs. If de soldiers wanted a chicken dey just killed it and someone cooked it for dem. I ain't never seen no one have so many chickens. De soldiers cussed de slaves like dogs. Dey was de Union soldiers, de blue coats.

"When de soldiers come de men folks just got up and flew. Dey taken to de woods. De soldiers come to get master's money and dey hunted everywhere. Dey asked me, 'Whar is de money?' I say, 'I don't know.' Dey say, 'You know d—well you do! I've a notion to cut your throat!' I knowed where it was 'cause I seen master when he done hid it but he told me he would whip me to death if I told and I thought de soldiers was foolin' but master meant it. De soldier said: (Here it is necessary to delete some of the most colorful words.) 'She is one of de ... stubbornest little black ... I ever seen! I've a notion to cut her throat!' (Marilda evidently enjoyed her reputation for ... stubbornness.) Another man say, 'Maybe she don't know. Children don't know things like dat. I wouldn't hurt her.' So dey went away. Dat was de truth, de children didn't know everything den like dey does now. Dey knows too much now!

"De morning we was set free we didn't have nothing. Mother had three little children and no place to go. De white folks told dem to 'git away from here' and we come on down to Williamsburg. We walked down de road in de snow, mother and de three little children. We went to de old mistress and mother asked her could we find some place to stay. She said, 'Yes, Louisa. I'll take care of you and de children. I would not have turned you out of doors.' She sure was good to us.

"I seen people turned across barrels and whipped. Dey was whipped 'cause de white people was mean. Sometimes dey tied dem to trees and whipped 'em. Dey didn't have no clothes on at all—dey was just like dey come into de world! Dey used a cowhide as big as my finger. It was made of two strips twisted together and was keen at de end. De master whipped when he could. When he couldn't do it, he called in de neighbors 'til you'd think dere was a meetin'. De poor darkies had a hard time!

"De patrollers (accent on the first syllable) used blacksnake whips. Dey was a lot of de neighbors dat were patrollers. When dey would meet de colored men out at night, dey would ask dem if dey had a pass. If dey didn't, de patrollers would get off de horses and whip dem. De colored men would slip out at night sometimes for a little pleasure. My daddy got tired of being whipped and he put out. He was gone clean away.

"De Ku Klux Klan come out and run de colored people away from home. Many a colored woman came to mother's house in de middle of de night with clothes covered with ice and snow to de waist and carrying her baby in her arms 'cause dey ran her away from home.

"We knowed who de men was. We'd hear dem say, 'Are you going out tonight?' 'Yas', I'se got a little cluckin' to do.' Goin' cluckin'! Huh! (Marilda fairly snorted with indignation and in some subtle way gave the impression that she did not approve of Klansmen.) Dose men would bus' de door down and run de people out. Run some of dem clean away.

"Dey was one colored man, named McPherson, dat told dem not to come pesterin' round his cabin. Dey come anyhow and he shot wid a double barreled shotgun. He killed a white man, too. Of course, he had to leave his home. He went to Illinois and I ain't never seen him since.

"Mother hired us out to Mr. Billy Arnold to buy a lot in Williamsburg and we built a little house dat was our home. I stayed dere until I married Henry Pethy and we went to de old Kidwell place south of Williamsburg. We lived dere twenty-five years. He worked for Taylor Arnold, feeding cattle and mules.

"We had eleven children. Four girls and one boy is still living. Dere are three girls and one boy dead. (Marilda's arithmetic may be faulty but it is excusable for she does not read or write.) My pension is a lot of help. I had a real nice garden but it's 'bout burned up now. Dese children think I'se too old to plant dat garden but I'll show dem. I can't do it all in one day but I can do it.

"I never went to no parties. Mother used to go but I better not look like I want to go. Dere's some people here in town dat can tell you lots 'bout slavery. Have you seen Albert Jones?"

SUSAN RHODES

Interview with Susan Rhodes,
St. Louis, Missouri.

She 'Members Stars Falling

Susan Davis Rhodes, more than 100 years old, a resident of St. Louis, lives at 915 O'Fallon Street in the rear with her married daughter, Susie West.

Susan is less than 5 ft. tall, weighs about 135 pounds and has mixed gray curly hair. Her memory and eyesight are exceptionally good for her years. Her small 3-room quarters are located in a very dilapidated old brick building, in the slum area of St. Louis.

Seated on her back porch, she cheerfully told the following story of her experiences.

"I was born in Jones County, North Carolina more than 100 years ago, I don't know exactly how old I is but goin' by de count I got on my children, dere ages and de war, and I even 'members de stars fallin', I do know I'se more'n 100, but how much more I can't tell you dat. My mother's name was Teeny Jones and my father's was Lott Davis. I 'member 15 of my mother's children, but she had a heap more of 'em dan dat. I just don't 'member 'em all. I am de mother of 10 children myself. I got 6 living children, 11 living grandchildren, and so many living great and great, great grandchildren I can't commence to count 'em.

"My first owner's name was Marse Edward Davis and his wife's name was Miss Susie, and I was de nurse girl, waitress and housemaid all my slave days. I was a good nigger and I never did get whipped much.

"I never did git no education in books neither, but did have common sense education and knew how to treat folks. People in my day didn't know book learning but dey studied how to protect each other, and save 'em from much misery as dey could. Dey didn't study trash and filth like this new day generation. I 'members when de stars fell, I tried to ketch some of 'em but I couldn't. I see'd in a dream a long time ago, honey, dat one of dese United States presidents was going to send folks around to get some of us slaves living to tell about our lives way back yonder, 'cause dey wants to know 'bout it from us ourselves and not what somebody else wants to say. And course de President was not old 'nough hisself to know, and he wants to learn de truth 'bout it all for hisself and he's right, honey. Yes, he is. I 'member well when de war first broke out de slave owners taken the little niggers from dere mammys, and hide 'em in all kind of places from de Yankees, so when de old niggers git der freedom, de white folks would have de children for slaves and dey wouldn't know nothing 'bout freedom. But de Yankees was smart 'nough to find out 'bout dat and freed us children and all.

"I 'member well when dey took Richmond, Va. I was nursing old Miss' baby, and she just hollered and cried 'cause she thought de Yankees done killed her husband. I was worse dan her. I thought dey done killed everybody and me too, I just was too scared to die. All dem soldiers coming in dere so mad dey didn't know what to do, and neither did we. Lord, I was glad when dat was done. Dem old Ku Klux folks in dem old hoods, would ketch us and beat us so bad. Dem was de meanest folks in all de world I do know. We sure did hate dem folks. Dey run off every one of my brothers. Den dere was dem nigger dogs. I guess you sure done heard 'bout dem, dey git on de niggers' tracks and run em down every time.

"Den my old Miss told my sister dat all de niggers was free now, go for herself, but she was going to keep de two youngest niggers. Dat was me and my baby sister, I don't know how old I was but I was big 'nough to do any kind of work most.

"But my sister stole us away. A white woman in another county hired my sister and gave her railroad fare to come to her place. My sister rolled up 3 of our baby sisters like a bundle in a quilt and told 'em don't move or cry and as soon as she could unroll 'em and let 'em have some air she would. So she got on de train with them three little niggers in a bundle and toted 'em up under her arms like dey was her clothes and belongings, and put 'em under her seat on de train. De bundle was so big every time de conductor passed it was in de way and he would kick it out of his way. Sister protected dem de best she could. Soon as he pass, she opened it and let 'em have some air. When she see him coming back, she wrap' em up again. Dey was all sure glad to git off dat train. Dey had been kicked so much and dasn't holler. So de white lady was mighty nice. She let us all stay dere till we could do better. Sister didn't have money 'nough to pay all us fare and she didn't want to leave us and we didn't want her to leave us. So dat was de best she could do. After a while she found our mother and daddy and they sent for us. My grandfather hid under de hills in de woods, hiding to keep from going to de war. Dey never did find him neither, but de boys all fought. After de war was over my father worked on farms, till he had made money 'nough to lease a piece of land at Fort Makin, North Carolina. I stayed dere with him until he was mustered out. I reckon I was 25 years old when I married, I don't know exactly. I farmed de whole time I was raising my children, clear up till I come up here to St. Louis and dat was over 20 years ago.

"My daughter, Susie, I am living here with lost her husband five years ago. She has worked at de nut factory every since she been here, till her health failed her. She is like me now. Neither one of us is no 'count, can't do nothing but sit here to home. One of my nephews, Sanders Randoll, is working on a W.P.A. job doing de best he can for us. De other nephew, Freeman Hollister, can't git nothing to do. De relief helped us some 'bout 18 months dat's all.

"I just look at dis new generation drinking and throwing parties every night, on der way to hell wid der eyes wide open. It's a pity, ain't no hopes for 'em. Der heads is too hard. I voted a Republican ticket one time in my life many years ago, dat was de only time I recollect voting. I don't even 'member de man I voted for.

"We old slaves use' to love to sing:

> When I can read my titles clear,
> To mansions in de sky,
> I'll bid fare well to every tear,
> And wipe my weeping eyes.
> Should earth against my soul engage,

And fiery darts be hurled,
Then can I smile at Satan's rage
And face a frowning world.
Let cares like a wild deluge come,
And storms of sorrow fall.
May I but safely reach my home,
My God, my Heaven, my all.
There shall I bathe my weary soul,
In seas of heavenly rest.
And not a wave of trouble roll
Across my peaceful breast.
Tis faith supports my feeble soul,
In times of deep distress,
When storms arise and billows roll,
Great God, I trust thy grace.
Thy powerful arm still bears me up,
Whatever grieves befall;
Thou art my life, my joy, my hope,
And thou my all in life.
Bereft of friends, beset with foes,
With dangers all around,
To thee, I all my fears disclose;
In thee my help is found.
In every want, in every strait,
To thee alone I fly;
When other comforters depart,
Thou art forever nigh
O! That I knew the secret place,
Where I might find my God;
I'd spread my wants before his face,
And pour my woes abroad.
My God will pity my complaints,
And heal my broken bones;

> He takes the meaning of his saints,
> The language of their groans.
> Arise my soul, from deep distress,
> And banish every fear;
> He calls thee to his throne of grace,
> To spread thy sorrows there.

"We used to steal off to de woods and have church, like de spirit moved us, sing and pray to our own liking and soul satisfaction and we sure did have good meetings, honey. Baptize in de river like God said. We had dem spirit filled meetins at night on de bank of de river and God met us dere. We was quiet 'nough so de white folks didn't know we was dere and what a glorious time we did have in de Lord. I am a member of St. Douglass Baptist Church on Laclede Avenue. Dey is de foot washing Baptists."

CHARLIE RICHARDSON

>Interview with Charlie Richardson,
Webb City, Missouri,
by Bernard Hinkle, Jasper
County, Joplin, Mo.

"Well, Charlie, let us sit right down here on this bench and chat awhile. Mr. Hal M. Wise, editor of 'The Sentinel' here in Webb City, told me about you. You won't mind if I ask you a few personal questions about the days of slavery will you?"

"No Sah' I'd be glad to tell you anything I know."

"Thank you Charlie. The first thing I would like to ask is; is your name Charles, Charlie or Charley?"

"Everybody calls me Charlie."

"Where were you born Charlie?"

"I was born at Warrensburg, Missouri."

"What year were you born in Charlie?"

"They always said I was born in March. Didn't never give no day. Jest March."

"How old were you when the Civil War broke out?"

"I don't remember exactly but I were seven they said."

"How old are you now?"

"The old-age pension man said I was 86 this year."

"Now Charlie, please give me the name of your parents and where they came from."

"My Ma's name was Ann Smith, the first time,'cause my Pappy was Charlie Smith. Then my Pappy died and my Ma married a man named Charlie Richardson. He was my step-Pappy so I took his name. Both my own Pappy and my step-Pappy were jest plain negroes and born in Warrensburg, but my Ma was a Black Hawk Indian girl, kinder light in color and purtty. Her Ma was a full-blooded Black Hawk and she married to Grandaddy Richard Dowle, which was my Ma's name 'fore she married."

"Tell me Charlie, did you have any brothers or sisters?"

"Yes Sah, I had two sisters and five brothers but none ain't here now."

"Describe your home and 'quarters' the best you can."

"Log Cabins, that's what they was. All in a long row—piles of 'em. They was made of good old Missouri logs daubed with mud and the chimney was made of sticks daubed with mud. Our beds was poles nailed to sticks standing on the floor with cross sticks to hold the straw ticks."

"How did most of you cook—in the cabins or in the 'big house'?"

"Most of the negroes cooked in the cabins but my Mammy was a house girl and lots of times fetched my breakfast from the Masters house. Most of the negroes, though, cooked in or near the cabins. They mostly used dog irons and skillets, but when they went to bile anything, they used tin buckets."

"What food did you like best Charlie. I mean, what was your favorite dish?"

"It warn't no dish. It ware jest plain hoe cake mostly. No dishes or dish like we has nowadays, No Sah! This here hoe cake was plain old white corn meal battered with salt and water. No grease. Not much grease, jest 'nough to keep it from stickin'. This here hoe cake was fried jest like flap-jacks, only it were not. Not flap-jacks I mean. When we didn't have hoe cake we had ash cake. Same as hoe cake only it was boiled. Made of corn meal, salt and water and a whole shuck, with the end tied with a string.

"We never had no flap-jacks in the cabins. No Sah! Flap-jacks was something special for only Marster Mat Warren and the Missis. That makes me remember a funny story about flap-jacks. My Ma brought some flap-jack stuff down to the cabin one day; you know, jest swiped it from the house where she worked. Well, Ma was frying away to git me something special like when she hears the Missis comin' with her parrot. So, Ma hides them flap-jacks right quick. Soon the Missis come in our cabin and was talkin' to my Mammy when that crazy old parrot he begin to get fussy like somethin' was wrong. He were a smart parrot and outside, generally called us all 'niggers, niggers'. Well Sah, he kept squaking and the Missis kept sayin', "shut up' shut up', what's the matter with you?" Purtty soon the Missis go over to sit in a chair Ma had with a big pad in it. And before the Missis could set down that crazy parrot begun to yell, 'Look out Mam, it's hot'. Look out'. Look out'. The Missis turned to my Ma and said 'What's the matter here?' My Ma answered,

'Tain't nothin' the matter Missie.' And then that fool parrot hollows agin, 'It's hot' It's hot'. And sure 'nough the missis she get a peek at a flap-jack stickin' through under the pad, where Ma hid them. And Ma almost got a good lickin' fer that.

"That parrot could out-talk Marster Warren and wouldn't eat anything we would give him 'cause he was afraid of being poisoned by is 'niggers'. They use to tie him out in the field to watch the negroes at work, and when he went in the house at night Ma said he would hollow and yell the most unholy lies about those 'niggers' and what they tried to do to him.

"Sometime we'd get him to drink some weigh milk, the Marster had given us when it was so sour it would make a hog squeal. The parrot would call us some awful names for doing that."

"What clothing did the older boys and men wear Charlie?"

"Big boys and gwon folks wore jeans and domestic shirts. Us little kids wore jest a gown. In the winter time we wore the same only with brogans with the brass toes."

"You said awhile ago that they gave you 'weigh' milk. That's a very poor grade of milk isn't it?"

"Yes Sah, It's the poorest kind of poor milk. It ain't even milk. It's what is left behind, when the milk is gone."

"And coffee. How about coffee. Didn't you have any coffee to drink?"

"We has coffee some time, but it ware made of burned corn meal. Once in awhile the slaves while makin' coffee for Marster Mat out of the wheat would burn a pan purposely and he would give it to them to make coffee with. That was purtty good coffee. Some time they got whupped for burnin' it, 'cause he knowed they burned it too much for his coffee, on purpose—jest so they'd git it."

"Now Charlie, you said you were born in Warrensburg, Missouri. Were you born on Mat Warren's place?"

"Yes Sah."

"How many slaves did Mr. Warren have?"

"150."

"I understand they sold off attractive women slaves and husky men. How is it they didn't sell your Mother?"

"She ware a house girl. Purtty and light in color, so they wanted to keep her for that job."

"Did they sell your father?"

"Yes Sah, they did. That is, they sold my step-Pappy as my own Pappy was dead."

"Speaking about your step-Pappy being sold reminds me: They say that the expression 'selling slaves on the block' is not true. That is, not always true."

"We never had no 'block' on Mat Warren's place. We calls it 'Puttin' 'em on the stump'. But the 'stump' were neither block nor stump, it were a box. Big wooden box."

"I have heard it said that some slaves brought big prices. Tell me, if you will, how much your step-Pappy was sold for."

"Well Sah, there was some buyers from south Texas was after to buy my step-Pappy for two years runnin', but the Marster would never sell him. So one time they comes up to our place at buying time (that was about once every year) and while buying other slaves they asked Mat Warren if he wouldn't sell my step-Pappy, 'cause he was a sure 'nough worker in the field—the best man he had and he could do more work than three ordinary men.

"But the Marster tried to git rid of that buyer agin by saying I don't take no old offer of $2,000 for Charlie, an' I won't sell under $2,055. The buyer he said right quick like. 'Sold right hare'. So that's how he come to leave us and we never seed him agin. Like to broke my Mammy up, but that's the way we slaves had it. We didn't let ourselves feel too bad, 'cause we knowed it would come that way some time. But my Ma she liked that Charlie and she feeled it mos'.

"We always knowed when they was going to sell, 'cause they would let them lay around and do nothin'. Jest feed them and git fat. They even smeared their faces with bacon rind to make 'em look greasy and well fed afore the sale. They never had no grease to eat only now and then Mat Warren he makes it look like them niggers is well fed and cared for. The buyers would a stick pins in 'em and examine their teeth like horses."

"By the way Charlie, what kind of jails did they have in those days?"

"They never had no jails. Your back was the jail. When you done something serious Marster Mat Warren called in the 'whuppers' and they made your back bleed and then rubbed salt into the skin. After that they chained you to a tree and let you suffer."

"What did you do as a child around the place?"

"I carried in the water and wood to the Missis house and helped Ma."

"What time did you all get up in the morning?"

"A big bell hanging in the center of all the cabins rang at 4 A.M. and then most of the grown folks worked from dawn till eleven at night. We never had no Saturdays off like they do now. Nor no Sundays off neither."

"What kind of house did the Master live in?"

"The Marster he have a very fine home. About ten rooms, built of common brick. It ware a very purtty house; great big like."

"What did you do, Charlie, after work at night?"

"Mostly, go to bed. We kids did early. But I wake up lots of times and hear my Ma and Pappy praying for freedom. They do that many times. I hear it said that Abraham Lincoln hears some slaves praying at a sneaked meetin' one time, askin' the Good Lord for freedom. And it is believed that Abraham Lincoln told them, that if he were President he would free them."

"Did you ever play any games or dance any?"

"No! No games, no play, only work. We had to be mighty careful we didn't use a pencil or any paper or read out where the Marster could see us. He would sure lick us fer that."

"What do you think of Abraham Lincoln?"

"I think he ware the greatest man in the world."

"Do you remember much about the war Charlie?"

"Not very much. I was only seven then, but I remembers that those Bushwackers came to steal my Marster's money but he wouldn't tell where he hid it. Said he didn't have any. They said he was telling a lie 'cause no man could have so many slaves and not have some money. He did have 150 slaves but he wouldn't tell where the money was hid. So they burned his feet, but he still wouldn't tell 'em he had hid it in the orchard. No Sah! He jest didn't tell.

"Them Bushwackers though, were not so bad as them Union soldiers. They took all our horses and left us old worn out nags; even took my horse I use to ride."

"What was the first thing you done after the war was over and you found yourself free, Charlie?"

"We went right next farm and rented land from Buck Towers and farmed until Ma died. Then I went to Fayetteville and worked at odd jobs there awhile. I worked too, on the Fayetteville College building. I stayed around Fayetteville 40 years. I was married when I first went there to a light colored woman. A Cherokee Indian. We had seven children, all girls. Only one is livin' now. She is the one I live with in Webb City, Missouri. I don't live with my wife now. My daughter's name is Mrs. Sam Cox. Her husband Sam Cox works at a garage in Webb. They have seven children too. Two girls, five boys, all living.

"When I was married I was a coachman and wore my

coach clothes—Begum hat (high silk hat), black double-breasted flap tailed coat and black broadcloth pants. My shoes were low and had beads all over the front. I looked like Booker T. Washington. And I like him most next to Abraham Lincoln.

"I use to work for Judge Brown in Fayetteville as coachman. Then I come here and worked for Mrs Louise Corn of Webb City for 13 years. I ain't workin' now, only firin' the boiler for the First National Bank in winter-time. My son-in-law Sam Cox, he works at the Bank on the side and I help him a little. Mostly, I'm jest man about town."

"Now, tell me in passing, Charlie, do you remember any men passing through your place in Warrensburg, looking for escaped slaves?"

"Yes I remember some tough men driving like mad through our place many times, with big chains rattling. We called them slave hunters. They always came in big bunches. Five and six together on horse back. Patrollers they was. They were almost as bad to us as them outlaws who used to come by and eat up all Marse Warren's chickens. There was some Texas bad men, too. John Reid, The Webb Boys, and Little Preston Smith.

"But, I'm sure glad it is all over now, but we didn't git nothin' out of it like we expected. We thought they was goin' to divide up the farms and give us some of it. No Sah! They was so mad at us for being freed that they got rid of us as soon as they could, and we was only too glad to go.

"I gits a small old-age pension now and live purtty

quiet like, but I tell you Sah, times ain't like they use to be. These yer young negroes—I don't think so much of anyhow."

MADISON FREDERICK ROSS

Interview with Madison Frederick Ross, Commerce, Missouri.

"Ah was bahn jes ninety year ago, two and one-half mile south of Commerce in Scott County. Mah Fathuh an' Mothuh was Jack an' Mary Ross. Ole Mastuh James Ross was a kind ole man, a'ways good to his cullud folks. Ole Missus died 'fore Ah was bahn. 'Nen dey was young Mastuhs James Jr., John an' William. Young Miss Francis married Joe Anderson.

"They was 'bout six hundred acres in de home place an' a hundred acres in de othuh fahm. Ole Mastuh had 25 or 30 slaves an we hed eight cabins built on three sides o' square with de big house on the othuh side. It was a big house, white with po'ches upstahs an' down. They was lotsa fruit trees 'roun' th' house, peaches, plums, pears, apples, an they was hollyhocks growin all roun' the yahd.

"Ouah cabin was jes one room with a big fiah place at one end. There was a'ways a big kittle a hangin in th' chimbly an' one o' them iron ovens a settin on the hawth. They was five in ouah fambly an' we had one big bed an' a trundle bed thet ud roll undah the othuh bed like that.

"Fethuh beds? Whew! Yessir! We hed the bigges' fethuh beds! You shoulda seen the big flock o' geese we hed. Hey, hey, hey—I'se thinkin' 'bout how us children a'ways crawled undah the house to gathuh the goose aigs. The geese a'ways laid undah th' house, an we'd crawl aroun' unduh there an git um an' when we's backin' out, the ole gander ud ketch us an' flog us. Many's the time he's wahmed the seat o' ouah pants.

"Somehow th' children was skeered o' Ole Mastuh, ah don' know why, 'cause he nevuh hit none o' us. Mastuh was tall an' thin,—an if we 'us sittin' roun' playin' an he come along we'd jump up an' run, an' if we 'ud look back—theuh he'd stan, jes shakin with laffin'. Ah spect he thought it war funny tuh have us skeered.

"Ever mornin' 'bout ten o'clock an' ever afternoon 'bout three all the chillern had tuh have they lunch. You know whut cahn pone is? Mmmm—thet's th' bes' bread! Jes make a sort a hole in th' hot embuhs, than pour it in an covuh it wuth mo' hot embuhs—an when ut's done jes wash ut off a bit. That sho was good bread! Well, each one o' us chillern hed to have a cahn pone—they was about 30 of us—an each take a tin pint cup an' foller the milk woman to the spring house. She'd fill ouah cups an' that was ouah lunch twice evah day.

"As a boy ah tended thuh cows an' sech like, an' built the fires in the fireplaces, later they let me plow an' ah thought ah sure had a big job. Ah wuz so proud at didden wanna stop for dinnah.

"'High Buck, Low Do' was one o' the games us boys usta play.

"My gran'fathuh was mos'ly Indian an he usta go out into the woods an' stay for days at a time. Ole Mastuh always called him Ole Yaller Abe—But one time he ran away—crossed the rivuh ovah heah an' went up tuh Canada. He usta write tuh Ole Mastuh an' he'd read the lettuhs tuh us. Mah fathuh was the shoe-maker, made all the shoes—for the white folks an' us too. We bought the leathuh from the tanyawd at the edge o town an We'd sell them tan-bark. Mah Mothuh was one o' the weavers. The loom an spinnin wheels was in a separate house—Ah usta watch the big warpin' bar go 'roun' an' wish ah could ride on ut but ah nevuh did.

"We had church foh the cullud folks an' lotsa white folks ud a'ways come an' lissen to the preachin'.

"We raised lotsa cattle an' horses, an mules—an in them days wheat was nevah less 'en $2.00 a bushel.

"The niggah buyahs usta come roun' ouah place but ah don' recollect any of ouah niggahs bein sold. They'd have slave sales ovah at Benton. One time young Mastuh bought home a thirteen yeah ole boy he paid a thousan' dollahs an' fifty cents for—We didden have no school fo' the cullud folks but young Mastuh William went to school an' in the evenin's he'd teach some o' us. In 'at way ah got as far as the fo'th grade.

"When the wah came on', 'cose we heared lots about it an sometime we'd see sojers. One time Gen'ral Grant come thru Commerce with about 40,000 men. They come down the rivuh in boats, an' camped here. The sojers 'ud come foragin' round ouah place but they nevah bothered much. They'd grind they swords on ouah grindstones an' show us how sharp they was by cuttin' the cahn stalks.

"One night in sixty-three, me an four othuhs ran away and went to the Cape an' joined the ahmy. Ah was in Co. H. 56th U.S. Cullud, unduh Col. Bentzoni.[2] We was in the Battle of Big Creek, Arkansas an in several skirmishes. Ah learned tuh play in the band, played second B-flat cahnet. We suah learned our do, re's.

[2] HW: Probably 56th Ohio Infantry (?) [TR: 56th U.S. Colored Infantry, Helena, Arkansas]

"Ouah Captain, Ole George Free, was a preacher an he'd have prayun meetin's in his tent. All the ole women from aroun' would come—an' we'd have big times on Sunday mahnin's. One time one o' the boys, Ed Johnson, got drunk an' the provost guahd put 'm in jail. Nex' mahnin, Capin Free go down theah to git him an' he raise so much racket Ol Cunnel say 'Turn im loose, Ole Cap'm go crazy 'bout his niggers.'

"We was stationed down in Helena, Arkansas, aftuh the fightin was ovah an' the officers sent up no'th fo' some teachers, to have school fo' us. They call it the Norman Institute an we each paid fifty cents a month to go. The teachers was Quakers an they never laughed or smiled. They a'ways seemed tuh be thinkin—seemed tuh think it was a sin to have fun. 'Ah kin still heah em—how they usta say, 'Thou shall get thy lessons ovah.' We was mustered out in St. Louis in 1866.

"Aftuh ah come back heah tuh Commerce Ah started a school, Ah called it 'Select School' an' they each paid fifty cents a month—grown folks come tuh mah school some o' em fifty an sixty year old an ah had all ah cud take caah of—Latuh, Ah taught school out in the country.

"Why do they call me doctuh? See that diploma on the wall! I got that fum a school of hypnotism. Yes'm a correspondence course. No'm, I nevuh practised it much, jes a little now an then for fun.

"One time the Ku Klux come aroun. They knock on the doah, then they say 'Please give me a drink, Ah ain't had a drink since the battle o' Shiloh.' What fo' they say that? Why, you see, they wants us tuh think they's the spirits a' the sojers killed at Shiloh an they been in hell so long they drinks all the water they kin git. This one man make us carry him five buckets of water, an' it look like he drink em but nex mahnin' theys a big mud puddle side thu doah."

United States. Work Projects Administration

ALICE SEWELL

Interview with Alice Sewell,
St. Louis, Missouri.

She Never Attended School

Never having attended school a day in her 86 years of life has not cramped the style of Alice Sewell, one of St. Louis' former Negro slaves. Alice lives with a married daughter, Mattie Hill, and a grandson, Henry Morse, at 329 South Ewing Avenue.

Spotlessly dressed, much after the fashion of a nurse, and weighing less than 100 pounds, Alice presents a pleasing picture as she chats interestingly with visitors. Her mind is keenly alive to what is going on in the world. She is much annoyed by the roistering younger folks, as she outlines in her observations in the following chat:

"I was born in Montgomery, Alabama, November 13, 1851, the daughter of Rhoda and Edmond Carey. I have three brothers and two sisters dead. I am the only child living. I ain't never been in a school house in my life and I never did learn how to read or write. I recollect three of my overseers. The first one's name Elik Clayton, the second one named Mofield and the third one named Pierson. I was 13 years old time de third one got me and de war had started, so we had to pack all de cotton up in bales, and in sun face houses and sun face cribs to be out of the weather. The seed cotton was kept in de gin house, 'cause dey didn't had no time to fool wid dat. Den dey up and bought spinning wheels and cards, so us women could spin it to make cloth, and make clothes at home, and would not have to go to de factory to buy clothes.

"Dey had to keep de money to care for de families de soldiers left behind, and send corn by de loads to de battlefield to feed de horses. Dey stopped raising cotton after de war started, and just raised food stuff 'cause dey had to send food to de battlefield for de soldiers. De poor white folks what lived up in de hilly country, too poor to own slaves, while de war was going on, had to come down out of de hilly country. Dey lived on government land and dey had to have food for dem and der children. Der men folks was taken away from dem to war. Dey was called counterscript soldiers, and if dey refused to go to war dey got shot down like a dog. So de most of 'em rather go on and take chances of de war missing 'em dan get shot widout a doubt. Dey use to say dey had to go and fight a rich man's war but dey couldn't help demselves no better'n us slaves could.

"My owner was very rich. He owned four plantations of slaves. He had two plantations on de Tallapoosa River, one named Jedkins upper ferry plantation and de other Jedkins Mill Place and the third plantation was called The Bradshaw Place. It was out from de river and de fourth one was called De High Log Plantation. He was always fairly kind to his slaves. He didn't believe in abusing dem less he couldn't help it, and when he'd find out de overseers beat 'em widout a cause, he'd fire 'em right away, and git somebody else. Dat's why he so prosperous, 'cause he was fair. He never even 'lowed overseers on his plantation what had grown boys, to be runnin' round 'mongst his slaves neither, no he didn't. He didn't believe in dat intermingling, 'deed he didn't. Dey didn't 'low us to sing on our plantation 'cause if we did we just sing ourselves happy and git to shouting and dat would settle de work, yes mam.

"Dey did 'low us to go to church on Sunday about two miles down de public road, and dey hired a white preacher to preach to us. He never did tell us nothing but be good servants, pick up old marse and old misses' things about de place, and don't steal no chickens or pigs and don't lie 'bout nothing. Den dey baptize you and call dat, you got religion. Never did say nothing 'bout a slave dying and going to heaven. When we die, dey bury us next day and you is just like any of de other cattle dying on de place. Dat's all 'tis to it and all 'tis of you. You is jest dead dat's all. De old lady dat raised my mother, she was a black mammy. She done all de burying of de niggers, said de funeral sayings by herself. She knew it by heart. Dey swapped my grandmother away 'cause she didn't bear children like dey wanted her to, so de man dey swapped her off to come back two months later and told our owner dat grandmamma was heavy with child. Den he wanted to buy her back 'cause she was a good worker, but her new owner would not let him have her back and she had thirteen children after dat. Our old owner surely was sick of dat swap. My mother was only three years old when dey sold her mother to another master and she never saw her agin 'till she had all dem thirteen children.

"Dis is how mother found grandmother. Our owner bought a slave what come off of a plantation dat my grandmother was on. She was turned over to dis slave owner to satisfy a gambling debt left unpaid by de dead husband. So she told my mother all about de deal and all de children mother had never seen. My mother had three children of her own, at dat time. De slave dat brought de news name was Elsie. So Elsie had lots of relatives on dis plantation she was sold off of. Well she had to have a pass everytime she want to go visit her folks. So she tells my mother next time I git a pass to go see my people, you ask old boss for you one too so you can go see you mamma and sisters and brothers you never seen. Mamma did and when mamma got to old John Beasley's plantation on Lime Creek mother didn't know grandmother Sallie and grandmother Sallie didn't know her daughter Rhoda till Elsie introduced 'em to each other. Dey was so glad dey just hugged and kissed plenty. De war was going on den and dey fought four years and two months.

"De first year after de war my father and mother kept us children and stayed right on with our old owner and done share cropping till father was able to buy stock of his own, but he did not buy no property. When I got 18 years old I married, but I stayed right on with my mother and father just de same and my children buried both my mother and father. My mother lived to be 100 years old and my father was between 80 and 90 when he died.

"I left Montgomery, Alabama de last of 1902 when Louis was only 11 years old and came to Morouse, Alabama and stayed five years after dat. I moved to Arkansas, stayed quite a while, don't know how long. All dat time I made my living washing and ironing and picking cotton from farm to farm. My husband died 28 years ago last March. I been in St. Louis now between 12 and 13 years.

"We used to slip off in de woods in de old slave days on Sunday evening way down in de swamps to sing and pray to our own liking. We prayed for dis day of freedom. We come from four and five miles away to pray together to God dat if we don't live to see it, do please let our chillun live to see a better day and be free, so dat dey can give honest and fair service to de Lord and all mankind everywhere. And we'd sing 'Our little meetin's 'bout to break, chillun we must part. We got to part in body, but hope not in mind. Our little meetin's bound to break.' Den we used to sing 'We walk about and shake hands, fare you well my sisters I am going home.'

"I never did hear nothing 'bout what de niggers specked from de white folks. We was so glad to get loose, we didn't speck nothing but git out of bondage. Dey didn't even give us time off to wash our clothes. We had to wash 'em at night when we ought to been resting our old backs what was so tired. We liked to go to de field clean in de mornings. Dat's de only way we had of doing it. I never been on relief in my life. I got my first pension last month. It was $17.50 old age pension. I sure was proud of dat.

"I never had no interest in politics till last year, dey come and got me and told me to vote de Republican ticket. I did what dey said do, but dey didn't git it after all. My oldest grandson works at a bakery where he been working nine years and takes care of me, his mother and brother. I think de biggest run of this late generation is ignorant. 'Course dey goes to school alright, but dey don't make no good of it. De people wid de Bible and God education is much better folks dan dis ignorant book learned fools. Dat's all dey is honey. Dey don't respect derself, God nor de devil. Dey jes' act like something wild raised, turned loose in de swamps. Dere schooling makes me wish I could walk de streets wid my ears stopped up and eyes blindfolded so I couldn't even hear nor see dis educated generation. Bless your soul honey, I don't care a scrap 'bout schooling dat don't teach decency or common respect. De knee way is all de education dat mounts to nothing no way. God's way is de only way. It makes you treat everybody in de world like you want to be treated by other folks and dat's right, and everything else's wrong by dat.

"But de time's on de way here, daughter, when we all be one people like God intended black and white de same. Course de end will be at hand when dat happens but it's sure coming. Den God will bless us all alike and everything we put our hands to will prosper. God's will is fast fulfilling and He is true to His word. We will walk with God some day, I won't be here I don't speck. But I am walking with God myself right now. I am a member of Southern Mission Church.

"I owned a nice home in Warren, Arkansas. I sold it to come up here. De folks down dere said dey would sure miss seeing me walking around down der wid my white apron on but I believed in immigration like de Bible said. So I just immigrated from de South up here to de North. God said de plantations would grow up and de hoot owls would have 'em and dey is doin it. Growin' up into wilderness. God planned dem slave prayers to free us like he did de Israelites, and dey did."

PERRY SHEPPARD

Interview with Perry Sheppard,
Aged 94, Fredericktown, Missouri.
Interviewed by J. Tom Miles.

"I'm hard of hearin'. I know I'm 94 years old; was born in Cape County. I was a slave till I was 20 years old. I was a house boy. De boss had a number of black men who did de work in de field. In warm weather we wore flax, an jeans, in de winter I had plenty of meat to eat. I can't read or write. Wish I could. My old mistress told me I was free when I was 20. Den I stayed there a while and worked on shares. De militia come an took a horse away from me on de road ten miles away from home and I had to walk home. But he fetched de hoss home after a while. I think slavery was a good thing. I never suffered for nothin'. Lincoln wanted every man to work for himself."

United States. Work Projects Administration

FRANK SIDES

Interview with Frank Sides,
Cape Girardeau, Missouri.

"Ah's jest a little feller when de war's over, jes' 'bout six year ole, ah wuz, an' ah don' rec'lect much 'bout dem days. Aaron an' Lucy Sides wuz mah daddy an' mammy, an' we belong to Mastuh Cato. Dey live near Fredericktown, ah don' membuh young 'Missus' name, an' dey neveh had no chillun. Dey had a big house, an' seems like we live in paht o' de white folks' house. De sojers come 'round sometime, but dey didden' bathuh us, jes' ask fo' a drink er suthin' to eat, an' go on.

"But de 'Bushwackers' wuz bad, dey go shootin' anybody, en' doin' devilment. I don' rec'lect nuthin' dey done roun' our place but one day a little bunch o' 'em stop dere fo' a drink. Ah's scared o' 'um, but ah gives 'em all a drink, an' de las' man takes his drink and t'rows de dippuh on de flo'.

"We didden' hab no school but ah learned to read an' write, but ah's not much of a scholar at dat.

"When de war's ovuh we move to 'Cape', an' we live fust one place, 'en 'nuther, doin' whut we could.

"One time ah's workin' wid a gang on a railroad bridge. Dey wuz a big gang of us. Oh, mebbe three or fo' hundred. De sleepin' cah wuz 'bout half mile down de track. Come mah time tuh turn in, ah starts down de track. It wuz bright moonlight an' ah's tired an' sleepy. Jes' as ah comes along whar de cattle gahd is, dere standin' in de middle o' de track is a big, tall man, all in black. He don' move, an' he's tall ag'in as ah is. It's so light ah kin see him plain. Ah stan's an' looks at him an' ah thinks: 'Shall ah run past? No, if ah does he'll git me sho'.' Den ah says, 'Shall ah climb dat bobwire fence an' go through de fiel'', but ah says, 'No, No!, spose mah pants gits hung on de bobwire, den whut happen?' Ah looks at him again an' he's twice as big ez he wuz befo', but he jes' stans dere. So ah goes jes' ez close to de fence ez ah could an' goes sideways pass' him, keepin' mah eye on him, but he don' move, jes' keep standin' dere. Nex' day ah goes tuh look at de place but don' see no sign o' him. Ah don' know why fo' he stan' dere 'till folks tell me dat, 'Bout a year befo', a man wuz killed right der'."

MOLLIE RENFRO SIDES

Interview with Mollie Renfro Sides,
Cape Girardeau, Missouri.

"Mah mammy wuz Rosie Renfro, an' we' un's blong to 'Massa' Tom B. English, an' Miss Sarah. We live neah Jackson. My daddy Spencer Renfro, he blong to 'Massa' Jack Renfro, en' de Cape Road.

"'Massa' English wouldn't sell us, an' 'Massa' Renfro woun' sell mah daddy, so dey jes' let mah daddy come tuh see us on Satudays.

"Our white folks, dey wuz all mighty nice people. Dey live in a big white house, an' dey has lotsa nice things. Mah mammy done de cookin' an' 'twen time she he'p weave on de loom, an' spin an' knit.

"Dey wuz jes' two o' us families. We lived in little ole log houses an' in tuther house dey wuz Ann, an' Nancy an' 'Aunt Dinah'.

"Den seems like dey wuz a 'nuddah house whar a bunch o' men stay 'at works in de fiel'. Dey wuz some field 'roun' de house, an' day wuz a 'nudder fiel' dey call 'mile fiel'. It were a mile big, evuh way. Dey raise lotsa wheat en' cahn an' sich-like, an' chickens an' cows, an' fruit, apples, an' peaches.

"Some o' de womans worked in de fiel' an' when dey comes in dey has tuh set down an' peel apples an' peaches fo' fryin' an' put 'em on big racks out in de sun an' when dey's dry, put 'em in bags, an' hang 'em up fo' wintuh.

"Ah wuzn' very big at dat time, jes' 'bout fo' yeah ole, but ah rec'lect how scared we is when de sojers come by. De men folks all hide out an' so de Missus, when we wants tuh hide too, she say, 'Run on out, run on out, and tell 'em nobody home'. Sometime dey hide unner de bed, 'hind de trunnel bed.

"An' ah 'membuh 'Miss Betty' died. She had pneumonya. Dar she wuz all pretty in huh coffin, an' dey had all de cullud folks come through de house tuh see her. Pore 'lil' Missis'! Dey buried huh in Jackson.

"When a 'body's sick, if yuh hears a hoot owl near de house, er a whipperwill dat's bad luck. Ah a'way's goes out an' tries tuh chase' em off. But ah guess ef dey's gonna bring bad luck, dey's already brung it."

JANE SIMPSON

> Interview with Jane Simpson,
> St. Louis, Missouri.

She Was Sold 6 Times

The subject of this sketch is Jane Simpson, familiarly known in her neighborhood as Aunt Jane. She is more than 90 years old but her exact age is not certain. She lives at 2712-1/2 Clark Avenue with her niece and family.

In a very poorly furnished old 3-room brick apartment, seated in the front bed room, was Jane Simpson, frail and slender, very light complexion with beautiful long white hair, well combed and neatly dressed. Owing to a recent illness, she was not able to do any housework. Jane very feebly tells the following story of her life:

"I was born more than 90 years ago down in Burkesville, Kentucky. My memory's not so good, 'cause I been sick more than 20 years, and just got up less than a week ago from a very bad spell. But I might tell my story scatterin' like. I'll do the best I can. I been sold six times in my life, first to Chris Ellis, second, to John Emerson and my third owner was Jessie Cook.

"I wasn't old enough to be much help, till I 'come the property of Marse Cook. Den I was big enough to pick up chunks in de field, set brush heap afire, burn up rubbish, pull weeds and de like. He sold me to Dr. Hart around de age of ten to be his house girl. De doctor kept me till de Civil War was in de air and dey started running de slaves to Texas 'cause dey thought de Yankees couldn't make it plum to Texas, but dey did. By de time we got as far as Crowley's Ridge, peace was declared. My father's owner was old Bill Cuington, de meanest slave owner in de county. Dey made him go to war, so when he come back, he told my papa dat he was as free as him now, and he could go if he wanted to, or stay, he didn't care which, but if he stayed he wouldn't git nothing for his work. So a white neighbor friend heard Marse Bill say it. He told my father to come to his place with him down de road apiece where he was clearing up land, but if he got caught, don't ever tell he helped him get away 'cause some of the land he was clearing up was owned by Cuington, and Cuington would fire him if he knowed he helped one of his ex-slaves in anyway.

"So papa taken my mother and us 4 children de route dis white friend helped him to go, to Clarington, Arkansas. He got us a job on a farm owned by his friend, Jerry Diles. Our whole family went to work on Mr. Diles farm and we made a good crop. Mama milked, I cooked, de rest of de family farmed and we stayed there more'n 4 years. When we left we had money enough to buy us a farm and stock of our own. I 'member well when I was a child how dey wouldn't 'low us chillun nothin' to eat but pumpkin and mush. We didn't own no clocks dem days. We just told de time by de sun in de day and de stars at night. If it was clouded we didn't know what time it was. De white folks didn't want to let de slaves have no time for der self, so de old folks used to let us chillun run and play at night, while de white folks sleep and dey watch de stars to tell about what time to call us in and put us to bed, 'fore de white folks know we was out.

"I been sold six times in my life, but, I never got more dan three or four whippings, but dey cut de blood out of me every one of dem times. If old miss got mad about something, just anything at all, she'd have you whipped, when maybe you had not done a thing, just to satisfy her spite feeling. I never can forget, I was sitting upstairs in old miss house quilting when de first Yankee army boat went to Vicksburg, Mississippi. Old miss made me git right up and go git her children out of school and bring 'em right home. She's scared to death most, but de boat went right on. It didn't even stop. I had to take her children back and forth to school every day. Dey was mighty nice children. Dem very white children taught me to read and write, but I been sick so bad and so long I done forgot every bit of it. My first old master never was married and he only bought 2 slaves in his whole life and had between 50 and 100 slaves, all kin folks. Dey raised children on his plantation worse dan flies. I never had a child in my life but I raised a host of other folks' chillun.

"Old master was a drunkard. He got drunk one night and fell off a rock and broke his hip. He died from dat fall. Before he died he told papa, he knew he was goin' to die, and he had been so mean to his old slaves dat he wanted to do somethin' for 'em, and no one never knew where he kept his money. My grandpapa, Meridie and grandmother, Juda, was de only 2 slaves he ever bought and all de rest come from dem 2. Old marse Chris told grandfather before he died, there was a keg buried at de foot of de cliff with all his money in it, for he was very rich. My old grandfather told de overseer 'bout it. Dey wouldn't dare to dig and find anything on de owner's plantation without de overseer let em, specially when de boss is dead, and de overseer of course said he looked for de keg and didn't find nothing.

"I had an uncle who was buying his freedom from marse Chris and was almost paid out when marse Chris died, but he didn't know nothing 'bout keeping receipts so he was put on the auction block and sold again. My mama and daddy had 13 children and they is everyone dead but me. My papa's name was Dave Bedford. He was 103 years old when he died in Holly Grove, Arkansas. My sister died and left 9 children and I raised everyone of dem. One boy is deaf and dumb, and lives in Little Rock, Arkansas and is one of the best paper hangers down there. My husband was a farmer. He has been dead so long, I can't tell when he died. My grand niece said he been dead 22 years, I don't know. My children I raised and my friends have been taking care of me, ever since my husband died, 'cause I can't take care of myself.

"While my husband lived we farmed all de time and lived well. When he died I had $4000 in de bank at Mound Bayou, Mississippi. De bank went down and I been a beggar every since. Never did get one penny of dat money. I been here in St. Louis so long, I don't know how long I been here.

"A Democrat offered my husband 80 acres of land if he would vote a Democrat ticket and get his friends to change from Republicans to Democrats and my husband told him he would suffer his right arm to be cut off before he would do that, and he didn't change either. I only voted once in my life dat was for a Republican President, I don't remember which one. De niggers didn't 'spect nothing from de white folks when dey got set free. Dey was so glad to get set free dey just glad to be loose.

"I never even heerd of white folks giving niggers nothing. Most of de time dey didn't even give 'em what dey 'spose to give 'em after dey was free. Dey was so mad 'cause dey had to set 'em free, dey just stayed mean as dey would 'low 'em to be anyhow, and is yet most of 'em. I used to hear old slaves pray and ask God when would de bottom rail be de top rail, and I wondered what on earth dey talkin' 'bout. Dey was talkin' 'bout when dey goin' to git from under bondage. Course I know now. I don't hardly know what to say 'bout dis new generation. Dey ain't nothing like when I come along, nor nothing like when you come along.

"You can just look at a person and tell whether dey is late day folks or not. Dey is de worse, ill mannered, biggody generation I ever heard of. Dey don't care for folks' feelings and jest as lazy and good for nothing as dey can be. Instead of being better 'cause der opportunities is better, dey is worse, and I feel so sorry about it. De old folks wanted to be free so bad dey use to sing a song named 'Free, Free My Lord, March on De Heavenly Way.' I can't remember none de other songs. I been sick so much. I wish I could go back to de Arkansas country where my mama and papa died. Dere is 11 children down dere right now what I raised and lot of my relatives, too. Dey would take care of me if I could get there, I would not have to live like I living here. I see better without glasses dan I do with dem, I don't read any way. I belong to de St. Paul A.M.E. Church, but haven't been able to go for six years but twice. I don't git no help from de relief and we need help de worst way. My grandniece tries to work when she can get it, but she is sick, too.

CLAY SMITH

Interview with Clay Smith,
Hannibal, Missouri.

Clay Has Vivid Memory

Clay (Carrie) Smith, now living at 612 Butler Street, Hannibal, Missouri, was born in slavery shortly before the Civil War on the farm of Joe Maupin about five miles west of Hannibal. Her present residence on Butler Street is part of the way up the hill overlooking Mark Twain Avenue (formerly Palmyra Avenue) and facing Cardiff Hill. Her mother's home was on Palmyra Avenue. Her mother's name was Luckett. Following is Clay's story as she told it:

"I was borned right here in Marion County. Dere was ten of us children in de family. We belonged to Joe Maupin and Sarah Ann Maupin. We called Mrs. Maupin 'Miss Spatsie'. Mother was brought here by de Maupins from Virginia. Father was born near New London in Ralls County. He belonged to de preacher priest. He was one of dose hardshelled, ironsides Baptists. Father run away to Illinois during de war and we ain't never saw him again.

"Three of my sisters was bound out to de Maupin children when dey was married and dey done moved somewhere in Monroe County. I knowed of only one slave in our family dat was sold, and dat was my Aunt Harriet. She was sold on de block down on Fourth Street right here in Hannibal. I was only five or six years old den.

"After de war my mother worked for Mr. Maupin for three years. Mother bought a house on Palmyra Avenue here in Hannibal den, and Mr. Maupin would help mother to make de payments by giving her work.

"Dere was only a few houses down on Palmyra Avenue den. Old Mrs. Vail had a hotel, or tavern dey called it in dem days, over across de street. Beyond de hill (Cardiff Hill) was all woods and we could see bears and deers and tigers over dere. (Of course this is untrue. That was Mark Twain's playground years before.)

"Dey didn't raise children den like dey does now. Dey don't mind at all now. When we was across de street and didn't mind we got a whippin' so dat we would fall over in de brush and when we come home we got another whippin',—we always got two whippins. Nowadays de youngsters runs 'round all over de town and dey don't pay no mind to nobody.

"Over on dat hill was a pes' house where dey took people with smallpox. Dey died thick and dey hauled 'em away at night. Dey carried torches and hauled 'em in wagons. When dey took someone by to the pes' house, old Man Cogner would go ahead and holler, 'Smallpox!' We would all run and hide 'cause we was scared. Dat was five or six years after we moved here.

"Dere was no houses 'round here den, but now I look out and see what de Lord has done. De Bible say de new would take place of de old and things would be changed.

"I worked in de old hotel down dere 'cross from de depot. It was de Ketrens Hotel den, for about fourteen years, and den I worked for de Claytons for about thirteen years. I can't do nothin' now, 'cause I is too old. I gets a small pension. Dis is my house, but dey is a mortgage on it and dey might come and take it away from me. I belongs to de Baptist Church on Center Street, but I don't go very often no more. My brother lives with me. He is dat one-legged man you sees in de City Park most of de time. He gets a pension, too. My oldest brother died last week. He was blind."

United States. Work Projects Administration

GUS SMITH

Interview with Gus Smith,
Rolla, Missouri.

Slaves Were Well Fed

"I was born in 1845, on de fourth of July, near Rich Fountain, Osage County, Mo., not far from Jefferson City. My father's name was Jim Messersmith, and my mother's maiden name was Martha Williams. I was called August Messersmith until I was old enough to vote, den I changed it to plain 'Gus Smith'. My friends nick-named me 'Chinie' and I am called dat today.

"My master's name was Bill Messersmith and he called hisself a Pennsylvania Dutchman. His father settled in Missouri, near Jefferson City many years before de war. He owned 1,500 acres of land. The old man, my master's father, had a good many slaves but de chillun didn't have so many after de old man died. Rufus, the old man's son and my master's brother took one of de Negro boys; his sister, Manisee, took a Negro girl. These two, Rufus and Manisee never married and lived with my master. Zennie, another sister, took a girl and a boy. She married a man by de name of Goodman and my master took my father and my mother.

"My master's father, before he died, told his chillun, dat at his death he wanted each child to put their slaves out to work until dey earned $800 a piece, to earn their own freedom, in dat way each slave paid it dem selves. He did not believe it was right to keep dem in slavery all their lives. But de war came and dey were free without having to work it out.

"We all wore home-spun clothes, made of wool mostly. Mother carded, spun and wove all our clothes. My master let us come and go pretty much as we pleased. In fact we had much more freedom dan de most of de slaves had in those days. He let us go to other places to work when we had nothing to do at home and we kept our money we earned, and spent it to suit ourselves. We had it so much better dan other slaves dat our neighbors would not let their slaves associate with us, for fear we would put devilment in their heads, for we had too much freedom. My father and mother had their own cabin to live in, with their family, but de rest of de slaves stayed with our mistress. My father's relation lived within ten miles of us. Dey came to see us but dat was about all de company we had.

"We used to sing all the old plantation songs, but my father and mother were not such good singers. We all had good times along with de work. During Christmas time, and de whole month of January, it was de rulin' to give de slaves a holiday in our part of de country. A whole month, to go and come as much as we pleased and go for miles as far as we wanted to, but we had better be back by de first of February. If we wanted to go through a territory where it was hard to travel, or get by, we got a pass from our master.

"We had quiltins, dancin', makin' rails, for days at a time. My goodness! We don't have nothin' to eat now like we did then. All kinds of game, wild ducks, geese, squirrels, rabbits, 'possum, pigeons and fried chicken. My! women in those days could cook. Great big 'pound cakes' a foot and a half high. You don't see such things, now-a-days.

"I remember my father shooting so many pigeons at once that my mother just fed dem to de hogs. Just shoot the game from our back yard. I have seen de wild pigeons so thick dey looked like storm clouds coming. I've seen dem so thick dey broke tree limbs down. Ducks and geese de same way. We could kill dem by tow sacks full, with clubs. White folks and colored folks came to these gatherings, from miles around, sat up all night dancin', eatin', and drinkin'. People kept whiskey by de barrel in those days. You see, Miss, in those days dey just loaded up ten or twelve bushel of corn, took it to de 'still-house' and traded it for a barrel of whiskey. Not much selling in those days, everything was traded, even to labor. Our folks would tell us to go and help so-and-so and we done it.

"Mother was de cook in those days at our place. De hewed log house we lived in was very big, about five or six rooms. In times of our holidays, we always had our own musicians. Sometimes we sent ten or twelve miles for a fiddler. He'd stay a week or so in one place and den he would go on to de next farm, maybe four or five miles away, and dey had a good time for a week. When we didn't have much work, we would get up about five o'clock every morning, but in busy season we had to be up and ready to work at daybreak. There was plenty of work for every one den, even to de little darkies, if only to pull weeds. We raised wheat, corn, cotton, tobacco, cabbage, potatoes, sheep, hogs and cattle. Had plenty of everything to eat.

"Our closest neighbors was de Thorntons. Ol' man Thornton did not allow his slaves to go no place. He was a rough man, a low heavy set fellow, weighed about one hundred and sixty pounds. He was mean to his slaves. He whupped dem all de time. I've seen their clothes sticking to their backs, from blood and scabs, being cut up with de cowhide. He just whupped dem because he could. He use to say he allus give his niggers a 'breakfast spell ever' mornin'! Dat is he whupped dem every morning. I remember he had a nigger woman about seventy years old on his place. De Thorntons did not feed their slaves, dey was nearly starved. One night that ol' woman was so hungry she stole a chicken from her master, ol' Thornton, and was cooking it in her cabin. He found it out some way and started to her cabin, and caught her, while she had it on boiling. He was so mad, he told her to get a spoon and eat every bite before she stopped. It was scalding hot but he made her do it. She died right away; her insides were burned.

"Why, ol' Thornton was dat mean dat he killed his own son. He just beat him to death with de whip-stock of dat cowhide, a whip made of buckskin. It was like dis. De boy had a girl he was courtin' in another town. He started to see her on Saturday noon. His daddy told him to be back by Sunday night. But de boy did not get back before Monday morning, ten o'clock. His father was in de field working and saw him coming down de road. He went to meet him and met him at de gate. He asked why he did not get back sooner and lit into beating him with de whip stock, de part dat should be de whip handle. He beat him so hard dat de boy died in about ten hours. It aroused de neighborhood and dey began to plan a lynching party. He got wind of it some way and got all his slaves together and pulled out. He left dat place and no one ever knowed where he went. Dat happened before de end of de war.

"There was a lot of run-a-way slaves in those days. I never saw any of dem but I heard de folks talk about dem. Many passed through our part of de country. In time of slavery, people were sold like cattle or hogs. There was no sale bills dat we seen, because folks in dem days was usually honest and did not have a lot of red tape in buying and selling. Our master would not sell any of us. He did not believe in separating us, and tried to keep us together. He didn't have any trouble with his slaves at all. He was as good a man as ever lived and we did pretty much as we pleased.

"He married before de war, but his first wife died a few months later. He married a year after his wife died. He went to Pennsylvania and came back and went to California for about a year. Before he left he made my father boss. My father stayed on de place and took care of everything. He was boss all during de war.

"When the battle of Wilson Creek was fought up near Springfield, most all de soldiers passed by our house. After dey passed den came de bushwhackers. Dey stole all de niggers dey could, running dem down south to sell. Dey came to our place in de morning; it must have been about 1862-63. De whole family of colored folks was home, 'cepting my father.

"Dey looked across de road and seen another house and asked us whose house it was. We told dem it was our master's house. Dey saw we had a mare in de yard and told us to saddle her up. And told my oldest brother to be ready to go with dem when dey come back. Dey went half way to my master's house and for some reason wheeled and came back. My mother looked out de door and seen them coming and said: 'Here they come.'

She said to my oldest brother, 'Get under dat puncheon floor, maybe dey won't take August,' meaning me. I was about 12 or 13 years old den. We had a great big hearth, de rocks and puncheon came right up to it. My mother raised de one end of a puncheon and my brother hid there under de floor. De bushwhackers came back to de house and searched everyplace, failed to find him, even raised de floor and looked under, but my brother had crawled so far up in de corner dey did not see him. Dey asked my mother where he was and said, 'By God! We want to know.' Mother answered and said she sent him down to de field to get some corn for de hogs and told me to run down there and look for him.

"Well I did. I run down in dat field and am going yet. I stayed out in dat woods for four days and nights with nothing to eat but what wild grapes and hazel nuts I could find. I knew better dan to go back dere, but I did not know where to go. I fell on a plan to go to my young missus, Zennie. Dey lived off de main road, two miles from where we lived. When I got to her home, it was in de evening about four o'clock. I saw my cousin, Melie, fifteen or sixteen years old, but was afraid to speak to her. I saw her out a piece from de barn, but I wouldn't let her see me. I stayed all night in de barn, but I wouldn't let her see me. I stayed all night in de barn and next morning I peeped out de window and saw her again. She was picking beans. I hollered and she recognized me and asked me if I wasn't August. I said yes. She told me to come on out and go with her, dat my mother and all of dem was at their house den.

My oldest brother, Jim, was there too. He was four years older dan me.

"Den I went down to de house and dey soon fixed me something to eat. But only a little because dey were afraid it might make me sick. My mother told me to stay with Miss Zennie. Miss Zennie had married de second time to a man by de name of George McGee. Her first husband, Dave Goodman, was killed right at de start of de war by a gang of robbers something like de bushwhackers, who went in gangs of ten and fifteen, stealing niggers or anything else dey could get their hands on.

"George McGee and my brother Jim hid out in de bluffs at Rollin's Ferry, a place where ferry boats ran. George McGee hid because he did not want to go in de army. So he takes my brother and hides in de bluffs. Dey both came to de house for provisions about twelve o'clock dat night and took me with dem. We camped out dat night and next morning dey said to me: 'You stay here. Dey is out of meat at de house.' So dey went back to de house and killed and dressed a young heifer and came back at night to get me. We had a good time, eating supper and playing. Along in de night I heard something like horses hoofs hitting de ground. I told my mother and she said, 'You don't hear nothin'.'

"George McGee, de young master said, 'Wait, he is right. I hears someting, too!'

"We jumped up and went out and down a steep holler and made it back to our camp dat night yet. Next morning we wondered who it could have been dat we heard. Dat night we went back to see how de folks was getting on and found out it was my own father and our own master who had come a hunting for us. If we had known, we would not have run.

"My master told his sister, Miss Zennie to keep us hid out of de way, that we were doing all right. I stayed in dat bluff about two years, until de close of de war, I never saw my father and master for over a year. I saw my mother every time I went to de house for something to eat, about twelve o'clock at night. My father had to hide out, too. He kept de stock out in de bushes, watching after de master's affairs while he was away.

"We stayed hid until dey took General Lee. Den we went back to ol' master's house and it was not long until peace was declared. Our house was about a quarter of a mile from de master's, on a farm he had bought from an old Dutchman, about one hundred and sixty acres. One morning, ol' master come over early and said: 'Jim, by God! You are a free man dis morning, as free as I am. I can't hold you any longer. Now take your family and go over on dat hundred and sixty acres I bought and go to work.' He was giving us all a chance to pay out de farm for ourselves a home. My father said: 'There's nothing to go with it to help clear it and live.' To which ol' master answered: 'There's de smoke-house, take all you want and I'll furnish you with everything else you need for a year, until you get a start.' He allowed us to use anything to work with, he had on his place.

"Den we went to work. Ol' master said, 'I've got all de land my heart could wish but none of it is cleared off. Go down dere with your boys and I'll send two men, both white (Irishmen, Jim and Tom Norman) and all of you clear off dat land. I'll give you five years lease to clear all you can. All you clear, you can have half." Well, we cleared fifty acres dat winter. We made rails, fenced it and put it all in corn dat first year. There was six of us to do dis, my cousin joined my father, brother, and myself, and de two white men.

"We had it cleared by the first of March—all ready to plow in 1865. My father raised his own sheep and cotton, and from dis my mother made our clothes. Father cleared thirty acres on his place de same year and sowed it all in wheat. De first year we got 817 bushel of wheat and 1500 bushel of corn, it was all new land. Corn really growed in dem days. We hoed it by hand. You don't see corn like dat now. We worked out every little weed. Every little darkey worked in dem days.

"My grandad, Godfry, owned a place called de old Potter's place, near Vichy Springs, Vichy, Missouri, not far from where we lived. He bought it from a man who used to make pottery. Grandfather made his own mill to grind grain for bread. In dose days there was no steam operated mills and few water mills. Sometimes we had to go as much as twenty miles to grind corn a bushel of corn. So grandfather made his own burr to grind corn and wheat. It was as big as any burr in de large mills, but it was turned by hand power. It was made of limestone rock, a great big stone about two and a half foot across. De top burr would probably weigh about three or four hundred pounds. Da bottom case would weigh a thousand pounds or more. There was a hole in de top stone, where de grain flowed freely to de bottom and ground out on the big thick stone below. I ground many a bushel of meal on it myself. I don't know how grandfather got de large stones in place, for it was there as long as I could remember. I just wonder if it isn't some place there yet. I would love to go and find out and see de old burr again.

"People call these hard times, shucks, they don't know what hard times is. Those were hard days, when folks had to go on foot twenty miles to mill. I remember in my early days, we used cattle for teams to haul, start at four o'clock in de morning, drive all day, stay over night and grind de next day. Sometimes de crowd ahead of us was so big we had to stay over for three or four days. Sometimes we would be until eleven or twelve at night getting home. Gone at least two days and one night. I had to make trips like dis many times.

"Sometimes we could take a couple of bushel of corn and go horseback, but twice a year, Spring and Fall, we would take eight or ten bushel of wheat, six and eight bushel of corn or according to what we needed and take de cattle and a old wooden axle wagon, walking and driving de cattle all de way there and back. We drove or led dem with only a rope around dem.

"De last trip I made millin', I drove for Bill Fannins, a yoke of young three-year old cattle. Wasn't even broke. Went twenty-five miles, drove all de way, walking, while he sat up in de wagon. Sometimes de wagon dragged in de mud, de old wooden axle burying so deep we couldn't hardly get it out, going through timber and dodging brush. Some folks went even further dan dat. Sometimes a mill might be four or five miles from you but dey got out of fix and you would have to go to another one. Maybe twenty-five miles or more.

"There was not many good doctors in those days, but my grandfather was an old fashioned herb doctor. I remember him well. I was about twenty-five years old when he died. Everybody knew him in dat country and he doctored among de white people, one of de best doctors of his kind. He went over thirty miles around to people who sent for him. He was seldom at home. Lots of cases dat other doctors gave up, he went and raised them. He could cure anything.

"When I was sick one time, I was den about eighteen or nineteen years old, my folks had Dr. Boles, from Lane's Prairie and Dr. Mayweather from Vichey, to come and tend me. Dey both gave me up. I had typhoid and pneumonia. Dese doctors were de best to be found but dey could do nothing and said I was as good as dead. My grandfather was gone, had come to Rolla, doctoring Charley Stroback's child whose clothes had caught fire and he was burned badly. Grandfather could 'blow out' fire.

"He got home about four o'clock in de morning after de doctors had done give me up. He felt my pulse and said he didn't know whether I was dead or alive. No pulse but he said I felt warm. He asked my grandmother if she had any light bread baked. She said yes and got it for him. He told her to butter it and lay the butter side down over my mouth and if it melted I was still living. She did this and soon she said, 'Yes, he is still alive. Now go to work and get a little whiskey and butter and beat it together good and drop just two drops in his mouth, and in four hours drop two more.'

"He sat beside me, layed his hands on my breast and about ten o'clock de next day I began to come around. I realized he was there and he asked me if I knew him which I did.

"In 'blowing fire', my grandfather simply blew on de burn and de fire and pain was gone. It was a secret charm, handed down from generation to generation. He said only one could be told. He told my Aunt Harriet and she could 'blow fire' de same as my grandfather.

"I remember one good old doctor in dis part of de country. Old Dr. Stark. He was as good a doctor, de finest we had in those days. He could chew tobacco and spit enough to drown a hog. A lot of de old herb remedies my grandfather used, I can still remember. He used one called 'white root'. It is a bush dat grows here. In de spring of de year, when its leaves bloom out, in de morning hours, when de sun shines on it, it looks just like bright tin. It has an awful bitter taste. It was used for mighty near any ailment. He had another herb, he used, called 'remedy weed'. It is a bright green looking weed dat grows around springs. It is also used for many ailments. Another one was sarsaparilla root. It grows here, lots of it. He went to de woods and gathered it all hisself getting wild cherry bark, ditney, penny royal, and camomile root. Others he gathered and dried some to make teas and others to put in whiskey.

"Dogwood buds, some kind of a medicine used as a laxative. Ginseng was another remedy. I do not know what it was used for, but it was powerful good, and one remedy he used was called 'spicewood'. It was also a healthful drink, like store tea. You gather it in de fall, using de stem or stocky part, break it up and dry it. I used it all de time while I worked on de river, at de tourist camps. It has a fine flavor and it's good for you.

"Indian turnip grows by de thousands in de woods here. Great places of it, looks like turnips, grows in big bunches and bright red. Colored folks used to use de Indian turnip in slave times. Dey would take dis and dry it, pulverize it and tie it in big quantities around their feet to keep off de trail of bloodhounds. No bloodhound could trail a bit further after smelling it. It was strong like red pepper, burns like everything and colored folks running away use it all de time.

"Grandfather also used 'butter nut root', some call it white walnut. You take one dose of dis and it will cure de worst case of chills, no matter how bad. Take two tablespoons for a dose. It is as severe as croton oil. By golly, it won't leave a thing in you, clears you out and one dose does de work. Oh, man, but it is bitter.

"He used golden seal, a medicine found in places here, very costly, worth $7 to $8 a pound now. I don't know what he used dem all for, but I do remember of him getting dem in their proper season, and kept dem always on hand.

"For sore throat or quinsy, he had some sort of tea. He used onion tea, too. He took an onion, roasted it in its hull in ashes, squeezed out de juice and added a little sugar and gave it to de patient. For rheumatism, he used poke root, dried it and put it in whiskey. De only thing dat is good for rheumatics. There were many more remedies, but I can't recall them now."

United States. Work Projects Administration

ANN STOKES

*Interview with "Aunt" Ann Stokes,
91 Years old, Caruthersville, Missouri.*

One of the most interesting characters of all Pemiscot County today is an old negro called "Aunt" Ann Stokes. She was born a slave "out hyar at Cottonwood Pint in 1844, a year of high water". Nineteen thirty-six brings her to her ninety third year; all of which have been spent in Pemiscot County, except for an occasional visit to relatives. In the early years of her life she was known as "a good hard workin' nigger". Now she takes things more quietly, especially since she has lost her eyesight and can only hear when you shout very loudly. All day long she does very little, just "sits and rocks." For a very old woman she is certainly fine looking. Most old people are usually wrinkled. Aunt Ann looks to be only in her sixties.

A sort of creepy feeling comes to one in the presence of this old negro. She always leans close to you as she speaks, lays her hand on your arm, now and then pointing her finger. Once and awhile she smiles showing her few remaining teeth in Graiae fashion. She speaks slowly in a high voice not at all shaky. Every story she tells is glorified and exaggerated. She is anxious to talk and likes to have visitors. Never does she fail to mention her first "schoolin'"; she tells, "I learnt my alphabet in de middle ob a field unnerneath a 'simmon tree. My cousin teached me, you know we weren't 'lowed to hab books in dem days. They didn't want us to know nothin'". When you mention the War Between the States, you have hit a favorite subject of hers. Especially, does she pride herself on her war stories.

At Cottonwood Point she remembers standing on the bank of the river to "see transpots goin' south. Done busted through up north here. Fom de steam ob de boats we was uz wet us if we'z a-standin' in a shower ob rain. Sa many soldiers dat dey wuz all standin aroun de pilot houses. Dey wuz goin' to Fort Pillar on a hill in Tennessee. Sech a shootin' as day was when dey turn dem cannons loose. Ize tol dat fur three mile down de river you couldn't tell if it's blood or water.

"An ol' soldier tol' me how dey capture Vicksburg. Dey put a man on a ol' skint-up mule an send him to de fort to spy. When he got thar he say he's a-runnin' way fom de Yankees. He's so pitiful lookin' an' so naked he couldn't hide his nakedness: so dey took him in. He stay aroun' de fort fur three days lookin' at everthing. He seen how it wuz all fixed. Den one mornin' he come up missin' and dey try to git on de track ob him. But it warn't no use 'cause one mornin' de man who'd been on de ol' skint-up mule come back wid sum Yanks an' took de fort."

"You cud allas hyar de Yankees at Kennett or Hornersville wen day's aroun'. One day I'ze over to see Melindy and I say: 'Melindy, does you all hyar sompin? Soun' like de Yankees, look out de winder and see if you sees anything.'

"She say, 'I don' see nothin'. Dey ain't no Yankees aroun' hyar.'

"Well, I jest sit thar 'till I caint stan' it no more. I gets up and looks out de winder myself. Thar dey come down de road and I knows theys Yanks 'cause I see de blue ob de coats. Pretty soon dey ride up to de house. Dey yell out: 'You all got any Gurrillers aroun' hyar?'

"Me an' Melindy stan' in de doah. I say, 'Melindy you go out dar an tell 'em.'

"Melindy start across de yard when de leader yell, 'I don' want you! De truf ain't in your yaller body.' (Melindy was a mulatto girl) 'Hey! you, you other girl, come hyar!'

"'Yes suh,' I say an' walk out de doah in de yard.

"'Got any Gurrillers aroun' hyar?', he yell.

"'No suh!' sez I, 'Taint non aroun' hyar.'

"'Know Mr. Douglass?', he say pointin' his finger to a house 'cross de prairie.

"'Yes suh,' siz I, 'I knows him wen I sees him.'

"'Has he got any Gurrillers thar?'

"'I don't know, suh.'

"'Wal, thars a collad girl thar ain't they?'

"'Yes suh, but I don' go round her no mo. We ain't speakin'. Reckon I ain't been on Mr. Douglasses place foah six month. I don't know nothin' 'bout it. You all better go see fur youshsevs.'

"He leab den an ride ovah to Douglasses place. I seen Bud come out in de yard. He call Bud ovah to de fence and talk to him. 'Bout dat time I see men comin' out de back ob de house an chargin' ovah de fence into de thicket whar warn't nothin' but lots ob trees, tare blanket, an blackberry bushes. Right den and dare dey had a scrummage. De Yanks set fire to ever' buildin' on de place. De blaze wuz a-goin' up to de elements! Not a thing did they take out ob de house ceptin' feather bed for a wounded Yankee.

"Mr. Douglass, he hear about de shootin'. He tuk to de woods an stay fur a spell."

"I ain't had nothin' scare me so bad as one time I went down to de lot to feed. A big ol' black cat run right in font ob me and jump up on de corn. Dar he sat, sech a big cat, good big twice! Wal, it scairt me so I started to bleedin' at de nose. I come back home as fas as I could. The ol' Doc he couldn't stop it, I couldn't stop it, seem like nobody can stop it. My blood bled so much it look de color ob sassafras tea. De second day Emma, she my daughter say, 'De black cat done gone. I cain't fin' it nowhere.'

"Den my nose stop bleedin!'"

"What's a cure fur Rheumitize you say? They's jus one cure for dat, I knows! Ain't I had it so bad I couln't raise up to step ovah a fence ral? Take a raw irish potato and pack it in your pocket. One day I'ze walkin' down de street an I meets Mr. Huffman. I say, 'Mr. Huffman, how's your Rheumatize?'

"He say, 'Aunt Ann, 'taint no better. I thinks I go down to Hot Springs fur a spell.'

"'Humph,' says I, 'Don' you go way down dar to git well. You don't hab to do dat. You git you a raw Irish potato and carry it wid you all de time. Wen you change yoah pants, change dat potato ober to de clean pants. Wen de potato git dry clean through, you won't hev no more Rheumatize.'

"Nex' time I see him he say hez fine. Now ain't dat proof enough dat potatoes cure Rheumitizm?"

"One mawnin' I gets up to make a fish in de stobe. It's fearful cold an de moon is still a-shinin'. I put on my coat an start to work. While de stove am heatin' up I looks out de winder. I see sompin' queer lookin' out in de garden, sompin' standin' 'bout knee high all bright and shiny. I wonder what kin' ob a ghost has got loose now. I takes a broom an sneaks out de doah. Kinda haf shets may eyes kaze I'ze scairt to death. Wham! I hits dat ting an scatters it all ovah de place. Warn't nothin' but an ol' cabbage, a po frozen cabbage!"

"Does I know Ol' Mexico Cole? Yessum, I reckon I do. He us a dawk man, a tolable dawk man, wid black hair an dawk eyes. He us what you say a medium built man. Yessah, Ol' Mexico Cole! He wuz a doctah. I 'member de night he wuz on his way home wen de storm cum up. De lighten lightened an de thunder thundered! Sho' wuz a powful storm! He'z a-ridin' along on his hoss wen all ob a sudden a big lim' done fall off a tree an smash him flat. Dat's mighty bad, I tell yo, mighty bad. Yessuh, ol' Mexico Cole, I 'members him.

"One time he walk on a tradin' boat an he see a bottle full ob sompin' he don't know what. He picks it up an smell a deep breaf. Dat really frowed him out fur a spell. Dey had to give 'em a half a bottle ob melted grease! Yessum, I 'members Ol' Mexico Cole."

Two of Aunt Ann's favorite songs are:

I

"By'm by don' you griebe atter me
(This line repeated four times)

II

Wen I'm gone don' you griebe atter me
" " " " " " " "
" " " " " " " "
By'm by don' you griebe atter me.

III

De Lawd has prepared de way an
has carried my soul away
(This line repeated three times)
By'm by don' you griebe atter me.

IV

Wen I'm dead don' you griebe atter me
(This line repeated three times)
By'm by don' you griebe atter me."

The second song is sung by a "mighty clevah woman" to her lover. The negro woman is at home rocking her baby, her husband is sitting not far away. A weird little whistle is heard. The negro woman sings to warn her lover of danger.

> "Oh, de win's in de wes',
> An' de cuckoo's in de nes',
> No lodgin' hyar foah you,
> By you baby by yoo.
>
> Oh, de devil's in de man,
> Cain't you unnerstan',
> No lodgin' hyar foah you,
> By you baby by yoo.
>
> (Repetition of the first verse.)"

United States. Work Projects Administration

EDWARD TAYLOR

> Interview with Edward Taylor,
> St. Louis, Missouri.
> (Written by Grace E. White,
> St. Louis, Mo.)

Born "Around 1812"

The subject of this sketch is Edward Taylor, exact age not known, but he is positive he is over 115 years old. He lives in a two room frame cottage in the rear of 8013 Dale Avenue, St. Louis County, Missouri, with his wife of less than twelve months and says she is in her 50's.

Taylor is a tall, slender, almost erect old man, looks well for his age, very hard of hearing, his hair well mingled with gray. He believes God has called him to preach holiness to the world, and it is a hard matter to keep his mind on an interview for his ex-slave experiences instead of preaching to his interviewer. His story follows:

"I was born in Cheneyville, Louisiana. I guess around 1812. But I don't know. I do know, I was owned by Marse William Chaney. He was a rich old slave owner. I thought in dem days white folks was God, didn't know no better.

"I 'member well when de stars fell, I saw 'em twixt midnight and day and tried to ketch some of 'em. I was grown, too, most. I wasn't scared 'cause I thought long as I staid where de white folks was, dey would protect me from all harm, even de stars in de elements, storms, or what not, just stay near de white folks and I had nothing to worry about. I thought white folks made de stars, sun and everything on de earth. I knowed nothing but to be driven and beat all de time. I seed em take de bottom rail out of de rail fences and stick de nigger's head in de hole den jam de balance of de fence down on his neck, and beat him till he's stiff. Den I seed 'em put 40 or 50 slaves in stock and as high as 300 at a time and punish 'em, till some of 'em died. It was terrible. Chaney done his slaves so bad when he taken down sick, he just suffered till de skin dropped off his bones. Nobody do any thing for him but me, everybody, even his own folks was scared of him, didn't want to touch him he looked and smelt so bad. But I just stuck hard by him till he died. I took care of Jeff Davis for years, long fore he ever got president of des United States. Yes sir, I did. When de stars fell people all runnin' and hollerin' judgment done come. I didn't see no need in all dat 'citement, as long as de white folks livin' I thought they could keep us niggers livin'.

"I used to hear de white folks readin' de paper 'bout de war, and readin' de Yankees beaten 'em, and I wondered what de world is Yankees. I thought dey talking 'bout birds of de air or sumpin'. After while Essex Gun Boat got all de South to Vicksburg. I found out den what Yankees was. Yes, sir, I did. My slave owners would make de blacksmith make buck horns and fasten 'em like a crown on de slave women's heads and brad 'em on dere so dey would know 'em by dat mark. Dey was so tight and heavy for dem women to carry around dey often times swell up dere head so dey couldn't hardly see out dere eyes.

"I worked naked most my time I didn't know nothing 'bout pride. Dey had looms some places to make hemp coats and jackets. I had to make rails, drive wagons, and make cross tires in a blacksmith shop. We had to have a pass to go any place. De patrollers would git us and make us show our pass, and we got to be in our cabin by 9 o'clock. I got one pound of fat meat a week. If you got sick de doctor tell you to not lie to the old Marse or old Miss and you git all right. After de war was over I had to cut two cords of wood at night and work all day for one penny, and we could buy a ginger cake long as I was tall nearly and it last us all week. You could git it for a penny and we called it a stage plank. It was long and thin. I never kin forgit when old Marse William Chaney died. We fell to his brother Marse George Chaney. De wife I married belonged to de same people owned me. Marse George chained a host of dem niggers together and sold 'em, and bought some more. He bought four wid my wife at one time but he sold 'em in droves. Marse William owned us by de hundreds. I 'member I was 30 years old when I married. My wife had two chillin but dey dead long ago. I don't know how old my wife was when I married her though. I know dis here wife I got now since she was a baby. We jes' been married less dan a year. I am de first colored man to own a piece a ground in Lincoln Terrace, and de oldest man, white or black, to ever apply for a marriage license in the State of Missouri. I owns dis whole block from Dale to Harter Avenue and am taking care of four families living on my property, dat don't pay me a penny, and haven't for years. I never been to school a day in my life. Just trustin' God for my gittin along, and my understandin'. An automobile run over me two years ago and I had another accident in Jefferson City, Missouri one year ago, but am still able to go and preach the word of God.

United States. Work Projects Administration

TISHEY TAYLOR

Interview with Mrs. Tishey Taylor, age 77, Poplar Bluff, Missouri.

"I wusn't very old during slave time but I worked, yes sir, I did, and my por 'mammy chile', it wus from daylight ta' dark, and on good light nights it wus way up in the night. Mah mammy's name was 'Katie', Katie-Cherry, an ma father wus William Walturf, or somethin' like 'at, never did know good 'cause he never stayed wif us in our cabin no how and we never knowed him much.

"Shap Phillips wus our marster and he brought my parents 'fore I wus bawn, frum Frank Parker, (we jus said 'Ol Parker',) and brought us from Woofalton to New Madrid County. 'Ol Man Shap', (that what we call him,) had two sons, one name 'Amos' and one name 'Little Murry'. I took care 'Little Murry' fer ma, 'Task' and I warn't much biggner him but did I let him git hurt? Not me chile!

"'Ole Man Shap' owned 'bout two, three hundred us slaves and he had cabins built all over and around his plantation. This house is por nuf' but then we jes had one little room and 'irt floos and no windas, sometime jus holes out.

"Some them slaves cooks in their cabin, not what they wanted but what 'Marse' gibd 'em, most times wus beans an' 'tators and corn bred and milk, and some times 'round hog killin' time he pass out the 'jowl meat'.

"I jest don' 'member but it seems we did eat three times a day. I wus allays so glad to hear dat bell ring else a horn blow. Youse seed that kind of shell like calded 'Konk horn'—and could that 'nigger' blow lowd!

"Mammy cooked in the big house for 'Marse', and then som' time when her work was done in there she was took to the fields and lef' me and my brother and sister by our selves 'till she come and som' time when she did com' she would run in scared-like and lock de door and motion us quiet and say, 'Dey will think I'se sleep'. I didn't understand all that stuff den but fore long I did understan' what I'se tellin yu.

"'Nother thing our beds wus poor stuff, but mammy said she wus allays 'dog tired' and could 'a slep on the ground. They wus straw ticks and hard. Law no, chile, we didn't known what springs wus.

"One day I 'member bad, 'Ol Man Shap' sol' granma, she was mammy's mammy and all we ever hear, she was sol' down souf. We knowed not to do no takin' on for if'n we did the hide would got tooken off us.

"Mammy used to card wool and cotton and spin, then she would weave goods. I 'member one time, I wus little, I played 'rat under de loom'. I would crawl up and grab mammy and say 'e-e-e-k', and pinch her. She say, 'I'll puts a stop to that "rat" bothering me when I got work to do!' That didn' stop me but she sho' make me wish it had the nex' time I do it.

"I never knowed Sunday from Monday, 'cept on Sunday the white man come and we are called out under the brush arbor, didn' have no work in the fiel' at day, and he stand up 'fore us and preach out a little green-back book; I didn't know what it was then, but I knows now it was a Bible. I 'member every 'preach day' he say, 'Mind you not to steal from Missis or Marster'. He was plenty strong on that part.

"Well do I 'member dat 'nigger' overseer, big, 'smart aleck'; he wus called de 'nigger driver'. He say 'hurry up there, you get the hide split on you lazy back'. I wusn't hardly big enouf but the bigger ones when they wus gib a task to do, they better do it in a hurry else they would get the 'hide split' and some time salt put on.

"I never had no book larnin' 'cept two, three times when Miss Fanny La Forge, she wus the white school teacher, and she tried to larn me, she didn' have much time and couldn' do much with it. But I allays says, 'Give me good ol' common horse sense', and not braggin, Miss, but I have got that; always did have. Mos' these educated ones are smarty, big head, smarty, and I never did want to be that way 'tall.

"If they wus jails then fo us slaves I never seed one, jes whippin' fo' punishin', some one wus gittin' it all the time.

"'Ole Parker' like mammy and all her people and he tol' 'Ol Man Shap' if'n he lashed my mammy and her family he would com' and take us back, 'cause we wus good and didn't need no punishment but that was the only reason that we wusn't lashed like the rest of them.

"I was tellin' you about Sunday meetin', none of us had a Bible 'cept the white man, and I don't know where he got it from. I never did have one 'cept once and it burned up in my house in Advance. I liked to look through it but I didn't know a word it said.

"Times it seems I can hear them sing, I didn't sing much at the meetin' 'cause I was too little, but the others sang, 'Hark From the Tomb', and 'I am a Soldier of the Cross'. When the preacher man shook he haid and stomp his feet and yell, I say to mammy: 'What that man mammy? What he doin?' And she say: 'Hush', and put her hand over my mouf. I knowed plenty well to stay hushed too. Any babtising went on I never seed any of it, never knowed nothin' 'bout anything lak that then.

"The older ones had some fun too about that time, maybe once week or more some one get 'mission' from his Marster and gib a 'hoe down!' (calls dance now.) Any one that went from all the close plantations got 'mission' from the Marster or overseer to go but they had to be home at a certain time or they would wish they hadn't went and some time they would slip off and go out mission', if ever they wus caught they got 'it', and plenty of it. I heard sister say, 'Mammy I would like to go to the hoedown tonight'. Mammy say: 'Think you can come back in time?' Sister say, 'Don' know mammy,' then mammy say, 'Better save your sef chile'. Then sister say, 'Well, I better go to bed then'. But you could hear the fiddle and the hollerin' all over, and 'twas hard to stay 'way.

"At Christmas time we knowd 'bout that and both of mammy's owners gib her a good time. 'Ol Man Shap' alluys gib us a pair of stockings and some candy and apples. For the men folks they sometimes get whiskey. New Year's was 'bout the same and I don' 'member no other holidays.

"When we got sick they was a white doctor way off somewhere that would come, if he wus sent fo', but mos' de time 'Old Uncle Nee John' and 'Uncle Jake' would conjure us; they was called 'Voo-Doo's'. One time sister stepped up in the meat house do'r and hurt her foot, don' know how, Mammy tell Marster and he say, 'Tell Jake he come', an' I wus allus' 'fraid of him and he say to sister, 'Gal, get up and walk'. She say: 'I cain't.' He set back down and go 'M-m-m-m-m', for a longtime and than say: 'Gal, I say get up and walk'. She say: 'I can't'. I was so scared and mammy say to me, 'Set still there Gal, he ain't gwine to hurt you no how', but he look so wild and mean and the next time he mumble words over her foot she get up and walk. He have us wear a dime around our necks fo' somethin'; don' know what tho'. I was allus such a fool 'bout money. I just liked to wear it and didn' care.

"When some one died we didn't know what wus don' with 'em but sometime they wus took out in the night and I heard some wus hauled off in a little push-thing and throwed in the river and some wus put in a hole with their clothes on.

"'Bout that time we begin to hear stories of bein' set free. The slaves sang at their work all day.

"'Thank God Almity, I'll be free some day', (there are 'bout all the words I can 'member). They sang this over and over and made a pretty song too. Nearer time for us to be freed, the owners get meaner all the time. Some took their slaves down in the cane brakes and hid them; others wus kept working. 'Ol Man Shap' tell some, 'When you get free I give you home and pay you for your work'. I guess he would too if'n he had stayed there.

"Them 'Blue Coats' (Northern Soldiers), wus lots meaner than the 'Brown Coats (Gray), in the South. Them 'Blue Coats' come in and steal your chickens and cook them over your fireplace and eat them right 'fore your eyes. I 'member one time the 'Brown Coats' come and wanted sister. I squalled like a panther. During and after the war, them 'Guerillas' was a sight, dey steal, kill, and tear up, everywhere. The 'K.K.K.' was a powerful, mean, bunch and dey would com' ater night and take people out and whip them; ah didn't know what for.

"I well 'member the day we wus freed, every one sang, 'Thank God Almity, I'm free at last, free at last, free at last, thank God Almity, I'm free at last, I'm free at last.'

"'Ol Man Shap' was mad and he whipped some of his slaves and de took him to de town jail, last I seed of him he wus sittin' in the town jail winder, maybe died there, I don' know. After we wus free there wus plenty of work, they couldn't whip nobody and had to pay us for the work. Mammy cooked for Mr. Hunter and 'Riley' and 'Dalton'. She kept me with her 'till I got 'old 'nouf to cook and then I lef' and got a job away from der somewhere.

"I got married 'bout 40-50 years ago to 'Baltimore' here. He is 105 years old now. He tells me his old Miz' thought he was an 'Angle' and he wus almost 36 years old when the war broke out. He wus from Lotterville County, Tennessee. He tell me people just thought bountiful of him and they seemed to be a welcome all over the world for him.

"He says he was called one of the finest barbers in the world, all was a natural gift and 'man out of sight'; he barbered thousands and thousands. His mother wus from Georgia and her name was 'Liza' and she married Jim Taylor. Me and 'Baltimore' had eleven children since we been married. They was Charlie, he dead, Martha, living, and not got any kids, and Tony, dead, and Louisa and Gussie, dead. How many that—five? Rosie dead, and left six children, part of them are here, 'Little Baltimore' and Henry are dead, Roosevelt is living and here at home and Robert is in a C.C. Camp, but David works in a fine hotel in St. Louis, don' know what one the name is.

"'Ol Man Abe Lincoln' was a fine ol' man, and I liked him, he never freed us; but tol' us how. But 'Booker', and Jefferson Davis wusn't no friend to the colored man that I knowed anything 'bout.

"It is best to be free if you carry your self right you'll be free all you days. I belongs to the Saints Church, t'aint the 'Holy Roller' and I allys wus 'ligious but I don' know much 'bout stuff, never put no study on it.

"Ise just a poor old 'nigger' slave that is waitin' for the Good Lord to come and take me home and it won't be long chile; no, 'Granny' ain't got long."

LOUIS THOMAS

Interview with Louis Thomas,
St. Louis, Missouri.

Slave Hitched To Plow

The subject of this sketch is Louis Thomas, 93 years of age who lives at 3007 Clark Avenue with his oldest daughter, Laura Richardson and family.

In the middle room of a 3-room brick apartment laid Louis Thomas, confined to his bed, with a severe cold, but kind enough to be interviewed by the writer. The old man was clean and quite composed and said he had been interviewed so often it was a common thing to him. He was 6 feet tall and weighed 174 when taken sick. The home was very poorly furnished but clean. He is of dark complexion with white hair. He said:

"I was born in Pickens County, Alabama, May 9, 1844. My mother's name was Tama and my father's was Thomas Windom. Our owner was Levy Windom. I had 2 sisters and 2 brothers. I married Caroline Windom. She was owned by the same folks I was, we had 11 children but only 2 is living. The oldest one, Laura Richardson, I am living with. The other daughter's name is Evergreen Richardson, living at 3100 Clark Avenue. Dey are both Richardson's but dere husbands are not related.

"I been living in St. Louis since 1923. When I was a slave, I had to plow barefooted, hooked to a double horse plow. For 8 or 10 years of dat time we had a white overseer in de summer. I did not only plow barefooted but naked as well. In de winter dey allowed me a few clothes but not many. I worked from daylight until dark, I didn't know nothing 'bout time.

"Making and gathering crop was my biggest task. We made 500 bales of cotton a year, besides growing wheat, potatoes and other vegetables for the hands. I stayed on de plantation till way after de Civil War was fought. If de slaves could get as near as East St. Louis and Ohio with out getting caught, dey would join de Yankees and help fight for freedom. But the Rebs wouldn't think of giving slaves any guns, as mean as they had been to us.

"Dey knew too well, we would shoot dem first thing. I remember well I was in Tuscaloosa, Alabama and dere was a speech made dere by General Forest on a Sunday. He said, 'Dere ain't a Yankee in 500 miles of Tuscaloosa, Alabama.' So de Rebs was so happy 'bout dat, dey started early de very next morning putting de flooring back in de bridge dey done took out so de Yankees couldn't cross and get to them.

"The following Tuesday night, de very next day I mean, don't you know, dem Yankees come in our town cross dat very bridge. That same night old Marse made us hitch up all his horses and git up all de flour, meat and everything we done raised, and carry it up Tom Bilby River. It was a swamp, to hide it from de Yankees. But, honey, dat didn't do a bit of good, dem Yankees got all our stuff and us, too, and destroyed everything he had. Us slaves was so mad at Old Marse, we helped 'em git rid of everything, den went on back home, we had no where else to go, and de war wasn't over and we hadn't nary a penny of money, child. No we didn't.

"I made my last crop in 1867 on dat very plantation where I lived all my days. Of course we was free den or supposed to be free. Dey promised to pay us, but we never got nothin', least not yet, Marse ain't paid me, and he's dead now. In March 1868 dey sent to de field for all us hands to come up to de house to sign a contract. We all went. We was so used to minding old Marse when he sent for us we just mind right on like it was still slavery. So I had always been mighty handy 'bout most things so he wanted me 'bove de others, so he took my hand, put it on his pen and held it right dere and signed my name hisself. I got mad as a wet hen 'bout dat agreement he read to me. So he tried to make me feel good saying he was goin' to give me half. I knowed better.

"I felt dere was going to be some trouble up to de house, so I had a pistol in my pocket, that had been dropped by the Yankees on purpose to help us slaves shoot our way out. So I just told my old boss I ain't goin' to do it, and when he raised up at me I just whipped out dat pistol and everything in sight got out of my way. I was mad a plenty, and I already always had plenty of temper. So while I had everybody scared and excited I left and never did go back. I went to Columbus, Mississippi, and stayed until 1923. All dat time I done share cropping farming and made good. When I left dere I came to St. Louis and have not worked since. I was too old for a job, but sister, I worked many a day for two bits a day and churned all day to get milk to drink 'cause I couldn't get no other food. I cut grass—mowed after share cropping days were over.

"I never had any schooling. What learning I got I

picked up hearing the children. I have 22 grandchildren, 9 great grandchildren. The first 3 years in St. Louis I lived with my daughter Evergreen Richardson at 3100 Clark Avenue. I am a member of The Church of God in Christ, on Leffingwell and Bernard Street."

JANE THOMPSON

>Interview with Mrs. Jane Thompson,
>Fredericktown, Missouri.

"I gets a pension from de Civil War. Wilson Thompson, my husband, fought for seven years. He fought de Indians in de west. I gets $40.00 a month. I have 21 grandchildren and 6 great grandchildren. I was de mother of 6.

"My first boss sold my mother and I can remember her climbin' upon de stile block made from de trunk of a gum tree. Dis was down in Zuca, Mississippi, and de trees grew big down there. My boss was my father, they claim. De boss was purty cruel. Our second boss did not believe in slavery but his wife did. One of de daughters of de boss married and I went with her as a slave. Then my boss, Burgess, was a Baptist preacher and he would travel 'round. I would pick cotton, den I did de house work.

"I had two uncles dat ran off and nebber came back. Dey joined de war. De Ku Klux Klan would come and claim dey could drink a bucket of water. That was done so dey could get us to come out to dem. They would be four or five in a gang. I 'member de soldiers comin' and killing chickens and throwing them in de kitchen an having us to cook dem.

"I 'member how de freedom come but we were taught fer a long time not to know anything 'bout slavery. De only thing I knew 'bout it was bad times. Even de boss would not let me stay in de house when he had family prayers. At night before bedtime I would have to seed cotton and I would nod from getting sleepy and den de boss would knock me over de head. But I'm so glad de good Lord let me stay here to do something. I've raised about 30 children. Most of my work as a slave was spent helping de mistress, picking up her hankerchief, cleaning up de house, etc. Sometimes I think slavery was a test dat de lord has us to go through. It was through God dat Lincoln was given de brains and de talent. I would find different friends to take me in after de war. Sometimes I would have only two dresses.

"I tell de old folks dat we is having slavery again. But de depression is not as hard as slavery 'cause de government is helping de people now. After de war we had parched wheat for coffee and corn meal with de husks in it. Old Burgess' children helped me to learn to spell. De Boss would make me spell words backwards. I remember a song, "Let's go down to de water an be baptized", and 'Bound fer de promised land'. My Uncle would play his guitar in his cabin at night. At Christmas dey would have a dance on de plantation. We used to hang up our stockings and get a little candy at Christmas time."

SARAH WAGGONER

> Interview with Aunt Sarah Waggoner,
> Savannah, Missouri.
> (Written by G.K. Bartlett of Kansas City Office
> from FC by Dovie Rose.)

A familiar figure in Savannah, Missouri is that of an aged, bent and withered Negro woman with a little patch of white whiskers on her chin, a cap on her head winter and summer; who is seen almost daily pulling a little red wagon along the streets.

"Aunt Sarah Waggoner", as she is called, lives alone in a small unpainted house, almost a hut, near the right-of-way of the Chicago Great Western Railroad; about three blocks southeast of the courthouse.

The yard as well as the house is cluttered with all kinds of junk, odds and ends which Aunt Sarah has picked up as she meanders through the town. She has been a fixture in Savannah for many years and has the friendship of the white people, who commend her faithfulness and religious fervor.

"How be you?" she asked pleasantly when answering my knock at her door. When it was explained that her recollections about slave life before the war were wanted, she beamed delightedly.

"Yes'm. Come on in an' set, an' soon's I fix the fire I'll tell you everything about slave times. Everything I kin remember."

She wiped off a chair for her visitor, then busied herself at the old wood and coal cook stove, where some vegetables were simmering in an antiquated iron kettle, and "fat meat" was frying in the skillet.

"I was a slave," she stated. "I was born in Kentucky. In Grayson or Hardin County. I don't know which 'zactly, 'cause we lived in both counties; an' I never did think to ask ole Miss Howard who raised me; and I forgot to ask my mother if she knowed, and I don't think she knowed." Sarah paused for a moment, then continued plaintively, "I wish I knowed for sure."

"Who was old Miss Howard?"

"She was white folks. I was raised by de Howards. Mr. and Mrs. Jim Howard. They owned me. We called him Pap, and her Old Miss. My mother's name was Waggoner. She belonged to Mr. Howard too. My father he belonged to another man and lived on a farm near us. No mam, no'm, we was never sold. I'll tell you how 'twas. You see, Mr. Howard's father—he came over from England. He called all his sons to his bedside at de last and gave each of them some of de colored people and told them to take good care of them and never to let them be sold. I had a cousin, June, who was sold here at de courthouse door in Savannah. Him and another boy was sold down South.

"The Howards brought me from Kentucky to Missouri. That was befo' de war. I've been here a long time. I'm 93 years old.

"Sure I know how old I is", she remonstrated.

"I's 93 years old right now (1937). And I knows my birthday too. I knows it for sure. It come on February

17th. I'se sure about dat, for it comes so close to dat of Abe Lincoln. His birthday is February 12th."

Memories of the past surged through Aunt Sarah's mind and awakened emotions. She rose to her feet, and speaking with the enraptured ecstasy of her race when roused by religious fervor, testified.

"I knowed about Abe Lincoln, 'cause his cousin Cap Lincoln; Yes, Cap Lincoln, lived right nigh us in Kentucky. And he sure was a fine man!

"I knowed about Abe Lincoln befo' he ever run for president. Long befo' he was 'sasinated. You see, I lived neighbor to some of his kin folks. Yes ma'am! Oh, yes, ma'am! Long befo' de war!"

"Yes, Oh Lord! Yes, ma'am!

"Abe Lincoln was jes' next to Jesus Christ.

"Yes, Oh Lord! Yes! Dat he was!

"Jes' next to Jesus Christ!

"I remember when I was freed!"

The exaltation of Aunt Sarah dimmed and faded, and with a quavering subdued voice she whispered:

"I wish I knowed. I wish I knowed. Abe Lincoln was born in Hardin County;[3] in the same month I was; almost the same day. I wish I knowed was I born in the same county he was, but I ain't never goin' to know. Yes ma'am, I was moved with the Howards from Kentucky," she continued, "right up to the Nodaway River, about ten miles from Savannah. It took us about six weeks to come with oxen. I saw the emigrant trains goin' through to Californy.

[3] *Abraham Lincoln was born in Larue County, Kentucky, February 12, 1809.*

"That was befo' de war. I'se been here a long time. I'm 93 years old. I'se been here since de woods burned, and I'm goin' to be here a long time yet, 'cause my mother was a hundred and fifteen 'fore she died.

"My, but the Indians was thick when I fust come here. And there was buffalo; and there was deer; and there was quail jes' thick. I wasn't skeered none of de Indians, and I ain't skeered of nothin' now. No, ma'am. 'Cause why? 'Cause de white folks put de fust clothes on me, and fed me; and they been doin' it ever since.

"You wants to know what kind of clothes did we wear in them days? I'm gwine to tell yer. I jes' had two dresses. De best one was made out of plain, white muslin. I went out in de woods and got walnut bark to color it brown.

"I allus had to wash it on Saturday, 'cause we all had to go to church on Sunday. Yes'm, I went to de white folks' church, and part of de time I was de only nigger gal there. Then I had another dress and a shirt. I made them jes' like Old Miss taught me. Dat was my work dress. It was made with a cord 'round de bottom, a cord as big as my little finger, so's I couldn't tear it; 'cause I went over fences like a deer.

"De shirt was made like a long petticoat. In de winter old Miss made us stockings out of yarn, and we had brogan shoes. Didn't you never see any brogan shoes?" queried Aunt Sarah. "Don't you know what dey looked like? Huh. Dey was neither lined or bound; and we used a peggin' awl to make holes for the laces. Some of 'em had copper toes."

"Didn't they hurt your feet?"

"Yes'm, but if dey did hurt, we had to wear 'em anyway. Dem old brogans; I'm sure glad they're gone.

"Durin' de war, old Miss keep tellin' me I had to help her put new cloth in de loom and when little Jane, tha's her little girl, wanted me to play, her mother would say, 'Sarey has to work fast now, 'cause she goin' to be free'.

"Oh Lord, Miss, Sarey will never be free. But I was freed. Now I am goin' to tell you about de home life.

"I worked in de house for old Miss, and we had plenty to do and plenty to eat. When de white folks was through eatin', I got a pan and got de grub, and set on de floor and et it. Oh Lordee, but I worked hard since I was twelve years old. But not in de fields. Old Miss she say dere was plenty for me to do in de house, and dere was, sure 'nough.

"I washed and cooked for all of us. And ironed too. I het de irons, great big old irons, in de fireplace. I ironed on a quilt spread out on de floor, and I ironed jes' as nice as anybody. I lived right in de house with de white folks. In summer we slept, my brother Henry and me, in a trundle bed in the kitchen; and in de winter made a pallet beside de fireplace.

"Old Pap was good to us. He kept up a fire all night when it was cold. I never saw a cookin' stove or a lace shoe until I was freed. We jes' had to burn our faces cookin' over de fireplace. I milked eight cows and den put de milk away. Dat took a long time. They didn't have no horses then, much. They had a yoke of oxen. Sometimes some of us was hired out to work but we didn't get no money for dat ourselves. Dey drawed de wages.

"No ma'am, dey didn't have no beauty parlors den. Huh. Old Miss never had her hair curled, or anything like that. We didn't know nothin' about face powder and primpin' up in dem days. Huh. Old Miss never used anything on her face 'ceptin' soap and water.

"Yes indeed. We sure did have good times, too. There was dances, and I liked to dance. Uh-huh. I was a regular king ruler at de dances. Many a time I danced till broad daylight, and den when I worked I was so sleepy I'd nod, and nod. Then old Pap he say: 'Go out dere and make Sarey go to bed'. Yes, indeedy, we had good times, too.

"Did I ever get whopped? I never was whopped — much. Old Miss never whopped me, 'cause Pap did all de whopping. He said if dere was any whopping to be done he'd do it. Anyway dey never whopped me—very often, — 'cause I done my work de bes' I could.

"I remember once, when Old Pap started off for St. Joseph, he rode back into de yard and said to old Miss. 'Don't whop Sarey, or let anybody else whop her, or I'll cut the hide off their backs when I gets back.'

"Yes'm, we allus called 'em Pap and Old Miss. Pap wouldn't let me take his name 'cause he was a Republican and believed dat de colored people ought to have their own laws and doctors and all. He was afraid folks would think he was a rebel and de soldiers might kill him. We didn't dare take his name so I took my father's name of Waggoner. He belonged to one of the neighbors in Kentucky and didn't come to Missouri when we did. Yes'm, I had two chilun during de war, a boy, Bob, and a girl, Mary; and later a girl, Minnie. Married? No'm, I never married. I never was married.

"Well, no'm, I didn't have a very hard time after I was freed. Slaves wasn't hardly ever allowed to look in de door of de school house, so we couldn't learn to read and write. When I was freed Pap tried to learn me evenin's to count my fingers. He made me sit by the fireplace and learn to count and learn about money so's de white folks couldn't cheat me after I was free. After I was free one of Mr. Howard's boys taught me my letters and helped me learn to read some.

"After I was freed I went to St. Joseph and did housework. Den I was a chambermaid. After while I came back to Savannah to work for de Price family. Dey was mighty rich and had a big home. Place is still here. I had a fine time there. I remember Mr. Ed. V. Price. He was just a boy when I went there to work, and he did plague me terrible some times. He'd run into the kitchen, grab a handful of cake dough and run outside laughin'.

"Then I got so I couldn't work no more, and he was a rich man, and he always helped me. And he left me in his will ten dollars every month for de res' of my life. Oh yes'm I'm to get my state pension every month. It's goin' to be twelve dollars. I ain't got it yet, but I will fore long. I ain't skeared. 'Cause de white folks put de fust clothes on me, and fed me; and dey been doin' it ever since."

With a weary, dimming of her eyes, old Sarah settled back in her chair, sighed and murmured:

"I been here a long time. I'm 93 years old."

MINKSIE (MINKSY) WALKER

Interview with Minksie (Minksy) Walker,
Poplar Bluff, Missouri.

The following interview pertaining to former slaves and the conditions under which they lived was obtained from Minksie (or Minksy) Walker, seventy-eight years old who lives at the end of Davis Street in a subdivision called New World, Poplar Bluff, Missouri.

"I was one year old when de war broke out and six years old when it closed. I don't remember the day or month I was born, but you can figure out how old I am. My mammy's name was Blanch Walker, de name Walker come from her belonging to Cannon Walker. He had two brothers, Sam and Jimmie, and all their ground run together. I well remembers dem boys and so does every one else. Dey was de best masters in all de south. Put all their slaves together, dey owned about two or three hundred. I don't know how much land dey had but it took a lot to keep all dat many niggers busy.

"I don't know where my parents was born, Old Virginia, I guess, but I was born in seven miles of Dyersburg, Tennessee. My father was Nat Parker and his master was 'Little Dan' Parker. He was kept on de Parker place but mammy got to see him every Sunday morning. Dey lived about five miles from us. Dey didn't get to talk in de evening 'cause de white folks preached for us then. We was called together in de brush arbor by a big bell dey rung.

De arbor was as big as a square block here in town, but dey was so many of us dat we filled it up pretty quick. De meeting was about like it is now 'cept we didn't know half de time what dey was talking about, we couldn't read and learn; had to listen to learn.

"I well remember after meeting mammy would stop and talk with women and she said, 'Minksy, dis is your aunt, my sister. You can walk along home with her'. I was little and I would catch hold her dress tail to keep up. She would meet other women and dey would start talking about de meetin'. First thing I would know dey would be jumpin' up and dancin' around and pattin' their hands until all de grass was wore off slick.

"I didn't have no chance to go to school, but I was a little tad and did not have to work very hard either. I wasn't big enough to hitch up de team of oxen but some big person would and then I sure could drive them, drove all day, and I can remember hauling tobacco to de barns all day. We had several barns tall as dat tree, yonder (tree about 75 feet high.) About all we raised was tobacco. Dat sure 'nough was tobacco country, a little corn for de stock and we raised what we eat.

"De only fighting I remember of during the war was on de farm of Dan Parker. De soldiers met right in de middle of his corn and tobacco field and when dey got through de tobacco was tramped in de ground and you couldn't find a double handful of de corn.

"I have always said I was like a shingle, not like a barrel of snakes. You never saw a crooked shingle and you will never see a straight snake. I have always practiced one thing and dat is telling de truth about all things.

Dat is why I can say I don't know much about de slavery times, I wasn't old enough. I was just a slave and dat is all. I said when I was a small boy, 'Lord, just give me de power to read de Bible, old blue back speller and the hymn book'. He done dis and I know de Bible by heart. I could preach for six years, and never tell all I know. I can't write a word or read anything but dese books. For a while I did preach. I traveled by mission. Didn't own a church of my own and didn't belong to any special one. I guess I must have preached about five years.

"I have been married twice, both my wives are dead. I don't know how old I was when I first married but I had been free many a day. I went to Dyersburg and bought de license. I got drunk and didn' get to Newbern, Tennessee, where my girl lived until de next day. We had two children, a boy and a girl. Dere names was George Earl and George Ella. Dere mother lived nine years and when she died I give them to their grandmother. I told her she could have dem and I would never bother around and I have never seen dem since. Guess they are grown by dis time if dey lived and are still alive, dey are the only kinfolks I have.

"I went to Clinton, Kentucky, and married again. Dat wife just lived a short time and then I moved to Arkansas and lived until thirty years ago when I moved to Butler County and Poplar Bluff. I have lived on dis hill all dat time and sometimes it gets lonesome but when it does I just gets my Bible and reads. I spend lots of time since my mule died, under the shade of dis tree, because I haven't anything to do anymore. I was just thinking de other day in slave times you never seed an old nigger man or woman allowed to rest in the shade. There was some work for dem. De old women took care of de kids and de old men kept clean around the master's door and barn yard.

"Where I was we fared extra fine during slave times. Our master, Cannon Walker, was a Union man. We had plenty pork meat to eat and fared fine. He bought us good clothes and paid all the doctor bills when we got sick. We had good houses too. We had to get up preety soon in de morning but we didn't know nothing then. Our old mistress wanted me to call her boy dat was de same age as me, Marster Tillie. I said, 'No, Mam, when he call me Marster Minksy then I call him Marster Tillie'. Master Cannon Walker did not allow any patrollers to boss his slaves when any of dem was stopped on de pike and ask who dey belonged to all dey had to say was Cannon, Sam or Jim Walker and dey never bothered them.

"My father and oldest brother run away with de Yankees during de war and we never heard of dem anymore. Our master give all de older men a place to raise chickens. He give others poplar trees to make charcoal and dey was allowed to make a little money on de side dis way. I remember hearing mammy tell dat one year he give all his men twenty bushels of corn a piece and dey took it to de still and had whiskey made out of it. They put de barrel in de field and she said there wasn't very much raised that year.

"De slaves did not have to fight in de war but sometimes one would go in to look after his young master. After de war and we was free, mammy hired out to our old master and we stayed on there two years. Den she married and we started moving from place to place. My step-father was a mean man. I couldn't have been more den ten years old when he started hiring me out by de day. I was hungry all de time because I had been used to plenty of pork meat and all he would let me eat was parched corn. One day I was working for Archie Dickerson, I was sick and he ask me what the matter with me. I told him I had been used to meat and my step-father would not let me have any. He called his wife and told her to feed me meat every day, I never will forget him.

"I didn't get any education but I don't care. Lawsy, dis is a free country now, you can either wear shoes or go barefooted. Slave times was alright before de war because we didn't know nothin' better, but I sho' wouldn't like it now. I am an old man now and I get de old age pension, so all I have to do is rest here under the tree and read my Bible."

United States. Work Projects Administration

JAMES WILSON

Interview with James Wilson,
St. Louis, Missouri.

James Lives Alone At 87

Living alone at the age of 87 probably is not a mode of existence that would appeal to many. However, James Wilson, a former slave living in a single room in the rear of 917 O'Fallon Street seemingly takes this little matter of a lonely existence in his stride. James stands quite erect, considering his years and his eyesight is good. His hair is white and he is about six feet tall.

When the writer called to interview him, both he and his room were spotlessly clean. Sitting outside the door of his quarters James' mind wandered back and forth through the years he has lived since he was born on Christmas day, 1850, and, piecing together the bits of information that he could recall, he told the following story:

"I was born in Charleston, South Carolina, December 25, 1850. John Wilson was my owner. He owned more than 700 slaves and a terrible big plantation where he raised cotton, rice, corn, and cattle. Bless your soul, daughter, he was a hard task master, yes he was. He owned big ships, both kinds, for freight and passengers. He kept me running on dem boats from de time I was 10 years old till I was 16. We sailed everywhere. From New York to Rome, Jerusalem, Sweden, France and everywhere under de sun transporting passengers, clothing, cotton, and everything from one country to another. I handled de sails. It certainly was hard work for me because I was so young, but I was an expert wid dem sails just de same. Yes, I was.

"But old President Abraham Lincoln taken me off dat boat, and I fought in de Civil War. I lacked two months of fighting five years. I never even married until 15 years ago, I married a woman 45 years old. After we was married, she decided I was too old for her, so she just went on off with a younger man. I never been de father of a child in my whole life. I git a $13 a month old age pension to live on. Since I been free, I made my living railroading, brakesman and steamboating.

"I voted many times in my life and just can't feel right to vote nothin' but a Republican ticket whether they ever get back in power again. I never did have a political job nor had no friends had any that I know of. I just can't explain how I feel 'bout this generation. Dey jes' ain't doing right, dat's all. Dey jes' doing everything dey is big enough to do. Don't regard nobody, don't care what dey say nor how dey act to their own parents nor nobody else's folks. Dey just sets me to worrying terrible sometimes, wonderin' what on dis earth gonna become of dis here sin-racked generation.

"Dem old Ku Klux was a bad lot of mongrels. Dey catch you out widout a pass dey cut you 100 lashes, and you feel like you ain't able to go nowhere again wid a pass or widout one. After de war was fought, I do know some of dem old slave owners to be nice enough to start der slaves off in freedom wid somethin' to live on till dey get on der feet, but dey wasn't in droves, I tell you dat now, just a mighty precious few. Den der was some others dat kept der slaves in bondage after de war, just like before de war and de slaves, never know till der dying day dat dey was free folks. Far as dat goes, down dere just below Sunflower, Mississippi, and lots of other countryside places in de deep South, dey got slavery right now. De only song I can think of we use to sing so much was: 'O, Lord Remember Me'.

"I can't remember none de other songs. I been all over de world, seen how different races are in dere own lands, and I often sits and wonder if maybe dese little fellows here now running about will see de equal rights dat gits talked about now and den. But, daughter, you and me will never see it. No we won't. I am a member of the Paradise Baptist Church."

United States. Work Projects Administration

MINTIE GILBERT WOOD

Interview with Mintie Wood,
St. Louis, Missouri.

Ex-slave Blind But Happy

The subject of this sketch is Mintie Gilbert Wood, 90 years old. She lives at 4321 West Belle Avenue, St. Louis, Missouri, with her widowed daughter, Emma Swift, 69 years old.

In the living room of a 10 room brick residence located in the better class section of the Negro district of the city, Mintie lives with her oldest daughter and two granddaughters. The old woman has been blind for 8 years. She is quite bent and shows the burden of her years. She is hard of hearing and her mind is no longer keen and alert. Her daughter claims a recent illness has caused the latter trouble. However, the ex-slave very feebly tells the following story.

"I was born down in Bethel, Giles County, Tennessee, September 9, 1847. Marse Carey Gilbert was my owner and I lived on his farm until 1892, when I moved to little Rock, Arkansas. Marse Carey was mighty nice to his slaves and he had a host of 'em. Can't begin to say how many. My old uncle was de overseer of us younguns, about 50 young darkies, and he trained us up till we get a certain age, then they turn us over to the grown up lot, where the white overseer took charge of us. I don't 'member every thing so good, but I do de best I can. I 'member when Marse Gilbert's daughter Miss Rebecca married Marse Maples, they lived 'bout 8 or 10 miles from her daddy's farm, and she use to come home ever so often to visit. She looked so fine de slaves working in de field see her coming dey all stop and rest on der hoe to look at her pass by on her way to see her mamma, and she would tell 'em, you niggers better pray my father never die. Cause if he died, I wouldn't 'low none you niggers to lift your heads from de time you go to work till you quit. My niggers work and never stop. Marse Gilbert gave her 4 slaves as a wedding present, and they had a hard time, but her parents was mighty fine.

"Dey owned so much land, cattle, corn, sorghum, tobacco, millet, barley and everything the very finest kind and the wealth was handed down from one generation of the Gilberts to the other. Dey was so rich dey didn't know how much dey was worth themselves, but dey was altogether different than most of dem slave owners. Dey was prosperous 'cause dey was better folks. When peace was declared everyone of Marse Gilbert's slaves dat had sense enough and did stay wid him, got half of everything they earned turned in on land and stock to be independent right der on de same spot where we had been a slave. And he had so many of his family and darkies, too, he has his own graveyard where everyone of us black or white dat ever been in de Gilbert family can be buried without costing us a penny.

"He owned so much I can't begin to tell it, and nobody else I don't expect. Right now a gang of his old slaves' children is livin' right there owning and working property their parents slaved on, de old Gilbert estate and his folks der wid' em, yes mam. None of us never cared for

Miss Rebecca. She made her slaves eat wid de hogs, even poured der milk in the hog trough and de hogs and slaves ate and drink together. She was worse dan de whole family of Gilberts. I get a blind pension.

"I never did learn to read or write, but my husband was a school teacher and he never was a slave. He was a soldier in the Rebel army. I had 6 children, 6 grandchildren, 3 great grand children and 3 great, great grandchildren. I liked to sew, knit and make quilts fore I was blind. I never used snuff or tobacco in my whole life. I have 2 sisters living, one 82 years old, one 84 years old and a brother 87 years old. Dey all live in Prospect Tennessee, where they were born and raised. My husband died in 1914. Den I went back to Tennessee to live with my father until 1916 when I came to St. Louis to live with my younger daughter Lydia King Davidson until 1920.

"Den I was called back home on account of the death of my father. After the funeral I went to Lonoke, Arkansas, to live with my oldest daughter, Emma Swift and been with her often and on ever since. I only eat 2 meals a day, that's breakfast around 7 o'clock and dinner between 1 and 2 o'clock, the rest of the time I drink plenty water all day and all through the night.

"We moved to St. Louis in the year 1922. I just can't get used to this younger generation. Dey sure is a reckless lot. Cause my life had plenty work 'tached to it. When I was coming along I split rails, hauled wood, raised de white folks family den turned right around and raised my own family.

"I believe in regular hours doing things, work, rest and everything else it takes to make up life. I worked as hard after freedom as I did in slavery. After all we got to work for a livin'. I don't believe in all dis gallivantin' around at night. You ain't fit for no work in de day when you don't rest at night. And I always believe in helping de fellow who needs help and can't help hisself, much as I can. I even ask my neighbors to save me all the old rags and bottles, anything they don't want no more so as I can sell it and git hol' of a little somethin' to help somebody, what ain't got some help like I got. I don't lose nothin' for that, and I get joy out of it. I always keeps my little old pocket book pinned in my pocket to put that little extra change in, and I got it here right now and some change in it, too. I never did vote, and never lived in Virginia nor know nothing about it. I do know de slaves 'spected a salary for der work when dey got free. Some of 'em got part of de promise, but most of 'em got nothin' but de promise. My owners was exceptions. Dere might of been some more like 'em but not many. At least I never heard of em. All my old favorite songs us slaves use to sing, I can't separate 'em anymore. I try to think of 'em, so I can sing 'em, but I jest find myself mixin' 'em up, and can't tell one from the other. Just singing. But the songs I like best dis day and time is 'Life Is Like A Mountain Railroad', 'God Will Take Care Of You', and 'I maybe blind, and I can not see, I may be crippled and I can not walk, But I'll meet you at the Station when the train comes along."

ELLAINE WRIGHT

Interview with Ellaine Wright,
Springfield, Missouri.

Ellaine Wright was born March 1, 1840 and is 97 years of age. Was born of slave parents just outside of Springfield, Missouri, and lived there at the beginning of the Civil War.

Her father and mother's name was Evanson taken after "Marse Tom" Evanson who owned both Ellaine's mother and father and sixty other slaves. Tom Evanson was a wealthy farmer and ran a big hog and cattle stock ranch.

Ellaine Wright, whose name was Evanson in slavery was married after the war in 1866 to Pete Wright. She remembers the "Wilson's Creek" fight between the Union and Confederacy and only a short time after that she, with all the other Evanson slaves, was hurriedly taken south. The Evanson slaves with many other of the district were shipped as far south as possible to hide them from the Unionists. Ellaine Wright told of a heartbreaking meeting between she and her slave mother when Ellaine was just four years of age. Her mother had been sold to a slave trader and was to be taken to another state.

They permitted the slaves to say good-bye to their children and Ellaine said she would never forget the few words her mother spoke to her just before they were separated. "Ellaine, honey mamma's gwan way off and ain't never goin to see her baby agin". "An I can see myself holdin onto my mamma and both of us crying—and then, she was gone and I never seed her since. I hopes I goin to see my good mamma some day, I do. Yes' I'se goin to do it son, I sure is, yes indeed."

Ellaine doesn't seem to remember anything concerning the Civil War. Just this one important thing clings to her memory—her parting with her mammy.

SIM YOUNGER

> Interview with Sim Younger,
> Sedalia, Missouri.
> Geo. K. Bartlett, Kansas City, Mo.
> Reference: FC by Kathleen Williams.

The two-story frame house, very plain in appearance, almost square in shape, located at 400 North Moniteau Street, Sedalia, is the home of Sim Younger, an interesting product of Negro slavery. He was born May 17, 1850, at Independence, Missouri; at the dawn of the "Golden Age of Steamboating on the Missouri River" and is a pensioned soldier of the Civil War.

Traditions and customs of the Old South have stamped their influence on the modest home. A porch extends across the front of the house and steps lead to the front door, but neither the porch nor front door are used much. They are for formal occasions.

However, home life begins with the smaller porch on the south side where bright flowered morning glory vines climb twine strings, their large green leaves bringing sheltering shadows to Sim's favorite resting place. Here is placed an old-fashioned hickory chair with woven cane seat which is his haven of peace and comfort.

The yard on this side of the house affords plenty of space for exercise and a large catalpa tree spreads grateful shade. It was here, under the catalpa tree that Sim Younger wanted his picture taken while seated in his favorite chair. There is a quiet, soldierly dignity about the old Negro that is striking and impressive. He is well preserved for all of his 87 years and his keen eyes require no glasses. The impress of his college education and soldierly training are evidenced by his conversation, bearing and the lack of Negro dialect in his speech.

He courteously expressed pleasure at the request for an interview on slavery and invited me into the house. The living room where we talked is large, the floor is covered with linoleum and a leather covered couch stands against the wall. In the center of the room is a large oak table. Other furniture consists of two plain oak chairs, but no rocking chairs.

Sim lives alone, and while we were talking a Negro brought in his breakfast; a pint of milk, an egg and two slices of toast. Although urged, Sim would not violate his code by eating in my presence.

"My father," he replied in answer to my question, "was Charles Younger, the originator of the Younger family in Missouri, and grand father of Cole, Bob, and Jim Younger. My father was my mother's master. She was a Simpson. I knew Cole Younger well."

Cole, Bob, and Jim Younger, known as "The Younger Brothers", were notorious outlaws. It is recorded that Sim's father was the Younger who operated a canoe ferry across the Missouri River from Randolph Bluffs, in 1821, to what is now Kansas City, then known as Chouteau's Landing.

"My father died when I was five years old, and left mother a farm on which my brothers and sisters are still living. Father arranged for my education and by the terms of his will I was sent to Oberlin, Ohio, where I was reared by Delia Sheppard, in whose care I was placed."

Sim Younger related that he attended Oberlin College, and graduated from there in 1870. He did not see his mother from the time he was five years old until he was the age of 21. When comment was made that he did not use Negro dialect, Sim explained, saying:

"That is due to my early training. Delia Sheppard gave me excellent training, and I remember everything she told me, even when I was a very little boy.

"I will always remember one thing she told me," he continued, fondly reminiscent. "I was just a little boy and she said, 'Sim, if, when visiting, you find a pin on the floor, put it up and call attention to it. It does not belong to you.'

"Yes, ma'am," he continued, "I was born in slavery and I enlisted in the Union Army, January 1, 1864, at Oberlin, Ohio, and according to the National Tribune, I was one of the youngest soldiers in the ranks.

"I was present at the battle of Petersburg, Virginia, July 30, 1864; one of the disasters to the Northern forces of the war, and present on June 15, 1864, at the initiatory battle of Deep Bottom, and also at Cold Harbor.

"I was in the Ninth Army Corps, under Burnside, and was transferred around, in front of Richmond, Virginia.

"General Butler went down to Fort Fisher and failed, which was the last open port of the Confederacy. Another expedition was organized and General Terry given command. We embarked on the night of December 31, 1864; landed the morning of January 13, 1865, on the peninsula. On the night of January 15, 1865, we captured Fort Fisher.

"We had a terrible, terrible time landing! There was an awful storm! I was told to jump overboard, and oh my! I swallowed a good deal of the Atlantic!"

He sat still a moment, living over in memory the thrilling events of that night at Fort Fisher, then, saddened by the pageant of the past evoked from memory's storehouse, he said:

"I want to tell you of one of the tragic things that happened during the war, and I was there and saw it.

"It was at the Southside railroad, at Petersburg, on September 27, 1865. I was put on picket duty. The 'Rebs' had built a fire and the wind was driving it toward us. They began to holler and cheer, very happy over the fact.

"All at once we could hear someone coming toward us. The pickets opened fire on what they thought were 'Rebs', and found out to their distress that it was a bunch of recruits from our own lines. Many were killed."

The shadow of this past grief faded from his countenance and in a brighter mood he exclaimed:

"If I could choose my weapons for the next war, I would choose doughnuts, to be thrown at each other across the Atlantic."[4]

[4] Bibliography: E. Miller, W.H., "History of Jackson County, Mo.", Kansas City, Mo., Union Hist. Co., 1881. 1006 pp., illus., map. Consultant: Pearly Smith English, Service Officer, American Legion, (colored), Nineteenth and Missouri Street, Sedalia, Mo.]

Transcriber's Note

Original spelling has been maintained; e.g. "stob—a short straight piece of wood, such as a stake" (American Heritage Dictionary).—The Works Progress Administration was renamed during 1939 as the Work Projects Administration (WPA).

www.ingramcontent.com/pod-product-compliance
Lightning Source LLC
Chambersburg PA
CBHW071646160426
43195CB00012B/1374